Praise for *Too Much Magic*

"Kunstler's writing is remarkably lucid, readable, incisive, accurate, and telling, making it the absolute non-fiction page turner of 2012 . . . It is a MUST READ! . . . The definitive book for anyone who is done with fairy tales and who is ready to meet the world where it really is."
—*Transition Voice*

"American journalist and novelist James Howard Kunstler has become widely known in urban planning and energy circles for his articulate and acerbic observations on contemporary American society and its sundry addictions, delusions and dysfunctions . . . a sharp critic of energy-sucking, big-box landscapes."
—*Winnipeg Free Press*

"Kunstler methodically skewers what he asserts is the misguided thinking of people like Ray Kurzweil (*The Singularity Is Near*) who reassure us we can somehow craft benign, inexpensive fixes that will permit us to continue in a lifestyle roughly resembling the one we enjoy today. . . . a disturbing picture of the decline of American society, as our current lifestyle collapses in upon itself."
—*Shelf Awareness*

"He's not claiming a crystal ball and isn't interested in specific prediction, nor does he have a tidy list of solutions. Instead, he points out that we can't expect to tackle problems until we recognize them."
—Media with Conscience

"I highly encourage you to read [*Too Much Magic*], and to check out Kunstler's other works."
—*Urban Times*

"Kunstler is refreshingly uninterested in spinning a bad situation. He is willing not only to read the data about resources without illusion but also to assess the state of the culture without the triumphalism so common in the affluent world."
—*Al Jazeera*

Too Much Magic

Wishful Thinking, Technology, and the Fate of the Nation

James Howard Kunstler

Grove Press
New York

Parts of this book appeared in a different form in *Orion Magazine*, July 2011,
and *Salmagundi*, a Quarterly of the Humanities and Social Sciences Nos.
168-9 Fall 2010–Winter 2011.

Published simultaneously in Canada
Printed in the United States of America

ISBN-13: 978-0-8021-2144-8

Grove Press
an imprint of Grove/Atlantic, Inc.
841 Broadway
New York, NY 10003

Distributed by Publishers Group West

www.groveatlantic.com

13 14   10 9 8 7 6 5 4 3 2 1

This book is for Wendy Anthony

CONTENTS

1. Where We're At   1

2. Farewell to the Drive-in Utopia   23

3. Cities of the Future: Yesterday's Tomorrow
    or Tomorrow's Yesterday?   43

4. The Dangers of Techno Narcissism, or: Frankenstein Release 2.0,
    How Ray Kurzweil's Singularity Aims to Replace the
    Old God with a New and Improved Version   65

5. The Futility of Party Politics in the Long Emergency   85

6. Going Broke the Hard Way: The End of Wall Street   111

7. The Energy Specter: Oil and Gas, Alternative Energy,
    and Waiting for Santa Claus   155

8. Insults to the Planet and the Planet's Reply   197

9. Social Relations and the Dilemmas of Difference   216

Coda: A Systematic Misunderstanding of Reality   241

Everybody's got a plan until they get punched in the mouth.
—Mike Tyson

ONE

WHERE WE'RE AT

"He went broke slowly, and then all at once."
— Ernest Hemingway

The episode in human history that I named in my 2005 book *The Long Emergency* is off to a good start. The cavalcade of fiascos within that shape-shifting monster we call the economy and its overgrown subsidiary capital finance is getting so bad as I write that by the time you read this an even more profound crisis than the crash of 2008 may be resetting the fundamental terms of your everyday life. Perhaps you are hungry tonight, with poor prospects for securing a meal.

We've blown past the defining mileposts for global peak oil — 2005 for conventional crude and 2008 if you include natural gas liquids, tar sand by-products, coal-based distillates, esoteric syncrudes, and other such stuff. In 2008 we had a nice demonstration of extreme volatility in the oil markets (predicted in *The Long Emergency*) with the price of crude zooming up to $147 a barrel and then crashing a few months later near $32. We're not so sure of ourselves these days. The British Petroleum company's 2010 Macondo well blowout in the Gulf of Mexico tempered the public's zest for risky deepwater drilling projects. Oil is back in the $100 range. The Fukushima nuclear meltdown in the following year sobered up many nations about the prospects for the only well-developed alternative energy method capable of powering whole cities. Whether you believe in climate change or not, or contest that it's man-made or is not, the weather is looking a little strange. In 2011 tornados of colossal scale tore through the American South, hurricane-induced five-hundred-year floods shredded Vermont, and Texas was so drought-stricken that Texans wondered if ranching there would even be possible in the years ahead. People have begun to notice a number of signals that reality is beaming out.

Whenever I venture out to the campuses and professional conferences people ask me, *What's your time frame for this long emergency?* I tell them we've entered the zone. It amazes me that that there is any question. Who can fail to notice all the obvious trouble our country is in? The middle class is dissolving. Americans have lost jobs they may never get back, in occupations that may cease to exist. They are getting tossed out of their houses at a rate never seen before. Government is broke at all levels, along with households and corporations. Foreign nations have gone bankrupt. Despite the mighty exertions of the U.S. Federal Reserve money is scarce, especially for loans, the lack of which is killing any enterprise that depends on revolving credit (meaning just about all enterprise). Times are hard and look like they will get a whole lot harder soon. Nothing is getting fixed, despite the pretenses of government. The public is ticked off, gathering up into political factions that did not exist in 2005, while the traditional Democrats and Republicans spiral into paralysis, irrelevance, and, perhaps most dangerous of all, loss of legitimacy. Wall Street and many other public places are being occupied by protesters, a different breed than those of yesteryear, hardened by economic calamity, battered in war, and low on idealism.

The most conspicuous feature of these times is our inability to construct a coherent consensus about what is happening to us and what we're going to do about it. Extremes in thinking and a vacuum in the middle where fact and reason used to dwell lately characterize the national state of mind. Conspiracy theories have gone mainstream — the New World Order, the Bilderbergs, the global elite, the Council on Foreign Relations, the Trilateral Commission, Freemasonry! This is the same paranoid ideology I first encountered at John Birch Society conventions I covered in the 1970s as a young newspaper reporter (with an affinity for the loony). It was a belief system relegated then to the margins, and deservedly. Today, people who appear to function normally in daily life fret over chem trails in the sky and the suspicion that Vice President Dick Cheney orchestrated the 9/11 attack on the World Trade Center. Some of this apocalyptic occultism is pretty elaborate, and probably requires some brains to traffic with, but that's doubly dispiriting because it means even informed people can lose track of reality. In such a cultural milieu it becomes difficult to scope out where stupidity ends and craziness takes over.

Wishful thinking is another symptom of our impaired consensus. I've encountered appalling displays of wishful groupthink in unlikely places around the United States. For two years running I was invited to the Aspen Environmental Forum. When the oil issue came up there, the chatter was all about how America was going to solve its motor fuel problem by "coming up with" a range of ingenious new ways for running automobile engines by other means than gasoline—electricity, natural gas, petro-algae excretions, compressed air. Apart from the unlikelihood that any of these systems might feasibly keep the national car and truck fleets running another decade at the current scale, note the Aspen group's basic assumption: that car dependency is perfectly okay, as long as you can find another way besides oil to run the vehicles. At the center of that strain of wishful thinking was the Rocky Mountain Institute and its founding chief, Amory Lovins, whose advanced econometric models managed to completely overlook their own diminishing returns, a mode of thinking that is one of the recurring themes in this book. Lovins's organization had been engaged for years on a "hypercar" project aimed at developing a vehicle that would get supernaturally high gas mileage, based on a belief that efficiency is a virtuous end in itself, and that somehow this virtuous efficiency would mitigate the many environmental problems stemming from the excessive burning of fossil fuels. The unintended consequence would be . . . more efficient car dependency! And continuing, increasing car dependency and, therefore, the continuing elaboration of suburban sprawl for car dependency to exist within. In short, the hypercar project was insane. It beat a path straight to Jevons paradox, the proposition that greater technological efficiencies achieved in using a given resource tend to increase the rate of its consumption.[1] The diminishing returns were obvious.

What it revealed about the Aspen cohort was how invested they were in the status quo of Happy Motoring. They wanted to solve the problems of CO_2 emissions, air pollution, and climate change without having to make behavioral changes. There was no talk whatsoever at the Environmental Forum about other strategies for dealing with the manifold predicaments of burning oil in cars—for instance, walkable neighborhoods or restoring the national passenger railroad system and other kinds of public transit. They were not interested, or these things had not occurred to them, so single-minded was their pursuit of techno-grandiose "solutions" for propping up the familiar comforts of daily life. The cream of America's green intellectuals convene at the Aspen Environmental Forum; if they can't think straight about this part of the problem to whom do you turn? NASCAR fans? Wall Street? Glenn Beck? The Mafia?

I encountered a similar odd groupthink when I was invited to give a talk on our energy quandary at the Google company's headquarters in Silicon Valley. First, stepping back a moment, I couldn't help noticing that the company's building itself was tricked out like a giant kindergarten or day-care center. The public areas were furnished with all manner of parlor games: Ping-Pong tables, knock hockey, billiards, video game consoles. Here and there were stacks of Lucite boxes and bins filled with Gummi bears, yogurt-covered pretzels, and

---

1. William Stanley Jevons (1835–82) based his proposition on observations about coal consumption in England, which soared with increasing progress in the efficiency of coal-burning steam engines. The better the engines performed, the more engines were applied to a diverse range of new tasks, and the more coal they used.

similar junk snacks. Not a few of the Google employees who came into the elegant new auditorium were dressed like teenaged skateboard rats in low-hanging ass-crack pants and sideways hats, and these were executives, senior programmers! After I gave my talk on the energy situation, some time had been reserved for questions and answers. There were no questions, only statements from several Googlers, and they all pretty much said the same thing, which might be summed up as *Like, dude, we've got technology* . . . (Subtext: *You're an asshole.*)

This informed me of something pretty scary: the executives and programmers at Google didn't know the difference between technology and energy. They assumed that these were interchangeable, that if you run out of one you just plug in the other, which is inconsistent with reality. Note that these were the top people in the leading high-tech corporate enterprise in the United States. If they don't know the difference between technology and energy, what might we expect of the salary mules in the U.S. Department of Transportation, or in ten thousand other offices in the land where people have to make decisions about how we live?

This encounter with delusional groupthink especially troubled my mind. As I reflected on it, though, I arrived at a possible explanation. In the age of the computer revolution, tech companies are valued for being *playfully creative,* thus the playtime incunabula deployed all around the Google headquarters, the games and the sugary snacks and also the childlike costumes worn by the executives and programmers. *We're childlike, therefore we're creative, therefore our company is that much more valuable, therefore see our share price go up.* The childlike thinking at Google was a logical extension of this corporate culture: the belief in magic, in this case the magic of high tech. A lot of the high-level employees I spoke to in the auditorium that day were people who had become millionaires before they had turned thirty (thanks to Google stock), mainly by pushing pixels around a screen with a mouse, that is, by making computer *magic.* They had magically become rich by making magic. Naturally, then, they were true believers in tech magic, and also, by extension, believers in the idea that any problem facing the human race could be fixed by applying tech magic.

This techno grandiosity (or techno triumphalism or techno narcissism) is one of the main impediments to thinking straight about the problems of the long emergency, which will also be a recurring theme in this book. There are other mental constructs that present obstacles to clear thinking about what is happening to us and what we can do about it. One is the belief that *when you wish upon a star your dreams come true*. I have previously labeled this the Jiminy Cricket syndrome—from the Walt Disney feature film cartoon *Pinocchio*. It gets additional reinforcement from the incessant programming of the advertising industry and also from factions within the psychological self-help movement, which have led people to believe that visualizing an outcome is likely to produce that outcome, that is, *Wishing makes it so!*

A companion to that idea is the belief that it is possible to get something for nothing. It is probably inherent in human nature that we're susceptible to this form of magical thinking, since we're always looking for shortcuts, bargains, for ways to minimize and even avoid the price we have to pay to get things in life. In Western culture, it took the full force of the Protestant ethic to override this tendency, and after a few hundred years that override seems to be wearing off. The something-for-nothing wish manifests in advertising tropes such as miracle diets and especially in the widespread legalization after 1970 of gambling, an industry firmly based on the wish for acquiring unearned riches, the most popular form of the something-for-nothing theme.

When you combine these two beliefs—*when you wish upon a star . . . you'll get something for nothing!*—you end up with a toxic psychology, which, I submit, has become baseline normal for the American public lately. It was exactly this magical thinking that came to infect the realm of capital finance and has so far come close to destroying it.

As I have traveled around America since 2005, with the public mood growing increasingly anxious over oil prices, Wall Street swindles, and a sputtering economy, I constantly heard a cry for solutions at every stop. This was partly an expression of anxiety over difficult problems, and just as often a form of censorious scolding aimed at bearers of bad news (me). "Give us *solutions*, not doom and gloom!" was the gist of a complaint I heard at every conference or college campus. I sensed that there was something not quite right with this complaint, partly because I was presenting all sorts of ideas for addressing the long emergency and my audiences seemed to be blocking them out. After a while I began to understand what lay behind this plea for "solutions." They were clamoring desperately for rescue remedies that would allow them to continue living exactly the way they were used to living, with all the accustomed comforts ranging from endless driving to universal air-conditioning, cheap fast food, reliable electric service, NASCAR, Disney World, Walmart, and *good jobs* with a guaranteed comfortable retirement. They didn't want to hear anything that suggested we might have to make other arrangements for everyday life in this country.

I certainly understand that people want to feel hopeful about their situation in this world, as well as their fear of losing what is familiar and comfortable. But I don't believe we can get through this long emergency without making other arrangements for a lot of the common activities of everyday life, or without giving up some familiar comforts and habits. When I hear people yelling for "solutions," I recognize that they are looking for ways to sustain the unsustainable. That's why I propose we begin by making a clear distinction between "solutions" and "intelligent responses" to the changing circumstances we face.

I don't believe there are any solutions that will allow our current economic arrangements to continue exactly as they are. But I do believe there are plenty of intelligent responses that will lead us in different directions toward different behavior and new ideas in new arrangements. I also believe that these new conditions will contain much that is familiar and even welcoming to us. They will derive from our own culture and national character as well as our regional and ethnic

7

backgrounds. They are likely to put us back in touch with elements of human experience that we thoughtlessly discarded in our heedless rush toward a chimerical techno nirvana—working together with people we know, spending time with friends and loved ones, sharing food with people we love, and enacting the other ceremonies of daily and seasonal life in story and song.

Mismanaging Contraction

One could as well say *decline* or *collapse* but we're not quite there yet. For now, I'll refer to the defining condition of these times as contraction. We've reached certain limits of planetary resources: of oil and natural gas, of uranium, of many common metal ores, of clean fresh water, of good soil, and most particularly the ability to pay for things with borrowed money. Much as we would like to think that there are alternative energy resources, or technological tricks for prestidigitating some equivalent, and perhaps other ways of getting at those vital minerals—mining the moon has been promoted, surely a symptom of techno grandiosity—it's more likely that we will *not* come up with any combination of alternative energy substances or systems that can replace the fabulous versatility and power density of the fossil fuels, nor is it likely that we will discover vast new deposits of first-rate ores, rare earths, or the phosphorus so indispensable for the kind of agriculture we practice. Peak oil is only part of a package of resource shortages that Richard Heinberg has correctly identified as "peak everything"[2]— though oil is the primary resource of our economy.

At the same time, we've achieved a global human population of about 7 billion as of this writing. Peak human population will surely

---

2. Richard Heinberg, *Peak Everything: Waking Up to the Century of Declines* (New Society Publishers, 2007).

lag behind peak oil and peak mineral resources until these conditions express themselves as food shortages. This means that the human population will continue to rise for a while, even as we begin to encounter these very strict resource limits. It's not possible to estimate how much the population will increase because the relationship between energy and mineral resources and food production is a very fragile equation, subject to any number of discontinuities. To these, add the complications of weather disasters arising from climate change, including drought, the spread of plant diseases, and so forth. This lagging further rise in human population will only make the inevitable contraction more acute, once food shortages begin. Anyway, 7 billion already amounts to a human population overshoot in relation to the planet earth's ecology. We're putting a strain on everything the earth has to offer us. While the combination of peak stuff and 7 billion humans is forcing the issue, I think the truth is that circumstances will now determine what happens, not policies or personalities.

This historical moment has arrived with stunning swiftness, one lifetime, really. When I was born, in 1948, overpopulation was a non-issue. Tens of millions of people had just died in the Second World War. Paul Ehrlich's 1968 book *The Population Bomb* gave the issue a platform. Meanwhile, along came the "green revolution" with oil economics and plant genetics applied to bump up grain yields world-wide and Malthusian thinkers were laughed at.[3] Now, a few decades later, world population has doubled and most sentient adults have some awareness that we have a problem with overpopulation, but it is still not a major political issue in the West. China instituted its one-child policy in 1979 but it is only marginally effective and likely to be overwhelmed by accelerating resource problems, especially water shortages leading to major food production shortfalls. (China became

3. After the Reverend Thomas Robert Malthus (1766–1834), author of *An Essay on the Principle of Population* (1798), which stated that the exponential growth of population would inevitably outpace the mathematical growth of food production.

a net food importer in 2008.) Several European nations have fallen below the demographic replacement level. Even so, their populations remain out of scale with their faster-declining resource base of the near future. The United States is still welcoming a large volume of immigrants and cannot overcome the national mythology associated with it. It's fair to say that in the West there is no interest in a one-child policy, nor in any other policy or protocol regarding population control (and we must make a distinction between population control and birth control for personal lifestyle reasons). The truth is, we don't intend to do anything about it. Population overshoot is therefore unlikely to yield to management. Rather, the usual suspects will enter the scene and do their thing: starvation, disease, and violence. (The fourth horseman is usually called death, which I have never understood because it just seems to be a consequence of the other three.)

As a more general economic matter, the crux of the problem is that peak oil implies an implacable limit to future growth, the kind of growth we've understood to be normal in the industrial age. From here on there will be no more growth defined as increased wealth from industrial production, only contraction. There is no credible model of a postindustrial economy that would permit our accustomed comfort and convenience to continue as is—apart from the wishes and fantasies of people who would like there to be one. Any way you cut it, the inability to increase energy inputs to the system limits what we can do in the system. We have no prior experience in human history running industrial economies in reverse. We know about the experience of other empires running up against resource limits, and the result of that has been collapse of one kind or another. But the complexity of ancient Rome can be likened to *The Flintstones* compared to what we've got going in the early twenty-first century with jet travel, gigantic electric grids, digital banking, and twelve-thousand-mile supply lines of food and manufactured goods, not to mention atomic arsenals and hundreds of other complex activities—all running under the aegis of computers. Rome took centuries to wind down and, even so, one might argue that Roman culture just shifted its center of gravity from Italy to Constantinople for a while and then migrated back to various locales in western Europe around 1500 in new and improved form during the Renaissance. Ancient Mesopotamia destroyed its soils with excessive irrigation and the population withered (until it became the modern oil state of Iraq three thousand years later). The Easter Islanders ran out of trees. After a good run of many centuries the Maya's cities melted back into the jungle when the weather changed. Each story is a little different but with resource limits at the center.

The industrial era differs from these prior episodes of civilizational failure in scale and complexity. Our complex systems are more complex, bigger, farther flung. These systems can be described succinctly and with precision: agriculture, commerce, manufacturing, transport, finance, the oil and gas and coal industry, the electric grid, and so on. These systems are currently in distress. They have all reached scales and levels of complexity that are no longer viable. But no industrial nation displays any overt consciousness of the need to deliberately downscale our systems, that is, to manage contraction, despite an array of intelligent responses that might avail in the situation. For one thing, neither the United States, Great Britain, France, nor Germany has officially articulated a recognition of peak oil, the heart of the matter. This denial itself is of a scale commensurate with the stupendous scale of the complex systems we're running.

The ineluctable limit of peak oil is a primary fault line threatening these systems with instability and failure. As these systems mutually ramify and amplify each other's failures, the process will only accelerate. As trouble with oil affects transportation, which will affect agriculture and commerce and finance, and so on, there won't be enough work, money, or power for us to run things the way we are used to running them. The financial system, based on banks tied together in a vast web of mutual obligations, is especially susceptible because the specter of no more growth means the end of our ability to generate meaningful new wealth as represented by money. There will be no new money (and the magic trick of central banks pretending to create it at this point will result only in the devaluing of existing money). Peak oil also happens to coincide with peak debt, and on the downward arc from the peak we will have less money with which to pay the interest on our gigantic outstanding debts, since our money is in fact loaned into existence and we have passed the point of being able to lend more. The direct implication of all this is a compressive deflationary contraction in which money (wealth) that will never be paid back vanishes into the black hole of default, from which it will never reemerge. The net effect of this sort of compressive contraction will drive civilization into penury and almost certainly lead to political turmoil and social disorder. It will destroy the legitimacy of institutions including political parties, the structures and operations of law, banks, schools, indeed anything that depends on vested authority. These failures are eventually joined by the failure of the system for producing and distributing food, and by the time that happens you have a society in severe hardship in which all bets are off.

We've done a terrible job of managing contraction so far. We can't face it. We pretend it's not happening. We're doing everything possible to defy it as a practical matter. But contraction is the essence of our reality right now. Faced with the likelihood that peak oil has already occurred, along with upheavals in finance, all we've done is mount a campaign to sustain the unsustainable, to attempt to reflate the deflating money supply, to try and ramp back up an orgy of borrowing that was insane in the first place and has already ended in tears once, to prop up the price of overpriced houses and use tax breaks to bribe more imprudent citizens to enter new mortgage contracts, to bail out failed companies and "socialize" their losses at the expense of the taxpayers, and to run up new public debts so extravagant they will impoverish generations to come. By the way, I say all this as a registered Democrat and not a right-winger.

One of the first things that the freshly inaugurated president Barack Obama did in 2009 was bail out General Motors and Chrysler and then direct hundreds of billions of dollars of so-called stimulus into "shovel-ready" public works projects, mostly highway building. This amounts to taking a huge chunk of our dwindling financial resources and investing it in a transportation system that has no future. Despite the mythology embedded in our culture that *what's good for General Motors is good for the country*, this was a very bad call. There is simply no way that we will be able to continue running the complex system I call Happy Motoring. It worked for about ninety years and now it's over. It was a lot of fun, especially in the early years when we were getting the system up and running. It was a great romantic adventure to take a car into the open countryside of this big gorgeous continent when the roads were new and there weren't so many other cars cluttering up the byways. It's easy to understand our sentimental attachment to all this. But it's over. Our own sovereign endowment of oil is running down so low that we have to import more than two-thirds of the oil we use, and the situation is only going to get worse. Anyway, it's not even mainly about oil anymore. A greater array of mutually ramifying system failures is now under way.

The financial hardships are taking an additional toll. Because so much money is vanishing into default, there is much less money for auto loans. This leaves a diminishing pool of borrowers who have some prospect of paying their loans back. Since taking out loans is the normal way that most Americans buy their cars, it is easy to see that fewer cars will be bought in the years ahead. Moving forward, there will be proportionately fewer motorists. This will feed political resentment as driving increasingly becomes a privileged activity and a broad class of former drivers are foreclosed from motoring. In short, it makes Happy Motoring less democratic, and the only reason it worked in the first place was that every American from the lowliest hamburger flipper to the greediest hedge fund manager could get in a car and drive somewhere at will.

We will also soon see the failure of the road system itself. The compressive deflationary contraction is bankrupting government at all levels, reducing revenue flows, destroying the efficacy of outstanding bonds, and discouraging the issuance of new ones. The result: municipalities, counties, states, and the federal government will be far less able to keep up with the massive maintenance required by the colossal road system. This system, which includes city streets, county and state highways, thousands upon thousands of bridges, and the fantastically expensive interstate system itself, was elaborated upon layer by layer, decade after decade, inviting layer upon layer of additional complexity, without any overarching thought about the future cost of maintaining it—especially if the American economic equation were to change in any substantial way. Now the equation *has* changed, and the American roadway is yet another complex system out of control. In 2010 we no longer have the money to keep all the pieces of it in repair. What's more, it is a fact well understood among highway engineers that the "level of service" (quality of the roadway) must be kept in immaculate condition or else the roads quickly deteriorate, especially in those parts of the nation where water freezes and thaws. Overlook road repair for a winter or two and pavements will soon be in hopeless condition. We may even be short of asphalt later in this decade. In Michigan, one of the country's most distressed states, it's now official policy to depave rural roads to save on maintenance. This policy will become infectious.

Faced with the compounding emergency he inherited in January 2009, President Obama could have made different choices with that stimulus money, which was borrowed money, of course, generated from treasury bonds that someone has to pay interest on. He could have taken the hundreds of billions and applied it to a restoration of the U.S. passenger railroad system. The United States is a continent-sized nation. One of the reasons we use so much oil is because our citizens routinely have to drive long distances. A hundred-mile daily commute is not uncommon. I drive from upstate New York to Boston at least five times a year because the train service is so abysmal. One train a day leaves Albany for Boston and it takes five to seven hours, compared to the three hours by car. And my situation is not so special. You can't travel by train from Cleveland to Columbus, Ohio, either, or Louisville to Nashville, or Denver to Albuquerque, or Minneapolis to St. Louis, or a thousand other fairly common routes.

We desperately need to restore passenger railroad service in the United States or we are not going to be able to get around this big country. It's as simple as that. Not only are the days of Happy Motoring numbered but the sun is setting on commercial aviation. All the major legacy airlines in the nation have gone bankrupt over the past decade, some more than once. (American Airlines was the latest, in the fall of 2011.) They continue operating as zombie enterprises, unable to generate profits. Their customer base is dwindling as the middle class shrinks. They may not survive further rounds of fuel price increases or market disruptions in anything like their current form. Mr. Obama made a tragic choice when he assigned all that stimulus money to highway projects and new airport runways. Only a tiny fraction of the stimulus was apportioned to Amtrak and to a couple of high-speed rail projects: one to connect the cities of California and another to run between Tampa and Orlando, Florida (based on the absurd premise that the economy will continue to depend on theme park visits), but the total amount of money committed to rail generally has been a joke. Anyway, the Tampa–Orlando system was summarily scratched in 2011 when new Florida governor Rick Scott refused the offered federal funding.

High-speed rail for the United States at this point is an exercise in techno grandiosity. We simply cannot afford to build a high-speed passenger rail network, not of the kinds that were built in previous decades before peak oil and peak debt by the European nations, Japan, and China. It is, unfortunately, too late for that here. We are broke. We don't have the ability to raise the necessary capital by additional borrowing. High-speed rail requires an entirely alternate set of tracks and rights of way from the existing rail networks. High-speed trains require different curve and grade ratios. We are unable to pay for a new, alternate rail network, even if we could overlay it on the interstate highway system and avoid problems of eminent domain in taking away people's property. The intelligent option, therefore, would be to rehabilitate the existing railroad tracks and outfit them with the appropriate rolling stock to run on them.

By the way, Mr. Obama could have bailed out General Motors by requiring them to get into the business of manufacturing locomotives and rolling stock for a restored U.S. passenger rail system, but that idea never made it into the policy arena. It might have been difficult for General Motors, perhaps, but it wasn't easy in 1941 for the automakers to shift from making cars to making tanks and airplanes either. They did what was necessary at the time. Had President Obama decided to restore the standard passenger rail system, he would have created hundreds of thousands of meaningful new jobs at all levels from labor to operations to management. And the American public would have been deliriously happy to be able to go from Albany to Boston or Memphis to Little Rock at seventy-five miles an hour if the trains ran on schedule. The last thing that the United States needed in the year 2009 was hundreds of miles of new freeways to maintain.

Now, this was not managing contraction wisely. We might ask ourselves why we are making such bad choices, and there are certainly ways of accounting for this collective fecklessness.

Joseph Tainter, an anthropologist at Utah State University, developed a comprehensive theory of collapse, which can be summarized in his formulation of "overinvestments in complexity with diminishing marginal returns."[4] In this book I will be concerned with diminishing returns as applied to many cultural as well as economic matters.

---

4. Jospeh A. Tainter, *The Collapse of Complex Societies* (Cambridge University Press, 1990).

Tainter's model plainly applies to the energy resource limits we face, but we are running so many interdependent complex systems at the same time that the public remains baffled by the interplay of mutually reinforcing diminishing returns between them. I aim to demonstrate exactly how they will ramify each other's failures, and the discussion will move to some less empirical concerns that also will be affected by these failures—matters of culture and even of our collective national spirit.

The American public is frustrated that the religion of progress can't seem to overcome the workings of entropy in this corner of the universe—although by and large, Americans are not acquainted with the concept of entropy as such. They just wonder why so many things are going wrong from sea to shining sea. Why is California dead broke? Why won't the oil stop leaking into the sea? Why can't I find a job eighteen months after the Acme Corporation handed me that pink slip? Nothing works anymore. Entropy, of course, is the condition in reality that makes time operate in one direction, makes hot coffee cool off, and tends to make things run down or fall apart eventually. Entropy is behind the idea that there is a beginning, a middle, and an end to all stories, including our lives and the societies we belong to. Entropy is responsible for the diminishing returns of the things we do and the way we live. Entropy never sleeps.

The American public remains in thrall to the constructed elegance of the mighty systems we are running by means of technological magic. The wonders of technology seemingly never cease. Alas, techno magic delivers some extra added features we did not figure on getting—for instance, buyer's remorse, a particular brand of ennui—but at least it never fails to reinforce the idea that there is no end to the magic, whatever else may be going on. The banking system may be a walking-dead system, but the Apple company just released a sleek new iPad that will enhance your social status down at the corner Starbucks, so who cares about the fate of capital? Peak oil got you down? "They" will come up with some new way to power Walmart, Disney World, and the Interstate Highway System. We'll run those iPads on an as yet undiscovered, inexhaustible, "renewable" means of power. Then we can become energy independent! Everybody will have electric cars and all-electric home heating! We will land a man on the moon before the decade is out. Oh, wait a minute, we did that already.

I happen to look at it another way. Maybe we've had too much magic. One big diminishing return of all this magic is that an awful lot of it stops seeming like magic after a while. When you turn on the giant flat-screen TV, does it really seem magical when Larry Kudlow's stately visage resolves in that matrix of glowing pixels and he begins yapping about "recovery"? Flying in airplanes these days feels as boring and tiresome as sitting in the dentist's waiting room yet you're shooting through the sky eight miles above the earth at 550 miles an hour to get from New York to Paris overnight (something the human race may never accomplish again). How many readers feel a special thrill these days when a switch is thrown at home and the lights go on? (Your great-grandparents might have been awestruck, but you'd be shocked only if the lights *didn't* go on.) Even YouTube begins to feel as mundane as watching rain drip off the roof.

A few years ago I was invited to give a talk at the glamorous TED conference in Monterey, California.[5] This popular annual shindig brings together a huge variety show of presenters who have carved out some niche in our culture, and they put on a three-day extravaganza for a self-selecting cohort of attendees who, by and large, come out of the high-tech industries of Silicon Valley and who pay thousands of dollars to attend the conference. Presenters are not paid to do their act, but they get to watch one another for free, plus free eats and a hotel room. The year I was there many distinguished characters were on hand: Daniel Gilbert, the "happiness" psychologist; Stewart Brand, impresario of the *Whole*

---

5. TED stands for Technology, Entertainment, and Design.

Earth Catalog and its offshoots; and prolific author Malcolm Gladwell and other interesting intellectuals, many of whom had something to say worth listening to. Yet a poll of attendees taken near the end of the event showed overwhelmingly that the most popular presentation was the one about flying cars. I happened to see it and it was the dumbest damned thing on the whole three-day bill, with ideas and illustrations straight out of a mid-1950s issue of *Popular Science* magazine. (The flying cars all looked like '56 Ford Fairlanes with wings). And yet this, of all the ideas presented, is what most thrilled the elite of Silicon Valley. What it told me was that even the brightest collection of souls in California could not overcome the idiocy of their own ingrained culture.

In the extremely unlikely event that a flying car system were to arise—and I must tell you the chances are microscopically minuscule to nil—I'm sure it would soon enough be as drained of all its magic as the Happy Motoring system eventually was. In many ways it would surely make our lives worse as it distributed the annoyance of the highway to every dooryard. Yet this is the sort of fantasy that excites people who ought to know better in these twilight days of the techno-triumphant empire. The infantilism is striking. Note, too, that this childlike delusion among the elites of technology, business, politics, and media is just as remarkable as anything you'd find among any World Federation of Wrestling audience. And it raises the question: how does the USA happen to find itself at a moment in history when it seems absolutely unable to think straight, let alone address its most pressing problems? This is the essential mystery of contemporary life that I'd like to plumb in this book.

Kingdom Come

I was amused to discover some years ago, on a visit to Disney's Magic Kingdom in Orlando, how much of the overarching metaphor employed in old Walt's kinetic semiology of thrill rides and wish fulfillment galleries revolved around the invocation of death (and its aftereffects). Right from the get-go there was the entry to the theme park by way of a ferryboat crossing a mysterious body of water to the front gate, an archetype so hoary and universal that everyone on the boat from the Indiana Presbyterians to the jangling tourists from New Delhi seemed to get it. Having mysteriously "died" somewhere in the parking lot, you're conveyed to "heaven," at least as represented by "Main Street USA," which, of course, was a cartoon rendition of Walt Disney's actual boyhood home of Marceline, Missouri (now a mere smudge of strip malls and big box outparcels on the fruited plain).

One can easily understand the nostalgia of someone born in the year 1901, as Walt Disney was. The nation had pretty much fully outfitted itself for modern life by the time he came into sentience (1908, let's say), with all kinds of additional promising marvels to come, and yet the automobile and suburbia had not yet messed up the everyday world of small town America. Walt's childhood was a kind of magical moment in history: the bridge years between the old times and modern times. By the mid-1950s, when Walt was deeply ensconced as a business mogul in Southern California and its pervasive ethos of cruisin' for burgers, the bygone small town of his childhood must have seemed like heaven to him, notwithstanding the fact that his own kinds of business activities were responsible for despoiling so much of what made Southern California lovely in the first place (the original Disneyland in Anaheim, California, actually borders the Santa Ana Freeway).

It was an odd condition of twentieth-century life that most people born in it usually lived to see the destruction, in one way or another, of the places they had loved or called home. The loss must have been deeply felt by many of the adults stepping off the magic ferryboat into Disney's Main Street USA, though the children of today's ubiquitous suburbia probably see it as just another shopping mall. It's sadly ironic that these same adults would return to their home places across the country and do everything possible — as planning board officials, Rotarians, car dealers, developers, etc. — to destroy the last vestiges of whatever had made their towns worth caring about, until the landscape of the nation became a futureless panorama of engineered anomie.

From Main Street, the Disney World visitor moves on to the many rides featuring brushes with death, haunted houses, animatronic corpses, holographic ghosts, screaming mummies, ghouls, skeletons, coffins, graveyards, and all the other stock trappings of our national bent for necromancy. The place is drenched in signifiers of mortality. Shrieking death is a payoff dispensed to Disney World guests as regularly as the reward pellets doled out to rats in experimental psych labs, so one begins to get the feeling that all those overfed Americans waddling so innocently about in their JC Penney casuals do share an intense subliminal yearning for death. This is especially curious given Disney World's emphasis on wholesome family fun and its place in the American mythology of childhood. But its thoroughgoing morbidity is not that much different in degree than, say, the morbidity of the Catholic Church, which has held children hostage for centuries and used that captivity to program them very successfully to become morbid adults living in terror of phantoms.

Extreme sentimentality sometimes beats a path straight to cultural suicide. The Nazis proved that nicely. The morbid sentimentality of Disney World is, after all, just the rectified essence of its greater context, the morbid American scene in general. Henry Miller's "air-conditioned nightmare," sixty-five years on, has entered a freefall to the furthest frontiers of entropy where homeostasis dwells in cold and darkness. Everything we do these days, our lust for ever more comfort, pleasure, and distraction, our refusals to engage with the mandates of reality, our fidelity to the cults of technology and limitless growth, our narcissistic national exceptionalism — all of this propels us toward the realm where souls abandon all hope. It's not the script that I favor and, given the chance, such as in the pages of this short book, I'd like the opportunity to recommend a different outcome, not necessarily a Hollywood happy ending but at least the carrying forward of a recognizably American civilization at lower amplitude, with the mendacity and idiocy purged from it and with our insults to the only planet we call our own put into a long-delayed reverse.

TWO

FAREWELL TO
THE DRIVE-IN UTOPIA

There are a lot of ways of referring to American-style suburbia, but these days I favor *the greatest misallocation of resources in the history of the world*. You can say this because it's clear we are not going to be able to run it in a very few years as the nation's oil supply gets more restricted (despite our fantasies about shale oil) and we have to face the disappointing reality that so-called alternative energy will not come close to offsetting our oil losses. Suburbia therefore represents a living arrangement with no future.

Pouring the vast accumulated capital treasure of the United States into building an infrastructure for daily life with no future is self-evidently a tragic misallocation of resources. There's no way to calculate exactly how much money we misspent building the far-flung housing tracts, strip malls, big box ensembles, office parks, muffler shop outparcels, giant centralized schools with gold-plated sports facilities, countless roadways of all sizes, vast water, sewer, and electric systems, and all the other accessories and furnishings of that development pattern, but anybody can tell it was an awful lot. And it came out of the richest society in the history of the world.

Now suburbia's time is over. We're done building any more of it. The stuff that already exists will increasingly lose value and usefulness. Most Americans don't know this yet. They are sure that suburbia is a permanent fixture of the human condition, just as Tom Friedman of the *New York Times* believes that the earth became permanently flat again in economic terms sometime in the 1990s. The frantic, atomizing quality of daily life in the suburban matrix probably even defeats any critical contemplation of it as Americans incessantly motor from home to work to mall to soccer field to burger barn in lives devoid of repose and tranquillity, the necessary conditions for reflection. A few wary citizens may sense that something feels increasingly wrong with the picture, but they're apt to draw the wrong conclusions, for instance, that a conspiracy exists involving some fantasized elite scheming to deprive middle-class Americans of their natural entitlements to a life of comfort and convenience. We'll have trouble otherwise accounting for the coming failure of our basic living arrangements. People facing dreadful losses commonly look for scapegoats to blame. The implications for political mischief along these lines are not very appetizing. There is no previous case in history of a civilization making capital investments as heedlessly as we did, of constructing what turns out to be a throwaway human habitat. The tragedy is impressive.

Nor was the great project of suburbia itself a conspiracy in the first place. Charismatic people in thought and action such as Frank Lloyd Wright and Robert Moses may have helped it along, but they certainly did not force suburbia on an unwitting American public. We opted for it collectively because it seemed like a good idea at the time and because we had the resources to do it. A consensus formed that building suburbia would produce many benefits for the American public, and that consensus proved to be so sturdy it has endured even in the face of growing evidence that the diminishing returns of living this way may become desperately problematic. Once the consensus was in place, and sets of standardized practices came together across a broad range of occupations, disciplines, and businesses—such as production home building, mortgage lending, highway engineering, land-use law, and automobile marketing—the project of suburbia rolled out as any emergent, self-organizing system will under the right conditions. It elaborated itself as neatly as an algorithm.

The United States was predisposed to a suburban living arrangement. The nation was poised to grow at the exact moment that the industrial age got up and running, and within a century of its start the country became the world's preeminent industrial power, with all of industry's obnoxious side effects on landscape and townscape. Our cities attained gigantism relatively quickly, something the human race had little prior experience with. Scant residue of their preindustrial beginnings survives. These cities were products of the industrial age. They were designed to serve all the most inhuman elements of industrial enterprise: the needs of machines, factories, transport infrastructures, and the efficiencies demanded by capital finance in its never-ending quest to maximize profit at the expense of other human values. This resulted in cities short on amenity and, especially in the decades after the Second World War, devoid of artistry. It turned out that gigantic, soulless cities lacking amenity and artistry were not very lovable, even to people of meager education, and a broad range of Americans developed an abiding hatred of them.

Along with this theme in the many-layered emerging American Dream narrative runs the counterpoint of rural romanticism, perhaps best embodied in Thomas Jefferson's ideal of the yeoman farmer utopia—the notion that the best social disposition of things was a polity made up of educated, independent farmers cultivating their own gardens, so to speak, competent to participate in governance and careful of their stake in freehold property. It was a model of existence that was consistent with settlement of the frontier using a system of land tenure laws—the fee-simple method of ownership—less onerous than the earlier English model. But in the long run Jefferson's agrarian vision wouldn't pan out as he'd imagined. It mutated into something that had nothing to do with working the land.

Because North America was such a large piece of real estate, sparsely settled by native peoples (who had experienced a severe dieback of their own populations in the initial encounters with Europeans), the new United States was able to accommodate large numbers of settlers. The numerous immigrants had their choice of where to settle: city, country, frontier. Even as the industrial cities ballooned in size, most of the U.S. population remained rural.[1] The peopling of a new nation on a recently discovered continent was a dynamic, anomalous, and relatively brief historical event, of course. Settlement of the lower forty-eight states was considered complete by the end of the nineteenth century, when Frederick Jackson Turner, in 1893, famously declared the frontier "closed" in a trope that resonated deeply among historians and cultural mythmakers.

The frontier experience and the domestication of the wild landscape generated a powerful romantic narrative that wove itself into the national mythology, especially as the industrial age, with all its discontents, quickly accelerated and vanquished many traditional arrangements. The more urban the nation became, the more nostalgia for rural life percolated through the collective psychology. Suburbia became the economic expression of that nostalgia, with the notion of country living proposed as the antidote to the obnoxious industrial city. Suburbia also coincided with the rise of mass production and mass consumer culture, merging into a mass demographic movement. Eventually, the new living arrangement outside the city, in a place that was not quite rural, was conflated with democracy itself as Americans of all classes joined in. It had three distinct iterations: the railroad suburb of the 1850s to 1890s (mainly for rich people), the streetcar suburb of the 1890s to the 1920s (now including the less-than-rich classes), and the automobile suburb from the 1920s thereafter (suburbia for everybody).

1. In 1910 the U.S. population was approximately 50 million rural versus 42 million urban (or 54.4 percent rural). In 1920, for the first time, the rural population was exceeded by the urban population.

Note that the United States developed the world's first oil industry in the late nineteenth century. Little oil had been discovered in Europe at that time (the North Sea fields not until the 1970s), the Arabian Peninsula was as yet unexplored, and a scramble was on for the oil fields of Persia and Indonesia by the European colonial powers. The United States was endowed with a generous supply, easy to get at and cheap to produce. We were finding more all the time. The U.S. oil industry was mature when car making was in its infancy. (Rockefeller's Standard Oil monopoly already had been broken up into smaller companies under the 1890 Sherman Antitrust Act by 1912 when Henry Ford first mass-produced his Model Ts.) The refineries were in place and easily re-jiggered to produce more gasoline (kerosene for lighting having been the industry's leading product for decades). This set the stage for the rapid development of cars, including Ford's assembly-line method of production, the mass-marketing to a broad customer base, the novelty of installment loans enabling people of meager savings to buy cars, the construction of paved roads financed by all levels of government, and the deployment of fueling stations. Pretty soon it became easy to leave the city behind, not just on a Sunday picnic in the cow pastures, and not just for rich people, but for clerks, accountants, even factory workers, to make a permanent home beyond the urban edge, in "the country." Undeveloped farmland outside the city was cheap and plentiful. In many regions west of the Mississippi the new car-based development template was handily imposed on a perfectly empty landscape — it was the only living arrangement they would ever know.

The new automobile suburbs allowed the spaces between the streetcar lines to be filled in. This occurred rapidly through the 1920s, and before long the competition for supremacy of the roadway between public trolleys and private cars ended in favor of the automobile. The streetcar age turned out to be very brief, and the wonderfully elaborate linked transit systems, which included the interurban light rail lines, were deliberately destroyed, in many cases, or allowed to wither away, representing a tremendous loss of capital investment that was written off as the price of progress. An arrant conspiracy by General Motors, Firestone, and others to buy up and destroy streetcar systems was later successfully prosecuted in the courts, but the destruction couldn't have occurred without a firm public consensus behind it. Americans wanted to go their own way and the car allowed them to do it.

The suburban building boom after the First World War was the impetus for the bubble economy of the roaring twenties. When that ended in tears with the crash of 1929 and a lingering crisis in the banking sector, the building trades were the industries hardest hit. The government ramped up great public works such as dams, parks, and roadways to stimulate the depressed economy, but very little in the private sector got built during the Great Depression, most particularly new suburban housing. Oil fell to under a dollar a barrel but money was extremely scarce and capital for lending was restricted. The suburban project lay suspended through the 1930s, and the Second World War kept it on ice through most of the 1940s.

In the awful wars and convulsions that racked the twentieth century, the United States escaped destruction due to the simple geographical luck of being insulated from the action by two oceans. We entered the Second World War in a depression and emerged from it perfectly positioned to dominate world trade and manufacturing for decades to come. Our factories, oil fields, and coal mines were untouched. We could make anything and lend our vanquished enemies and bankrupt allies money to buy whatever we made. By the mid-1950s we felt financially secure for the first time in decades. The suburban expansion resumed with a vengeance. Suburbia was the present we gave ourselves for surviving the depression and winning the war. It was a gift that kept on giving, too, in the sense that the more suburbia we built, the more a new economy elaborated itself in the activities needed to sustain it.

A victorious general, Dwight Eisenhower, moved into the White House in 1953. The lingering war production mentality animated a highly regimented workforce of battle-hardened young men mustered out of the military. For many, who had grown up in the Depression, this was their first experience of a normal peacetime economy and they were highly motivated to ride the new wave of prosperity. Interstate highway building got under way in 1955, the greatest public works project ever attempted, opening vast new frontiers of real estate development beyond every urban fringe. Men such as William Levitt learned to turn out little Cape Cod–style bungalows as if they were armored personnel carriers and then named new towns after themselves. (Housing subdivisions, of course, were not towns in any previously known sense, but rather one-dimensional monocultures organized under the rules of single-use zoning, itself a highly abstract, diagrammatic, and inorganic methodology for organizing the landscape in a regime of cheap oil.)

Alfred Taubman, son of a Midwestern failed fruit farmer, soon pioneered the suburban shopping mall, a monoculture of commerce that would obviate the need to visit the old city center to go shopping or watch a movie. The profit potential in all this was out of this world. The unlovable old cities of the industrial heartland were dingy and dreary after two decades of depression and war, and many fell deeper into decay even as their hinterlands boomed. Cleveland, Detroit, St. Louis, Milwaukee, Kansas City, and many other cities entered declines so severe they would seem virtually terminal. The cult of technological progress had the public convinced that the suburban template was the superior way to live, the envy of the world, the rectified essence of democracy and American exceptionalism. They had no idea how provisional it all was.

The High Tide

The more that people and investment fled the cities, the worse those cities got and the more self-evidently normal and desirable suburban life seemed in the dominant collective imagination. It was a classic self-reinforcing feedback loop in which bad conditions multiply negative outcomes. Those left behind in the industrial cities happened to be the people who had migrated there last, namely a generation of agricultural peasants who had fled the southern United States after the development of the mechanical cotton picker in the late 1940s. They were not all African American but the demographic was heavily weighted that way. They came to places such as Cleveland and Detroit to work in heavy industry and within a couple of decades those factories were shutting down. Thus they not only faced the successive dissolution of two economic systems—sharecropping and then factory labor—they also successively endured the failure first of their rural way of life and then their urban way of life, until nothing was working out for them. It is perhaps from the trauma associated with these misfortunes that the behavior we associate with the ghetto had arisen, including high levels of drug and alcohol abuse, unstable family relations, and violent crime; it was just as much of a self-reinforcing feedback loop as the rise of suburbia: bad conditions generating more bad conditions.

By the 1960s it is unclear whether Americans actually loved the new postwar suburbs or had just made the best of a freakish accident of history that had placed so many of them in it. In any case, a dynamic system evolved so quickly it became an overwhelming juggernaut and Americans submitted to it, even merged their national identity with it. The reciprocal relations between the builders, the bankers, the municipal planning officials, and the road builders were fine-tuned to deliver maximum profit and to defeat any other method of building new things, so that the suburban development pattern came to seem by many to be mandated by God, an implacable force of nature, unopposable, the fundamental reality of the times.

There was no evading the necessity of car ownership. After 1960 public transit ranged from laughable to nonexistent in many places. If you wanted to function normally, you'd better have a car . . . end of story. Increasingly, suburban families were induced to own two cars, in theory one for each adult in the household, making revolving install-ment loans (i.e., loans that were never fully paid off) a standard acces-sory of the life. The suburban package of a single-family house on a quarter-acre lot seemed like a good deal. It was affordable. You could heat it economically enough on America's own oil. There was light, air, birdsong, the chance to plant some flowers, grass for a dog to run around on. The kids had their own play space—though beyond the age of seven, when healthy children need to interact with a wider world, the tract housing layouts would constrict their personal development.

Most of all, the suburbia of the 1960s seemed safe and predictable for the people who bought into it, and especially for those who built it, sold it, and financed it. The procedures were all worked out and operating smoothly. The school buses ran on time, the real estate values increased steadily, if not dramatically, over the years. The predictability made it easy to swap property during the frequent compulsory moves from one job to another, so that the suburban asteroid belts of Kansas City, for instance, were composed of the same beige split levels as those suburbs in the outlands of Baltimore. This featureless flattening of everyday life was accepted, even celebrated, as the growth medium for the vaunted consumer economy. It didn't make for much of a life but it kept itself going and, given the vicissitudes of recent history, apparently that was not so bad.

The End of the Road

Going back to the early postwar period, suburban life was mocked and disparaged even by those who lived in it, though the exact reason was never very clearly articulated. The reason was that suburbia never did amount to what it promised, what it advertised itself to be: country liv-ing. It evolved from a simulacrum of country living, an unsatisfactory substitute for it, into something worse: a cartoon of country living, a simulacrum with all the sincerity and conviction leached out of it. In its worst incarnations it became a cartoon of country living in a cartoon of a house in a cartoonized rural landscape. The fraudulence increased steadily and insidiously over the years as all the details of design, assembly, and marketing got stripped down to their most elemental signifiers until almost nothing in the whole picture signified anything real—including the eleven-dollar plastic eagle over the garage door, which any sentient soul would have to regard as the final insult.

It was no small matter that these cartoon habitats evolved into places not worth caring about. But after many years the ambient falsity of it all apparently ceased to matter to a public subject to incessant attempts to manipulate its moods and appetites. Many people simply stopped caring that they didn't care about the places where they lived. The vacuum of meaninglessness could be filled with consumer products, not just big flashy toys such as cars and boats but the thousands of putative necessities of daily life.

In the early post–World War II period men were kept busy enough in the role of breadwinner, ensuring the flow of products and services into their American Dream households. By the 1960s, though, many women had reached the harsh conclusion that overseeing a household of labor-saving appliances was not as satisfying as advertised. For one thing, the appliances did not save much labor. Vacuum cleaners seemed nifty, actually even indispensible in houses lined with wall-to-wall carpets (another postwar novelty), but you still had to run the damn thing all around the house and it was rather tiresome work. Laundry was advertised to be "a snap" using a mechanical washer and dryer, but then there was the whole job of sorting, folding, and ironing. Hadn't it been easier a generation earlier to just stuff a bag with dirty clothes and bring it over to the commercial laundry down the street? Or, better yet, have them pick it up and deliver it? Now the revolution in home appliances was under way (boosting the GDP!) and creating new jobs in manufacturing, marketing, transport, and sales. The diminishing returns of this bustling economy expressed themselves insidiously. In suburbia, everyone was induced to run the equivalent of a commercial laundry in each house, and each housewife was its sole employee. Some of them began to notice that this was not what they'd bargained for. The more affluent "homemakers" who could afford maids were left with something even more dismaying than drudgery: a vortex of purposelessness. The more intelligent among them chafed angrily at the program and the set of vapid obligations and diversions ranging from PTA meetings to Tupperware parties that made up the consolation prize. It's interesting to note that the rebellion against all this, loosely called "women's liberation," coincided perfectly with the exact moment when it became imperative for women to quit the housewife role and join the workforce anyway. This was the period, entering the 1970s, when wages through much of the middle class began to stagnate and it was no longer possible to operate a household on the income of one adult. It was the point where even two wage earners might not cover household costs and the difference was made up in the assumption of ever increasing debt loads. This was also the decade when the divorce rate doubled and women found themselves living in single-parent households, a misfortune that turned the entire mythos of the suburban happy family utopia into a sick joke, especially for children.

At the more practical level, suburbia presented an array of short-comings that had not existed in the traditional urban or rural milieu. People without cars could not get around this environment. Without the assistance of the family chauffeur (mom), children were marooned in the housing monocultures. For kids between eight and, say, seventeen (when full motoring privileges were conferred by the DMV), the hours out of school became a prison of restriction (not that school was much better but that's another story). Suburban children did not get to casually circulate in the places of commerce and work, that is, the realm of what we think of as normal human life. They did not see adults going about their daily business, as previous generations of kids had. As the geographical spaces rapidly filled in with ever more subdivisions and strip malls, even the scraps of undeveloped landscape were erased as casual play areas. Boys especially were prevented from the adventures of roaming and discovery that are so crucial to their development as sovereign personalities. They could not easily venture beyond the obstacles of the six-lane connector boulevards; even if they did, what was there to discover besides the parking lots and other bewildering subdivisions of identical houses? Too often, on perfectly sunny afternoons, they were relegated to television and its menu of stupid fantasies—increasingly grandiose and supernatural as the decades went by—and the everyday reality of society faded further into the shadows.

Is it no wonder the first generation of suburban children, the so-called baby boomers, retreated into mind-altering drugs? And it was not surprising that the boomers then programmed their own children with so many organized activities, from soccer leagues to music lessons, to keep them relentlessly busy. Meanwhile, the magic of spontaneity was programmed out of them, replaced by the sociopathic labyrinths of commercial video gaming, premature sexual titillation, and an unhealthy preoccupation with status and dominance. The emulation of occupational roles—say, wanting to be a fireman—was supplanted by predatory fantasies of having superpowers to hunt down and destroy other people or blow things up.

For adults, especially those who had actually been raised in authentic towns and neighborhoods or genuine rural settings, the suburbs induced an anxiety around the missing sense of community, a vague complaint nonetheless felt keenly among those who perhaps could not articulate it more precisely. Surely a lot of this derived from the sheer physical disaggregation of activities mandated under single-use zoning. Just as a child could not casually roam or meet his friends without a formal playdate arranged by adults, a grown person could not stroll down to a corner pub or café and spend time casually with adults from outside the family. And not just for their personal mental health.

When you reflect on Tocqueville's notes about the rich associational nature of American life in the 1830s, the social poverty of suburbia in our time becomes more impressive, not to mention the impoverishment of politics in a democracy as face-to-face association was replaced by the coercive mechanisms of political advertising piped through television into the home. So it is fair to say that this broadly sensed loss of community is in effect a loss of association. Suburbia, despite its own advertising, proved to be a very lonely place.

Another loss was the demise of locally based economies that characterized the pre-suburban operations of all towns, villages, and neighborhoods in which the adults often played two roles: a business role and a social one. The fine-grained networks of economic interdependency were ceded to the national chains, and with that went the taking of responsibility for other people and for material things in a community. In traditional towns, local merchants had taken care of the buildings they did business in, as well as the one they lived in. Local businessmen employed local people and directly supported local institutions from Little League to libraries. Their realm of responsibility extended beyond their own families and their authority was not subject to myriad potential litigation. The loss of these relations—too often lumped into a shallow conception called "the patriarchy"—accounts for a range of social disorders from the inability to construct credible political agendas to the failed personal development of young men into responsibly honest adults.

Yet another problem with suburbia—related to its unworthiness of affection—was its horrifying mutability. Suburbs changed so dramatically from one year to the next that adults came home to find the places where they grew up unrecognizable, and almost always for the worse, often because some beloved patch of woods or other vestige of original landscape had finally yielded to the bulldozers. Life is precarious enough and there are some things in this world about which people need to feel a sense of permanence. Familial love and a place called home probably top the list, and we became a whole nation of souls whose home places were lost or mutilated beyond recognition. This sad condition, so common now, has surely worked even to the detriment of family relations, so that we've succeeded in undermining the two elements most crucial to healthy functioning personalities: place and family. It's ironic that as our home places became consistently mutating suburban cartoons (places less and less worth caring about), the word "home" slyly came to replace "house" in the jargon of the real estate industry so that one no longer had to consider the larger context of where that home happened to exist.

A lagging consequence of this horrifying mutability was the rise of nimbyism, the "not in my backyard" revolt against further development of any established place once a certain threshold had been reached. By the 1980s the very concept of development, as in *land* development, had taken on negative connotations. The public distrusted anything new, for the excellent reason that practically everything delivered in the second half of the twentieth century by the development industry was, in one way or another, ugly, degrading, insulting, or meaningless. In particular, new houses, even expensive ones, slapped together by the so-called production home builders in hundred-unit batches, were artifacts so obviously lacking in conviction that they gave neighbors the heebie-jeebies — even neighbors who lived in houses identically graceless. They didn't want another new one built anywhere near them.

The good news is that it's over. We're done. The suburban project is now complete. America does not know it and will not believe it until way beyond the point where it is self-evident. The people in the industries that brought us suburbia, especially, will resist the recognition that it's over. As I write, well into the compressive deflationary depression that I call the long emergency, the production home builders, the realtors, the municipal planning officials, the mortgage lenders are all waiting on the sidelines for this fugitive thing they call "the bottom" to be "in." By that they mean the point where the collapse in real estate prices, begun in 2005, will have reached its lowest limit and begun to climb back up the slope of hope toward a glorious new day of rising house prices and returning business activity, including a full-bore resumption of suburban expansion.

They wait in vain. But the psychological hangover is understandable. Given the deeply ingrained habits and practices of these industries for more than half a century, Americans can hardly conceive of building a human habitat differently.

The Destiny of Suburbia

The New Urbanists attempted a severe reformation of suburbia for two decades beginning in the 1990s. They were a group of architects, builders, visionary land developers, academics, municipal officials, and urban theorists, led by a cohort of baby boomers including Andrés Duany and Elizabeth Plater-Zyberk, Stefanos Polyzoides, Elizabeth Moule, Peter Calthorpe, Raymond Gindroz, Victor Dover, and Léon Krier, among others, who had grown up with the sickening spectacle of the voracious suburbs gobbling up the landscape, and with America's cities and towns rotting away, and were determined to do something about it. They formed an official professional group in 1993, the Congress for the New Urbanism, and undertook dozens of demonstration projects across the land to make their point that Americans could live in much better designed, more satisfying, walkable neighborhoods if they paid some attention to principle, tradition, and common sense rather than just relying on the rigorous stupidities of the embedded building and zoning codes.

The demonstration projects they collaborated on, from whole new towns such as Seaside, Florida, to substantial downtown rehabilitation projects such as Winter Park, Florida, and "downcity" Providence, Rhode Island, were wonderful achievements. But their greatest contribution was in the retrieval of lost information concerning the design and assembly of places worth caring about and worth living in. For two decades they engaged in a fierce ideological battle with the conventional suburban developers, as represented, for instance, by the rival professional group called the Urban Land Institute, which Andrés Duany constantly referred to in public as "the United Lemmings Institute." The whole planning officialdom of America resisted, and the mandarins of architecture disdained these new urbanists as reactionaries, though nothing had come to be as retrograde as stultifying offshoots of postmodernism.

Less than one percent of all the things built in those twenty years could be described as New Urbanist, but their projects got a lot of attention and, saleswise, uniformly outperformed conventional suburban projects in comparable locations. Sadly, as their work gained attention they were also co-opted by wannabes and fakers who applied a few New Urbanist elements to otherwise conventional subdivisions without fully understanding the principles of good design in any coherent way, and the results of those projects damaged the movement's reputation.

Ultimately, the New Urbanists won the ideological war but lost personally and professionally when the housing bubble economy tanked beginning in 2005. Not a few of them had hitched their fortunes to the production home builders in ambitious projects on large tracts of land that were, in effect, suburban subdivisions reconfigured as new towns. Some of them were excellent creations, but they came in for a lot of criticism, especially from environmentalists, for being "greenfield" development—that is, for popping up on meadows, cornfields, and forests. To some extent, the New Urbanists were hostages to the practices of their time, especially to the paradigm of perpetual growth, which expressed itself as continual expansion of human settlement into rural territories. History will probably show that they were a transitional movement, a bridge between the profligate Happy Motoring age and the radical change of behavior that followed when the perpetual growth model turned into contraction.

The housing bubble ended up subsuming what was left of the economy after manufacturing eloped elsewhere. In effect, the building of ever more suburbia became the basis of the U.S. economy from about 1990 on. We lied to ourselves saying we had a "postindustrial" economy, an "information" economy, a "service" economy, and so on, but what we really had was a suburban sprawl-building economy, including all the accessories and furnishings that came with it. Since suburbia had to be understood by definition as a way of life with no future, all that activity represented a massive misinvestment in more stuff with no future. How tragic was that? Even the shenanigans on Wall Street involving mortgage-backed securities and derivative-related swindles were made possible in the first place by a seemingly endless supply of new chumps signing contracts for mortgages that were unlikely to be paid. Meanwhile, the originators and underwriters of all these nonperforming loans made fortunes pawning off the dodgy debt to hapless investors in every corner of the globe, from pension funds in faraway lands desperate for yield, to their fellow underwriters the banks themselves (e.g., Lehman Brothers, which choked to death on mortgage-backed securities and their derivative offshoots in 2008).

Why any of these institutions held on to these toxic securities is anybody's guess. There may have been just too much of the stuff to pawn off on suckers before the racket came to grief in the end-of-musical-chairs summer of 2008. Perhaps the banks were hoping to collect on credit default swaps, positions that amounted to bets against each other's real estate–derived securities, only to find themselves stuck in a daisy chain of swindles so hopelessly interconnected that they could trigger a banking Armageddon of cascading defaults if, after a certain point, a single claim were ever made on the obligations concerned. So the banks lobbied for the TARP bill—the infamous bailouts of 2008–9—and allowed the Federal Reserve to vacuum up a hefty portion of the bad paper, with no legal requirements to truthfully report what was held stashed deep in their vaults.[2] There, so many of the bad mortgages and their evil derivative spawn reside to this day, though the too-big-to-fail bank holding companies still have plenty left in their own vaults. In some dim future, bottom feeders will vie to purchase all these impaired so-called investments for pennies on the dollar and then they will comb the landscape to see about the foreclosed properties these defaulted mortgages represent and deal with the people squatting in them. It will be a hazardous business, but there is no shortage of tough guys and shakedown artists in this world. And it may be a better sort of employment than the hard agricultural labor that awaits so many unprepared for the shocking changes ahead.

As I write in 2011, banks are broadly ignoring foreclosures in order to avoid declaring losses on their books and thus facing the wrath of the regulators, who could close them down if their balance sheets show impairment. Many suburban denizens are taking advantage of the situation by living free for years in houses they no longer own or pay rent on. How long that continues is unknown, but if it goes on indefinitely it would tend to fatally subvert both the rule of law and the functioning of a financial system. One way or another it removes the responsibilities of ownership from the picture. It suggests that things will fall apart and people will walk away. The case is similar for commercial real estate in foreclosure, though the retail tenants of failed strip malls generally do not stick around. Questions of title also linger ominously due to the multiple resale of mortgages bundled into bonds. Your mortgage may be the property of a civil service pension fund in Denmark. Or, worse, no one may be able to locate it at all. The sorting out of legal disputes surrounding these issues could take forever and meantime the uncertainty as to who owns what will be yet another thing subverting

2. As a result of a Freedom of Information Act lawsuit brought by the Bloomberg News organization, it was discovered in October of 2011 that total bailouts to banks in the crisis months of 2008–9 (including foreign banks) had amounted to $7.7 trillion.

the rule of law, the functioning of the economy, and the legitimacy of American institutions. The process has only begun, and a nation that identifies itself as suburban by birthright is going to resist the collapse of its favored living arrangement, at least psychologically, even in the face of obvious systemic failure.

Suburban living was a comfortable way to inhabit the landscape while conditions were right, and when the conditions that made it possible change, that will be the end of it. It doesn't matter whether people liked it, though this has been the pro-suburbia position of the public intellectuals Professor Robert Bruegmann, urban theorist Joel Kotkin, and right-wing anti-environmentalist (from *Forbes* magazine) Peter Huber, who argued repeatedly over the years that suburbia would prevail because Americans seemed to like it. The fatuous circularity of their reasoning itself said a lot about the quality of American intellectual life of our time: a species of thinking that guaranteed the complete failure to address the problems we had created for ourselves.

One way or another, we're facing a dramatic demographic shift as the age of cheap oil and easy credit morphs into the long emergency. Lots of people will be moving from one part of the country to other regions. I covered this in detail in my 2005 book and will not reiterate it here except to say we will be inhabiting the terrain of North America in a different way. If we are lucky, we will redevelop towns and cities that are more compact, dense, and integral (mixed use) than in their current incarnations. Most of our settlements were founded on sites of geographical importance, and many will remain important. The coastal harbors may drown due to climate change (assuming it heads in the direction of global warming and not toward an ice age) but the towns along our inland waterways will still be here, and as globalism dwindles and our economies are forced to shift for themselves they will regain roles that were lost, or given up on, in our time. They will become centers again for trade in this or that commodity, and we will find ways to make things in many of them too.

Other writers often remark on how relatively new everything is in North America compared to other lands, how recently our cities were built, how fresh the nonnative imprint on the land is, how quickly the whole gosh darn extravaganza came together into its righteous cruising-for-burgers glory. Right. This isn't Europe, with its echoes of Greece and Rome, or China, with its plangent memories of the old dynasties, or India, where time actually seems to have slipped its bonds altogether. Nathaniel Hawthorne, for instance, griped about the absence of palpable history to hang his prose artistry on, though he did a pretty good job with the paltry materials at hand in the form of the Puritan saga and prerevolutionary Massachusetts. The wonderful American painters of the mid-nineteenth century despaired over the lack of material ruins and journeyed to Italy to marvel at and paint the crumbling aqueducts and remnants of the classical orders. It's perhaps a little disappointing that our ruins, in contrast, will be the Kmarts and the hamburger shacks of various persuasions. It ought to be embarrassing, shameful even, but I rather expect the nostalgia for it all to wax pretty thick and gooey. That is, if we retain any capacity at all to remember it.

THREE

CITIES OF THE FUTURE: YESTERDAY'S TOMORROW OR TOMORROW'S YESTERDAY?

How You May Live and Travel in the City of 1950

Future city streets, says Mr. Corbett, will be in four levels: The top level for pedestrians; the next lower level for slow motor traffic; the next for fast motor traffic, and the lowest for electric trains. Great blocks of terraced skyscrapers half a mile high will house offices, schools, homes, and playgrounds in successive levels, while the roofs will be aircraft landing-fields, according to the architect's plan

I love those cities-of-the-future illustrations from the old pop culture bin. They always get things so wonderfully wrong in *yesterday's tomorrow*.

One of my favorites, from the August 1925 issue of *Popular Science Monthly*, depicts a heroic cross section of New York's Park Avenue looking south from around Forty-seventh Street in the far-off sci fi future of 1950. "Aircraft landing fields" are denoted on the roof of a building that has replaced the familiar Grand Central Station tower at the end of the vista, and it's not the former Pan Am (now Met Life) building either. A zeppelin hovers over a row of quaint airplanes stashed up there. Park Avenue itself has become a pedestrian mall, not a honking Checker cab in sight. They're all down in a three-level underground tunnel system: one level for "slow motor traffic," one for fast, and the lowest for trains and subways. "Spiral escalators" connect all the levels to the street above and turntable-equipped parking garages occupy the basements of the "half a mile high" skyscrapers that line the avenue. It's not clear exactly how all those people up on vehicle-free Park Avenue hail a cab.

The illustration is a beautifully rendered black-and-white lithograph and the layout of this future New York is impeccably rational down to the pneumatic "freight tubes" in the lowest subbasement of the buildings. It expresses every wish of its era about optimal city life to absolute perfection, the engineered efficiency breathtaking. Of course, this vision didn't come to pass. Among other things, it failed to anticipate the effects of the Great Depression, the Second World War, and the massive shift to suburbia afterward, which decanted so much wealth (and so many well-off citizens) out of the cities. About the only thing it got right was that the buildings lining Park Avenue would eventually become a lot bigger.

Another favorite of mine in this genre, from the mid-1950s portraying the far-off year 2000, depicts a city of towers cut through with swooping superduper highways. So far, so good. It could be Houston or Atlanta today. The amusing part is that the cars depicted all have giant tail fins because people were cuckoo for tail fins that year. So, naturally, the future would be all about tail fins!

In other words, most visions of the future are in fact less about the future and more about what's happening now. Extrapolation tends toward exaggeration of what we already know. Today, there are two such basic themes competing in the collective imagination: the dazzling megacity of megastructures, Dubai on steroids, let's say, versus something I'll call Thanatopolis, the city of the dead, of androids, zombies, vampires—various transhumans—and of ashes, ruins, and remnants (*Blade Runner*, *City of Men*, *The Book of Eli*, et cetera). At some risk of making the same mistakes, I will now venture to lay out my own version of how we'll inhabit the landscape going forward a few decades or so. It must be obvious that this question is tied into some pretty urgent issues of our time—climate change, peak oil, ecological destruction, the crisis of banking and money, population overshoot, war. Add to this the virtual certainty of the nonlinear playing out of events and you're soon in the realm of pure conceit. But assuming the human race will carry on (and I do) we'll have to live somewhere, and in some manner, and lots of plans are being made now anyway. So as someone who has written three previous books on the subject of cities and suburbs, I'll toss in my two cents.

No More More, No Bigger Bigger

I depart from a lot of current thinking on the subject. For instance, many people seem to think that there will be more of everything—more people, taller skyscrapers, bigger airplanes, more slums, larger metro regions. I don't go along with this bundle of ideas at all. Conditions will not be the same everywhere in the world, of course. But I think the general theme going forward, certainly in the United States, will be contraction. We are heading into a major reset of daily life, a phase of history I have been calling *the long emergency*.

I see our cities getting smaller, denser, with fewer people, and lower, with the skyscraper obsolete, travel greatly reduced, and the rural edge growing more distinct. The energy inputs to our economies will decrease. A lot. And probably in ways that prove very destabilizing. The first manifestations of climate change will be food shortages, and these will quickly affect the arc of world population growth downward, from the poorer margins inward to the developed center, with stark implications for politics and civil order. The crisis of money is already hampering the operation of cities and soon will critically impede the repair of water systems, paved streets, bridges and tunnels, electric service, and other vital infrastructure. Tomorrow will be a whole lot more like yesteryear in terms of comforts, the range of commerce, and scale.

A major theme of mine over the years has been the fiasco of suburbia, where more than half of the U.S. population lives. It was not produced by a conspiracy but because it seemed like a good idea at the time, given the confluences of history. But now its time has gone by. The global oil predicament and accompanying disorders of capital formation will finish it off, probably sooner rather than later. Laying aside the fine points of its design shortcomings, the logistical drawbacks will leave suburbia harshly devalued. That process is already under way in the aftermath of the housing bubble. In the past decade house buyers were told to "drive till you qualify," meaning far enough into the exurban asteroid belts where land was still cheap and you could borrow enough mortgage money to buy something. Those are exactly the houses that are now losing value the fastest as the long-term prospects for motoring dim.

All suburbs have a problematic destiny. Some will do better than others, based on idiosyncrasies of geography and politics. Some will be retrofitted into towns and villages. I don't think many will be transformed into garden communities—Beaver Cleaver meets Mr. Green Jeans—because a shortage of money for police and other services could easily lead to problems with public safety, food theft, and people's health. Suburbia's characteristic lack of civic armature suggests a lack of community cohesion to compensate for government service failures when trouble starts. I expect many suburbs will become slums, ruins, and salvage yards because we will have to reuse many materials that were energy intensive to make, all kinds of stuff, ranging from aluminum trusses to concrete blocks to Sheetrock to screw fasteners.

A lot of young people already have no use or affection for suburbia, and they've been moving into the big cities for a while. When our problems with energy get more traction, look for some surprising changes in the trend. A recognition that a whole new disposition of things is under way will prompt demographic shifts into our smaller cities and small towns, especially places that have some relationship with the local food production, water power, and water transport. Our smaller cities and towns are scaled better for the energy realties of the future. Most of these places are in sad shape now after decades of disinvestment, but they are sitting there waiting to be repopulated and reactivated.

Farming will require much more human attention than in the era now ending when roughly 2 percent of the population produces all the food for everyone else. This agricultural landscape will be organized differently, with smaller farms. More people will live on or near them. We'll run fewer big machines and have access to less fossil fuel liquids. We may have to use more working animals again, and they'll need care and feeding—lots of acreage will have to be devoted to growing their feeds. Food production will come closer to the center of our economy than it has for generations.

Meanwhile, our big metroplex cities will get into as much trouble as the suburbs, but for somewhat different reasons. Categorically, they are not scaled to the energy realities of the future. Our giant cities are products of the cheap energy age. The arc of their explosive growth since 1945 is self-evident. At present they're simply too large and too complex. Everything about them is designed to run on endless supplies of cheap fossil fuels and the resources and by-products made possible by them: steel, copper, cement, plastic, asphalt. They require long supply chains keyed to complex transport systems in order to support daily life. We are entering an era of reduced complexity and many of the systems we depend on now, from factory farming to the warehouse-on-wheels, just-in-time goods distribution method, won't exist anymore.

These large complex cities will contract and densify around their old centers, and around their waterfronts, if they are lucky to have them. Remember, cities generally exist where they do because they occupy important geographical sites: rivers, harbors, rail lines, and places of strategic importance, for instance, Detroit's position on a short stretch of river between two great lakes. Some kind of human settlement will continue to exist in most of these places, but not in exactly the form we're familiar with. They will be urban in the traditional sense of the word, compact, dense, mixed-use, composed of neighborhoods based on the quarter-mile walk from center to edge, the five-minute walk, a transcultural norm found everywhere in preautomobile urban areas. The pattern is scalable. One neighborhood is the equivalent of a village, several neighborhoods and a commercial district make a town, and many neighborhoods will make up a city—not necessarily a big one. What I describe is not a diagrammatic, abstract urban theory. It is essentially traditional urban design based on successful historical precedent. Rather, it is our recent experience with the cheap energy megacity that is anomalous.

The decline of cheap fuels will lead straight to the demise of the trucking system and commercial aviation. Forget about biodiesel, algae oil, and similar fantasies. They don't scale up beyond the "science project" level. We'll have to move more stuff (and people) by rail and boat. Waterfronts and harbors will become much more important in daily life, and in North America this applies especially to our inland waterways, the linked Mississippi and Missouri and Ohio rivers, the most extensive network in the world, plus the St. Lawrence, the Hudson / Erie canal system, and the Great Lakes. The inland waterways will be threatened less by changes in sea level than the saltwater harbors and, as the global economy withers, economic activity is likely to become much more internally focused.

It remains to be seen what climate change will do to the great ocean port cities. New York, San Francisco, Boston, and Baltimore have some topography to protect them, even though they could lose a lot of real estate if sea levels rise significantly. The picture is a lot swampier for Miami, Jacksonville, Charleston, Norfolk, New Orleans, and Houston. For decades we've been redeveloping America's decrepit waterfronts with condo towers, festival marketplaces, concert stages, bikeways, and other lifestyle attractions that will prove to have been tragic misallocations of capital. Now, we have to go back and restore the infrastructure for waterborne trade: the landings, the warehouses, dry docks, even the sleazy accommodations for sailors. Places such as Pittsburgh, Cincinnati, St. Louis, Kansas City, as well as many other currently sclerotic cities will regain relative importance, though I emphasize they will probably do it at a smaller scale than before now.

A number of newer U.S. cities occupy unfavorable sites and they will just go out of business. Phoenix will collapse without mass motoring and cheap air-conditioning. You can't grow food there without heroic irrigation efforts and all its water comes from elsewhere and at great expense. Over in Las Vegas the excitement will be over for the same reasons. Plus, it will be a hard place to get to for a hard-up population. I'd even go so far as to predict that the American people will eventually be disgusted by the notion that it's possible to get something for nothing, and that gambling will once again become a marginal activity, perhaps even illegal in many places. Denver exists in the first place only because of the logistics of cattle ranching and railroads and mining operations that are now played out. If the Southwest gets drier, as predicted, that city may wither. Its proximity to the winter sports nirvana of the Rocky Mountains will lose appeal also, for skiing is strictly a cheap-oil sport.

The cities that are composed largely of suburban sprawl face a less fortunate future as well. That's most of what exists in the Sunbelt, the part of the United States that grew explosively after the Second World War. Atlanta, Orlando, Dallas, Houston, Charlotte, and other sprawl cities are hugely disadvantaged. On top of a bad development pattern, recent construction quality is atrocious—chipboard, vinyl, and "innovative" spray-on stucco finishes. In the humid Southeast air-conditioning vies with the heat on exterior walls to condense moisture in the framing and buildings rot from the inside out. Mold and mildew can render them uninhabitable. In Florida, foreclosed houses left unlived in are often ruined in months as humidity infiltrates the Sheetrock and toxic mold grows. People who seek refuge in the Sunbelt states once our energy problems get under way in earnest may be disappointed by how things work out there. As air-conditioning becomes incrementally unaffordable to broad classes of Americans, perhaps even unavailable, Sunbelt city denizens will rediscover how punishing their climate is and why these places were backwaters of civilization until fairly recently.

Since the wealth of these newer cities is represented largely by sprawl, much political and financial capital will be tragically squandered trying to prop it up, amounting to a futile campaign to sustain the unsustainable. It's already happening in enormous government financial life support to the housing industry and stimulus dollars poured into highway projects, instead of going toward fixing the passenger rail network or developing local public transit.

Southern California is in a category of its own, with dire water politics on top of the liabilities of suburban sprawl and a simmering demographic stew of contesting ethnic groups. Much has been made of the relatively high population density of Los Angeles, which owes more to statistical legerdemain than to niceties of urban design. There are pockets of LA that have appealing urban qualities, though these are somewhat deceptive. For instance, the streets of West Hollywood between Santa Monica Boulevard and Melrose Avenue (east of La Cienega) contain many multiunit buildings (some quite handsome) generally under five stories (good!) that stand shoulder to shoulder on blocks well detailed with sidewalks and street trees. It's a dense neighborhood, schematically. But few people actually walk anywhere. The sidewalks are strikingly empty, even during the morning rush hour. Why is that? As it happens, each apartment house is built over its own underground garage so that the residents can zip out to be part of LA's implacable car culture with its armies of parking valets. This cultural habit defeats all the other earnest efforts to compose good urbanism in the city.

LA seems to work okay for the moment but beneath the whirring surface lies a set of disturbing criticalities—just as below all the asphalt pavement lurks a fragile geology of tectonic fault lines. Looking ahead, the city is just too big, too spread out, too car addicted, too thirsty, too primed for ethnic friction, and too dependent on supplies of everything from elsewhere to present a plausible picture in the energy-scarcer economy of the future. A favorable outcome for Los Angeles would be as a network of much smaller municipalities connected by public transit, kind of what LA evolved out of in the first place—except that history is not symmetrical and the sheer inertia of disintegration might drag LA beyond any desirable reset point.

San Diego's position at the Mexican border makes it even more vulnerable to a contest between cultures. First, there will be a fight over who gets to occupy the terrain. After a while it'll become clear that the terrain will not support substantial populations of *any* cultural group. Eventually, Southern California will be a ghost of an urban colossus, just like other lost empires of yore.

The Sky Is No Longer the Limit

One big surprise awaiting us is the recognition that the skyscraper is obsolete. They have already categorically exceeded their sell-by date

but we have not received the message. Even the architecture establishment does not recognize the problem. It's not primarily because
of the issues of heating and air-conditioning, or about running all the
elevators, though electric service may be a lot less reliable in the United
States a decade from now. It's because these buildings will never be
renovated. They have one generation of life in them and then they are
done. Buildings take a beating day after day and eventually all of them
need to be thoroughly renovated. Note that the duration of time from
completion of a building to first renovation has lessened significantly
over the past hundred years due to added complexity and the use of
"innovative" materials whose properties over time—response to stress,
weather, ultraviolet light, and more—are unknown and untried.

Reduced energy supplies means proportionately reduced capital
available for anything. We'll be painfully short of financial resources
and also of fabricated, modular materials—everything from steel to the
silicon gaskets needed to seal glass curtain walls. The cities that are
overburdened with skyscrapers will discover that they are liabilities, not
assets. The skyscrapers deemed most innovative today—the ones most
dependent on high-tech materials and complex internal systems—will
be the most disappointing. This includes many so-called green buildings. Cities cannot be made of buildings that have no potential for
adaptive reuse. We can easily see in this predicament another diminishing return of having lived through an age of cheap energy and easy
miracles: innovative things by nature have no track record of long-term
success, and sometimes don't work out, especially as basic economic
conditions change. Innovation cannot be an end in itself, and we have
made ourselves prisoners to a cult of innovation.

Like suburbia, skyscrapers seemed like a good idea at the time.
Alas, at the time, we never considered the possibility that technological
progress would hit a resource road bump and that so many of what had
become the common benefits of late industrialism might be impossible
to carry on. It's even likely that in the decades ahead work will no longer

be organized in the way that made the skyscraper necessary, as it seemed, let's say, back in the 1990s when the *Economist* cover story proclaimed that the world was "drowning in oil," and Wall Street USA ramped up its operations for the final chapter of massive capital accumulation, and spending one's day in a cubicle sixty stories above the street was, for a large class of people, the most normal thing in the world. As events ride the flux of evolution, we lose track of what reality may afford us, of what "normal" is, until one morning we get up and everything has changed.

In October 2004, *New Yorker* staff writer David Owen published a hugely influential piece called "Green Manhattan." In it Owen wrote, "New York is the greenest community in the United States, and one of the greenest in the world." By this, I suppose, he meant the most ecologically fit. He went on to say that this was due to the various efficiencies of apartment towers and the ability to get around on foot. While I'd agree that dense, walkable urbanism is very important looking ahead, it's a mistake to suppose that stacking people in skyscrapers is a good idea, for reasons I've already stated about that type of structure. Owen's econometric arguments were also too limited to the household energy savings of apartment life versus freestanding houses, as well as the benefits of not driving, and did not include the many other costs of supplying the city of stacked apartment dwellers with food, water, and everything else they need from outside the city limits.

Like Owen, the Harvard economist Edward Glaeser presents a similar view in his 2011 book *Triumph of the City*. His triumphalism is consistent with the techno grandiosity that tragically pervades the places where Americans affect to think these days. Glaeser is wholly oriented toward a rearview mirror theory of history, an extrapolationist who supposes that the future will amount to what we've already got, but much more of it. If anything, he is even more adamant than Owen about the necessity for skyscrapers and nothing but skyscrapers as the only feasible outcome for the urban condition. He sees little value in urban life as represented by, say, the Greenwich Village of Jane Jacobs.

The "triumphant" New York that Glaeser admires so much—home of too-big-to-fail banking, global corporations in fatal over-stretch, and luxurious power lunches for Harvard-based consultants like himself—is already a catastrophe. It has far exceeded the scale of a healthy urban organism to meet the realities of the future. It has suffered deadly hypertrophy something like the unfortunate circus sideshow giant with a runaway endocrine system. It is too big and too tall. It will lose the ability to service and repair its colossal infrastructures or to gather the massive daily inputs of what it requires to keep itself going.

By the way, central Chicago has similar problems. Most other cities in the United States have limited skyscraper districts of a dozen blocks or so, and in most of those—Atlanta, Houston, Minneapolis—the skyscraper districts are sterile and lifeless anyway, especially at night, when the cubicle serfs depart for other quarters. But these tower districts will all fail as infrastructures for daily life. From a strict real estate investment point of view (and within the context of late fossil fuel industrialism) it's easy to understand the economic appeal of skyscrapers. The temptation to maximize profits on the floor-to-area ratio of buildings—the number of stories you can stack on a given building lot—is irresistible. But it had the unintended consequence of producing too many tall buildings with an unsound future. All our big cities will contract, but in cities with lots of skyscrapers this will be especially traumatic. We have no idea what we're going to do about it. There's no public awareness whatsoever.

I saw a preview of coming attractions of this problem in Johannesburg, South Africa, in 2009. The *process* was not the same as the long emergency will be in the United States, but the *outcome* surely was: a city center of dead and dying buildings. When apartheid ended in 1993 and a black African majority government took over administrative power, virtually all of corporate Johannesburg moved out of the old skyscraper district at the center of town and decamped to new, fortified suburban headquarters on the northern fringe of town. The skyscraper district, a collection of 1960s and '70s vintage blocky towers—perhaps comparable in size to downtown Denver, Colorado—came under new ownership and before long turned into a set of vertical slums. The new owners didn't convert the offices into proper apartments, you understand. They just moved poor people into the old office floors with jerry-rigged partitions here and there and the same old bathrooms out in the hallway and casual cooking arrangements with improvised equipment. It was like camping, only in a skyscraper. The people inside could customize their quarters on an ad hoc basis but no ongoing structural building maintenance occurred. Here and there plumbing failed and the inhabitants had to deal with it as best they could, but don't bother calling the landlord. Curtain wall windows fell out occasionally as fasteners and gaskets failed. (Look out below!) The elevators worked erratically, if at all. Imagine trudging upstairs twenty-seven stories when you need to get a few groceries.

One by one, the buildings in downtown Johannesburg got so battered by the rigors of daily use, with no routine maintenance, that they were condemned as public safety hazards. When I was there, several towers stood in desolation, all the copper and other stuff of value stripped out, with razor wire around their ground-floor perimeters to keep people out, though I was told that squatters easily found their way inside; they just had to make do completely without electricity, plumbing, or elevators. The owners of these buildings had no incentive to invest in renovating them for any purpose. There was no sign that corporate tenants wished to return to the city center, and poor slum dwellers couldn't possibly pay enough rent to justify the installation of properly equipped apartments (that is, with a shower, a basic kitchen, and actual rooms). There was no incentive to maintain the buildings up to even the low standards of slum occupancy, nor was it cost effective to demolish the darn things. Operating these structures was the equivalent of strip mining, except instead of extracting wealth from the ground you extract it from a building, until there is no more value to be gotten from it. Finally, the building can only be abandoned, like a played-out open pit copper mine, a liability for future generations to deal with.

The Fantasists

So many of our current city-of-the-future ideas are preposterous fantasies that are only going to disappoint us. For example, consider the proposal called "Aerotropolis" contained in a book by that title published in 2011. The scheme was generated by a professor of business from the University of North Carolina named John D. Kasarda, with writing help from the journalist Greg Lindsay. Kasarda noticed that the Federal Express company revitalized the dying economy of Memphis, Tennessee, two decades ago, so he concluded that any successful city of the future must be organized around an airport. Aerotropolis is yesterday's tomorrow all over again, another rearview vision of things to come that have actually already come and gone. The authors seem to have no idea how the global oil predicament is already affecting commercial aviation, and what that bodes for the future. Airlines in the United States have been contracting for a decade, merging, dropping routes, firing so many employees that it is nearly impossible to find one nowadays in an airport concourse, and having an extremely tough time staying in business. I wouldn't assume that the future of commerce in this country will be all about mail order off the Internet with stuff shipped everywhere in aircraft. It assumes that cheap transport is a reliable constant as far ahead as we can see, which I doubt. It also assumes that the Internet is a permanent fixture in daily life when its fate hinges on absolutely dependable electric service.

The situation is only going to get worse, not better. There's even a fair chance that commercial aviation will not exist at all in twenty years. There are no other known types of airplanes that run on anything besides liquid hydrocarbon aviation fuel. We have fantasies about running them on stuff like distilled coal liquids because, people say, Germany powered the Luftwaffe with coal liquids toward the end of the Second World War. As usual with alt-energy arguments, it's a matter of scale. Running the Luftwaffe through all of 1944–45 probably required less fuel altogether than running trucks in and out of Providence, Rhode Island, during any given week today. Likewise, Virgin Airlines' proposed aim of running its fleet on biofuels in the years ahead is another absurdity conjured up to garner green brownie points. American cities will be lucky in the twenty-first century if they can organize their activities around railroads and waterways. File *Aerotropolis* in the folder labeled "Complete Fucking Nonsense."

Another powerfully silly idea is embodied in the proposal for farming in skyscrapers. Many fantasies are being spun around this notion lately as commodity prices rise steeply against a background of peak oil, overpopulation, failing capital management systems, mass unemployment, and supermarket checkout shock, while people everywhere start to worry about how they will feed their families. Growing more of our food locally is certainly very urgent, but farming in skyscrapers represents a set of misunderstandings about how this might be accomplished. It emanates from basic confusion about how the landscape, and the human habitat within it, is successfully organized. The fiasco of suburbia provoked most of this confusion by muddling the distinction between what was urban and what was rural so completely that we are facing a very uncertain future poorly prepared even to imagine how we might inhabit the planet without killing it altogether or just going out of business as a species. Hence the idea that we should focus our resources on growing food in the center of the city in high-tech towers, so-called vertical farming.

The problems we face with skyscrapers in terms of capital resources argue against this in the first place. Add to that the need to provide either artificial lighting for plants stacked under many layers of ceilings or the energy to mechanically rotate them around the outer walls in order to expose them to sunlight. These methods look particularly dumb when you consider that there is a practical relationship between cities and their agricultural hinterlands in traditional farming, where crops can be grown horizontally, on the earth, without elaborate structures, artificial lighting, or high-tech gadgetry. The vertical farming idea is a demonstration of how extreme our techno grandiosity has become. The wish to resort to techno magic trumps time-tested methods based on knowledge and experience.

The nineteenth-century urban market gardens of Paris occupied 6 percent of the real estate of the city and kept Paris supplied with fresh vegetables year round. The system was composed of plots that averaged less than two acres. It required a lot of human hand labor. It employed cold frames, glass cloches, walls for tempering wind, and large quantities of horse manure—abundantly available in that day—both to fertilize and as a heat source banked under and around cold frame boxes. The system was self-sustaining and called for much thoughtful deployment of material resources, but not what we would consider today high tech in the sense of automated, mechanized, computerized fantasies dependent on lavish quantities of electricity. The Parisian small-plot market garden system was abandoned when mechanical tilling and chemical fertilizers took food production up to greater scale in the early twentieth century, along with the hypergrowth of the city itself, which made centrally located real estate much more profitable for revenue-generating buildings. We are surely headed in the opposite direction now in this period of comprehensive contraction, and we have to rethink the relationship between where we live and how society organizes itself around food production.

Urban dooryard and backyard kitchen gardens are historically quite normal. Roof-top gardening is a fine, traditional practice (though without heroic engineering to deal with the weight of soil and water and the water runoff you'd better stick to growing things in pots). Community gardens on otherwise empty lots are a natural response to underutilized resources, but often they are carried out in a half-assed manner in which most of the produce rots because the labor is disorganized and poorly incentivized (usually for moral, political, or self-esteem purposes) and there are no viable market operations to absorb surplus production. That could very well change in the decades ahead. It is certainly one of the elements of daily life that is well understood, with plenty of precedence.

Yet gardening is not quite farming. The staples of civilizations are grain crops, and these don't lend themselves to the urban garden format. Even when a lot more of our food will have to be grown locally, it will have to come from the agricultural hinterland, outside the center of town. Some activities are essentially rural and some urban, and we need to reestablish the distinction. In any case, all food production will require a lot more human labor, and that may be the vocational destiny for classes of people who are currently idle, restless, bored, and indigent.

Some confusion about these issues shows up lately in the many proposals to turn Detroit into farmland. Detroit is so far gone, people think, that the only conceivable use for all that abandoned real estate is to re-ruralize it. This speaks to our lack of confidence in the urbanism and the broad failures of land-use law and architecture, which proceed from the diminishing returns of overinvestments in complexity. It's not so hard to see where this comes from: the decades-long inability of architecture to provide buildings worthy of our affection; city planners unable to conceive and execute the creation of urban neighborhoods that are worth living in; the environmental movement's focus on wilderness and wildlife and disdain for human activities; and, of course, suburbia itself, which prompts people to categorically despise the human imprint on the landscape. The end result is the fetishization of abstract, cartoonish ideas about nature that dishonor human intelligence and make the future seem fearsome.

Detroit is rotting from the inside out. The inside, the old city center, the part closest to the river, is destined to be the urban site of highest value in the future, even though Detroit will never be exactly the city it was in 1955. We have plenty of skill and knowledge available to make the necessary repairs. We can develop modes of urban gardening that take place without grandiose interventions. And they can be integrated with the world-class farmlands outside Detroit in rural Michigan and elsewhere in the Midwest to support a civilized future. In the meantime we are wasting our dwindling capital and human resources in thrall to preposterous high-tech fantasies.

When Fashion Goes Out of Fashion

The Congress for the New Urbanism coalesced as a formal organization in 1993 as a response to the suburban fiasco, especially as a movement to reform the embedded municipal planning and zoning laws that mandated suburban sprawl all over America. As a combat of ideas, the New Urbanists eventually won by default when the housing bubble bust put an end to the project of suburban sprawl. Since the New Urbanism was always based on traditional practice, it is now simply urbanism, period, though it will take more time for the morphology to sort itself out. So I'll continue to refer to it as the New Urbanism for the sake of this argument. There are no viable alternatives for the design and assembly of places for people to live. There is no other body of coherent principle that can produce human habitats that have a plausible future. Still, sheer human perversity manages to generate opposition from predictable interest groups. Harvard has been battling the New Urbanists for two decades on the grounds that traditional urban design is insufficiently avant-garde, intellectually unadventurous, politically retrograde, nostalgic, technologically naive, and lacking in sex appeal.

The mandarin headquarters of modernist ideology, Harvard's Graduate School of Design (GSD), having gone to war with the New Urbanist movement, is now pushing a dubious new practice called

Landscape Urbanism. Don't be fooled again. Under the fashionable green rubric it's simply another version of the misuse of nature as the default remedy for failed urban places, a rejection of genuine urbanism, per se. It hijacks a sentimental notion of nature in order to hold it hostage on moral high ground for the purpose of status seeking in a moralistic, politically correct culture.

Landscape Urbanism, so called, incorporates lots of high-tech "magic" infrastructure for directing water flows and requires massive, costly, complex site interventions. It's explicitly against density and vehemently pro automobile. In effect, it's just superhigh-tech suburbia in the guise of environmentally avant-garde high art. Its hidden agenda is to generate big fees for site-planning firms (which will employ Harvard GSD graduates, of whom there are too many in the world for available jobs) while it does nothing to prepare this society for a post-oil economy. Naturally it comes with heaps of opaque theory, designed to mystify and impress the nonelect. But the United States doesn't need more architectural fashion statements or high art stunts. It needs places to live that are worth caring about and compatible with the capital and material resources that we can expect to retain access to, which are liable to be fewer and scarcer than what we're used to. The United States doesn't need any more mendacious ideologies meant to confound the public about the operation of cities and the things in them so that star architects ("starchitects") can appear to be a type of wizard genius (and so garner star-power commissions).

The United States *does* need a body of principle and skill that will allow us to assemble places with a future, and the New Urbanists laboriously retrieved this information from the dumpster of history where it was carelessly tossed by two generations in thrall to the phantom of limitless expansion. The New Urbanists recognized the resource limits we are now up against and the threats posed by climate change. They were keenly aware of the need to reintegrate local food production into the landscape in an appropriate relationship with the places where people live. They were the only group of design practitioners on the scene capable of delivering a vision of the future that is consistent with the reality of the future.

Rather than abstract theory, New Urbanist practice is based on principle, that is, on truthful propositions about what human beings require in the way of places to live, and what it is possible to provide them with at a particular point in history. The New Urbanism is especially concerned with the emulation of patterns and relationships in urban design that have a history of success, of producing places that can adapt to economic change and endure through time, in short, places that have a future. The New Urbanism does not indulge in innovation for its own sake, or as a pretense to fashion or high art. By this, don't make the mistake of thinking that the New Urbanism is just about supplying the minimum or that it is only for wealthy people. Those accusations are, curiously, a psychological projection by the guardians of modernism of what they themselves have been supplying the world with for nearly a century, which is why so many people despise despotic modernist architecture and sterile modernist urban environments.

The New Urbanism is not about style—another accusation hurled at it by those preoccupied with style—and certainly not about forcing a nostalgic return to any *particular* historical style. We like our buildings to stand up and remain plumb as long as possible, and many traditional devices of architecture are designed to accomplish that: arches, columns, bays, and such. Human neurology seeks to be satisfied in a sense of being sheltered, in relationships between the inside and the outside as represented by windows, doors, and balconies, in the comfortable proportioning of rooms so that people do not feel cramped, lost in space, buried, or squashed, and to be reminded that the human project is a worthwhile enterprise. Many people, for instance, like a verandah on a house not for the sake of nostalgia but because they like a sheltered place to relax that is connected to the outdoors.

That one might want to decorate the elements of a building is also a well-understood human inclination. Often, what appear to be decorations are practical devices: brackets to support spans, a cornice to direct water away from the walls. (Buildings in the modernist mode and its offshoots are notorious for a basic failure to keep water out.) The decoration of buildings has been worked out in every culture in many styles over many centuries. As a Western culture derived from Greco-Roman roots, ours has some time-tested ways of decorating our building elements. People like to use them because they are proven, understood, and pleasing. There are plenty of other ways to handle the ornamentation of buildings, and many of these were employed in the exuberant style wars of the nineteenth century, what Americans generally refer to when they use the term "Victorian."

Of course, if you are coming from a position that to ornament a building is forbidden, which has been a fundamental rule of modernism dating back to the architect Adolf Loos's declaration that "ornament is a crime" (1908), then naturally any mode of design other than modernist must be ruled out. But the style issue is a canard, flung out by those themselves hopelessly hung up on their own style. In fact, modernist interventions in American cities are the places most in need of repair and rehabilitation, especially now that we face circumstances such as the demise of mass motoring, which implies the obsolescence of a lot of infrastructure that was hooked up to freeways.

In any case, the style argument is just a distraction from the far more important task of how we deploy buildings in meaningful ensembles of streets and blocks in such a way that the activities of everyday life can be optimally carried on. That is what a town or a city is. This task now becomes supremely important as our common car-dependent infrastructures for living fail. We cherish many techno-magic fantasies about this that will leave us disappointed. For instance, it's unlikely that all the functions of everyday life will shift to cyberspace. We have not yet absorbed the lesson that the virtual is not an adequate substitute for the authentic. By the time we do learn this lesson we may find ourselves in a world of far more limited electric service, perhaps none at all, something that is apt to nullify our fantasies about cyberlife. So I would not bet on that future, or anything related to it, such as Internet shopping as a permanent way to do commerce.

I don't think there's any question that we must return to traditional ways of occupying the landscape: walkable cities, towns, and villages, located on waterways and, if we are truly fortunate, connected by rail lines. These urban places will exist on a much smaller scale than what is familiar to us now, built on a much finer grain. They will have to be connected to farming and food-growing places. A return to human scale will surely lead to a restored regard for artistry in building, since the streetscape will be experienced at walking speed. The requirements for this will be fairly straightforward. It will not require "critical theory," as the grad schools style metaphysical thinking these days, but rather practical skill and something like common sense. Too much magic in the futuristic visions of techno rapturists has paradoxically produced places with no magic, no power to enchant the human spirit beyond the awe, often actually sickening, of seeing things made very big, or very high, or very slick. It turns out that the human spirit needs texture, not sleekness in everything, and it needs things human-sized to feel human, and despite all the striving to escape it that is exactly what we're going to get.

FOUR

The Dangers of Techno Narcissism, or: Frankenstein Release 2.0, How Ray Kurzweil's Singularity Aims to Replace the Old God with a New and Improved Version

"Yes, well, we'll have to be careful about that, won't we?"
–R.K.

So as not to be misunderstood about what follows, I need to make a few things clear from the get-go.

I'm not what you might call a religious person and this is not a religious argument. I am not an atheist, and certainly not a crusading one. I don't call myself agnostic, though an auditor might think so. It is true that I was raised in a religion-free household, escaped any sort of childhood indoctrination, and hardly concern myself with metaphysical matters beyond *truth* and *beauty*—making no claims to deep scholarship in them. I don't pretend to be a scientist, either, but I observe that the universe appears to follow some rules and is organized elegantly, perhaps with something we understand to be intelligence.

But that's enough about me. The point here is to discuss Ray Kurzweil and his *singularity* ideas.

Ray Kurzweil is an American computer scientist, inventor, businessman, and futurist. He is a very smart fellow and seems to be a buoyant, happy spirit, with a sense of humor, empathy for other people, and plenty of equipment to be a socially successful human being. He has been involved with an impressive range of techno ventures from optical recognition software and programmable musical instruments (Kurzweil keyboards) to medical products, longevity-promoting nutritional supplements, and popular books about where technology is taking us. We were born in the same year, 1948. I'm not sure we have much else in common.

Ray Kurzweil is an amazing scientific polymath with a record of signal accomplishment, especially as an entrepreneur. He thinks very large thoughts, about as large as one can imagine. He writes pretty well, too, and his book of Really Big Ideas, called *The Singularity Is Near*, made a big splash in 2005 the same year that my own book *The Long Emergency* was published. His book spins out a story about the future of the human race in the twenty-first century (and beyond) that is about as opposed to the ideas in my book about the same period of time as you could possibly find. His credentials suggest that he is a person who must be taken seriously and is not somebody to be mocked, so I am serious and absolutely straightforward when I say that Ray Kurzweil's ideas represent the major leagues of techno grandiosity. They embody what is most purblind about our overinvestments in complexity and the danger we are getting ourselves into as a result. He strikes me as the very soul of a mad scientist. *The Singularity Is Near* is to extreme technophiles what Ayn Rand's *Atlas Shrugged* is to extreme libertarians. I hope, though, that Kurzweil's book does not cause as much mischief in the world as Ayn Rand's book did.

Now, to Kurzweil's ideas. I will try to summarize them and then get into the particulars.

The singularity is the idea that human beings will join with artificial intelligence (AI) in machines and will allow us to transcend biology. Computer AI will multiply exponentially in a very short time, the next half century, and will replicate itself until the solar system is turned on as a kind of cosmic self-aware AI computer, and then this uberintelligence will make another rapid leap and light up the entire universe and by and by it may go down wormholes and light up additional universes until everything you can conceive and way beyond is occupied by human-spawned cybernetic machine intelligence. This will be achieved via genetic engineering, nanotechnology, and robotics, the GNE alliance.

Genetic engineering ought to be self-explanatory. Nanotechnology involves the manipulation of quantum particles—atoms, molecules—into teeny-weeny engineered machines that can be combined, arrayed, and programmed. Robotics is also what it sounds like: machines that perform tasks. If you make robots with nanotechnology you can send tiny machines, nanobots, into human bodies to perform tasks such as repairing organs. They can also (theoretically) perform tasks outside bodies, in what we call the environment, for instance in making solar energy arrays of nanotubes: stacks of atoms with hardly any weight that can be easily deployed above the earth's atmosphere and beam useful energy back here to the surface (again, in theory). Nanobots can be programmed to self-replicate, to make infinite copies of themselves. Eventually, they can permeate the world, the universe, and countless other universes. In the process of all this, human existence (or existence per se) will become a melding of human consciousness and AI until the boundaries between the two dissolve.

(I am reminded here of Kurt Vonnegut's 1963 novel *Cat's Cradle*, in which a mad scientist invents a substance called "ice-nine," which turns any water that it touches into a crystal substance, threatening to destroy all life on earth. The story was meant to frighten readers about runaway technology. I am also reminded here of Myron Scholes, the

Nobel Prize–winning economist who helped build the Long-Term Capital Management fund in the 1990s. Scholes boasted that the supposedly risk-free formulas he had worked out for making money *could not fail in the life of this universe or many universes like it*. LTCM failed inside of forty-eight months and had to be bailed out by a consortium of Wall Street banks.)

The Conundrum of Eternal Life, or: When Is a Worm Hole Like a Rabbit Hole?

In Kurzweil's singularity theory, individual death is considered an avoidable catastrophe. It is probably safe to say that few of us relish the prospect of our own moment of transition to the ether, though it does seem to represent a form of merging back into the essences of the universe, perhaps even a gateway to someplace else. Who knows? In any case, Kurzweil seeks to vanquish death by means of the aforementioned nanotechnology. One of his many businesses sells nutritional supplements aimed at super–life extension. Those of us who manage to keep going for around three more decades will make the cut, so to speak, for eternal life, because by that time, he says, technology will exist to keep us going forever. The regenerative nanobots will be sent forth into our collapsing veins and go to work rebuilding all of our tissues. We will choose to be whatever optimum age we prefer. Do you want the body of an eighteen-year-old? Fine. Want to be a more mature thirty? You pick. It gets better, or at least more complicated. Given the exponential explosion of knowledge and technology we will shortly be off on a kind of permanent LSD trip that grants us mind-blowing consciousness expansion, sensory satisfactions, and transformational experiences.

The boundaries between the virtual and the authentic will dissolve. We will be able to enjoy virtual sex with any incarnation of any god or goddess entity imaginable (porn star, supermodel, movie star, cartoon character) or trade places with our sex partners—becoming the other—or become anyone, or anything, beyond any CGI dreamed up by James Cameron. This would seem to raise the question right away: under such a proposed regime why would anyone do anything else but live in an endless orgasm? What other activity would interest us more? Collectibles? Entomology? Drypoint etching? Politics? Obviously, even orgasms as we know them would get boring if existence consisted of nothing but orgasms. But given the exponential theme of his singularity we must assume that Kurzweil has in mind an endless range of diversions from cosmic Sudoku to intermultiverse tourism. This may refute any prior fundamental understanding of human happiness as a dynamic range of contrasting experiences between pain and pleasure, but there you have it: bliss eternal, more or less.

How that particular nirvana-like state differs from death itself I don't know. A life of nothing but pleasure would hardly seem pleasurable, though it is difficult to argue with Kurzweil's suggestion that the dispositions of things in the singularity are so far beyond our current dim human ken that there is no point in straining our walnut brains to try and work it out within the bounds of standard philosophical discourse (which Kurzweil does, of course, but his is not a standard-issue human mind). I am suspicious of any system founded on the basis of "hockey stick"–type exponential growth, that is, of conditions that can be depicted on a graphical chart as turning up toward infinity. Though I have not journeyed there to gather evidence, I suspect that infinity is not a good place to be, since it is the flip side of nothing. In mythology, the seeking after infinite states always leads to hubris and destruction. The analog presently for industrial societies is that the yearning for infinite industrial expansion beats a path to economic collapse.

Kurzweil's colorful yarn likewise suggests that the destiny of the human race is to use computing power to become what we commonly call God, the all-pervading regulating presence of the place we seem to be living in, whose local address is the planet earth. It does raise the question as to whether the mere *possibility* of something called God is better or worse than the proposed *certainty* of human-spawned technology behaving as if it were God, in effect *being* God. Does the singularity occupy the God space of the universe (or multiverse or cosmos)? Does it shove the current God aside (assuming there is one)? If Kurzweil's new and improved god comes on to do its thing at the same time that the actual God turns out to be there, do they come into conflict and perhaps battle for supremacy of . . . everything? What happens to the vanquished god entity? Where does it crawl off to? And what does it do there? What happens to the stuff back in the space it used to govern, which it has presumably created, including whatever the human race has morphed into? Or if there was no original God in the first place, are we better off with a god contrived by human engineering? Would it be as indifferent to us as the current version of God seems to be? Or would it take sides? If so, against what? (Not death, which no longer exists.) Would the universe be occupied by nothing but human-made creations? One of the peculiar side effects of reading *The Singularity Is Near* is that it makes the notion of God seem much more plausible, even for those of us lacking in certain religious impulses.

Don't Worry, Be Happy

What about evil, or whatever you want to call the willful malice that the human race has proved itself so well equipped for? Kurzweil doesn't make much provision for it. Terrorism is AWOL in his scheme of things and he gives rather short shrift to the issues around war. He touches on computer weaponry and may even have had a hand in concepts currently under development by the U.S. military: swarming nanobots, bee-sized (or even dust-sized) aircraft, various "smart weapons" (e.g., guns that can shoot around corners). He maintains that battlefield deaths have been decreasing in the various conflicts staged around the world since the calamity of World War II, but he leaves out the proposition well known among even cadets that the pendulum of warfare has swung back and forth between offensive and defensive advantage for centuries, and the current situation may just be another phase of that. He brings up the fact that for some years now the United States has been prosecuting war in Central Asia with drone (unmanned) aircraft equipped with computer-guided weapons that allow a soldier sitting in Nevada to kill people half a world away and then go out for lunch at the strip mall. He readily admits that this is very much like a computer game, and I would imagine that at least some of the soldiers do not make much of a distinction between gaming and warfare. I just hope they are not jacked up on Red Bull and marijuana when they are sitting at their consoles and slapping high fives after every "hit." The result so far has been an impressive amount of collateral damage—wedding parties blown up and other targeting mishaps. One can't help but think it seems cowardly to slaughter people as if they were just pixels on a screen. I'm sure if another nation were doing it to us we would say so.

What if the warfare of the next thirty years turns out to be low-grade and internal, the warfare of a country breaking apart, civil war, with all sorts of amateurs and half-assed militias running around trying to kill each other? Contrary to the Big Brother fears of many, America's federal government may only grow less capable of controlling our lives and managing the affairs of state. It could bankrupt itself and become irrelevant, even dissolve de facto if not officially. States and regions could be left functionally on their own. This was one of the more extreme outcomes I sketched in *The Long Emergency* and in my *World Made by Hand* novels. We've seen coming attractions of that scenario in the collapse of Yugoslavia and in many ongoing insurgencies around the world. Even if some remnant of the U.S. military managed to carry on, it might be neutralized by asymmetrical "fourth generation" (local insurgent) warfare as the Viet Cong did to the U.S. forces in Vietnam and the mujahideen did to the Soviets in Afghanistan. A relative few motivated warriors supplied with small arms can very effectively paralyze much better endowed military machines. Then there is the question as to how a bankrupt nation can maintain its armed forces. In the former Soviet Union, many soldiers just walked away when they no longer got paid and the mess hall stopped serving meals. On top of money worries, the United States has to be concerned about fueling its military machine, which is the single biggest institutional consumer of oil in the world. Its overreliance on motor vehicles is just another instance of overinvestment in complexity. In 2010 gasoline used by American forces in Afghanistan cost $400 a gallon, when all the delivery costs were figured in.

The development of ever more sophisticated high-tech weaponry currently under way is nevertheless worrisome. Kurzweil assumes that technologies would develop to neutralize any weapons dreamed up. That gets back to the seesaw of offense-defense and the concept of asymmetrical warfare. Events may not hinge on how and what big bureaucratized armies might or might not develop but on the millions of small arms loose in the world in the hands of many people who are very angry about the disposition of things in a situation of increasing competition for scarce goods. But then what if they got their hands on something really nasty? We're already sweating out the security of nuclear weapons owned by Pakistan and North Korea and perhaps others.

Kurzweil's insouciant optimism that technology will solve the problems spawned by technology is yet another facet of our general drift toward overinvestments in complexity with diminishing returns, implying a high probability of failure. Jaron Lanier has made the point that while Moore's law[1] may ensure ever more fabulous hardware, software tends to lag badly behind, because programs are created within their own developmental bubbles and will expect the computer world to

---

1. That the speed of computer circuitry doubles every two years.

conform to them. The result, Lanier says, is "a fractured mess of data and modeling fiefdoms."

If Moore's Law is upheld for another twenty or thirty years, there will not only be a vast amount of computation going on on Planet Earth, but also the maintenance of that computation will consume the efforts of almost every living person. We're talking about a planet of helpdesks.[2]

Think of this applied to the military. Before long, the U.S. Army would be one giant IT division. Kurzweil seems to have no sense of the diminishing returns of technology, nor of unintended consequences. In fact, what he calls the "accelerating returns" of technological change (as an extension of biological evolution) are assumed to be capable of defeating the second law of thermodynamics. Anyway, without stating this explicitly, Kurzweil suggests that beyond a certain point of rapid technological development the human race (or its hybrid human-machine successor) will be so preoccupied by other things, like sex with virtual supermodels, that we won't have time for war, or it will be irrelevant. That would seem to be a baseless supposition, especially if the capacity for everything among sentient beings were to increase, including the amount of temporal space available for doing anything. The idea that warfare is heading in a direction that would make it bloodless, mere score keeping as in a video game, seems rather silly, given the various purposes of war, which are not just about the control of terrain, populations, or resources but include the darker motives lurking in human psyches: vengeance, hatred, jealousy, greed, religious fantasies aimed at extermination of enemies. This may prove especially problematic in the coming period of resource scarcity when nations

2. "One-Half of a Manifesto," Jaron Lanier: http://www.edge.org/3rd_culture/lanier/lanier_index.html.

become desperate. But the weapons of the future might be crossbows and poleaxes.

The Ghost of Ned Ludd

Kurzweil is well acquainted with the phenomenon of Luddism, named after the quasi-mythical figure Ned Ludd (possibly Ludlam), a British weaver of the late eighteenth century who was said to have smashed knitting machinery in a textile factory after being mistreated by his employer. His followers were called Luddites, and the term has been applied ever since to anyone considered to be against technological innovation. Luddism has served a useful purpose as a fitting regard for the downside of what we call progress, a governor on the very kind of boundless, cheerful techno narcissism evinced by Ray Kurzweil. The Luddite sentiment has some foundation in the way things have actually worked out for us. The industrial revolution still cannot be considered an unqualified success, for all the comfort and convenience enjoyed by a minority of people in the world. Where we stand now is the brink of unprecedented damage to the ecology of the only habitable planet in the only universe we know of, and I refer not just to climate change—which may or may not be caused by human activity—but to all the other insults and injuries we've done to the biosphere. While industrialism led to the formation of a prosperous middle class, it also plunged millions of people into the grimmest kind of regimented quasi-slavery in conditions that were arguably no improvement over their grandparents' lives as agricultural peasants (or their distant ancestors as hunter-gatherers).

Industrialism hasn't been an abiding set of activities in any particular place but rather a dynamic cycle, of takeoff, peak, and ebb. It has rotated from region to region and country to country, along the way disposing of whole classes of people when it was through with them, chewing through habitats, resources, political systems, and landscapes. The working classes of Europe and America had their decades of factory life and the scene has shifted to Asia, which may be peaking now in the face of constraints on fossil fuels. In the United States the cultural memory lingers on of the brief, ecstatic period after the Second World War when men on the automobile assembly lines made better salaries than college professors and factory workers enjoyed all the blandishments of suburban living. But of course that was the very peak of the cycle in America. The same class of people is now on the scrap heap, reduced to minimum-wage service jobs at best, or relegated to the cottage industry in outlawed drugs, with the gaps filled by subsidized idleness. Great Britain is a similar story, with Germany and France less eager to surrender their manufacturing.

After about thirty years of becoming the world's cheap-labor workshop China is faced with the demand to raise wages for its huge and disgruntled factory class — and this at the same time that its customers in the West lose jobs and incomes, suffer falling standards of living, and run out of money for purchasing cheap Chinese goods. China entered the industrial cycle very late in the game, on the eve of peak oil, when available net energy worldwide is in decline, something that has direct implications for what is commonly called "growth." Any halt to China's industrial expansion could prove precarious for that country's unelected political elites, who have not seen a serious challenge to their legitimacy in forty years. Labor unrest combined with disturbances in China's opaque banking system signal the onset of intractable problems there. We'll have plenty of our own problems here too.

Kurzweil offers a nod of recognition to the leading Luddite of the computer age, the so-called Unabomber, Ted Kaczynski, quoting his notorious manifesto "Industrial Society and Its Future," which was published in leading newspapers with the hope that doing so would induce Kaczynski to discontinue his bombing campaign — he had explicitly stated as much in letters to the news media. Kaczynski's biography reveals a clearly antisocial personality, though he was also a Harvard math whiz and a prize-winning academic before he walked away from a plum job at the University of California, Berkeley, campus in 1969 for life alone in the Montana woods. Yet apart from his criminal activities his arguments against technology were not casually dismissed by American academics and intellectuals, and Kurzweil politely entertains Kaczynski's complaints—if only to dispose of them—without doing the honor of listing their author in the index to *The Singularity Is Near*. In terms of temperament, Kaczynski is the flip side of Kurzweil's ebullient confidence that turning the universe (and its nether reaches) into a colossal computer can only be a good thing.

Ray Kurzweil's singularity is an apt fantasy for this dicey juncture in the story of human culture and its relationship with the place it calls home. The more comfortable we have become with the blandishments of industrial technology, the more complexity we are burdened with—as the BP oil blowout and the Fukushima nuclear meltdown remind us—and the more likely we are to meet the very fate we are desperately trying to avoid: our rendezvous with entropy.

Let the Nanobots Figure It Out

It should be obvious that my own view of the future is in conflict with Kurzweil's too, though I think that circumstances will determine our future, not a campaign of violence against technology. I believe we're heading into a time-out from technology, and that it will commence far short of the mind-blowing advances that Kurzweil predicts. I believe this time-out is not only inevitable but also necessary. I do not wholeheartedly subscribe to James Lovelock and Lynn Margulis's quasi-religious Gaia theory, appealing as it may be to think of the earth as a metaconscious, self-regulating living organism, but surely one may suppose that all the troubles we are having with economy and ecology in our time are nature's way of telling us to step back and reflect a while on what we are doing. It looks to me like we'll soon have that opportunity, whether we like it or not. The singularity is fraught with internal contradictions but also some good jokes. Kurzweil is hostage to his own times and our present reality, much like previous futurists, for instance the American author Edward Bellamy (1850–98), who published a very popular utopian novel, *Looking Backward*, in 1888. His story was set in the yesterday's tomorrow of the far-off year 1950 in a future city (Boston) that is a Beaux Arts urban paradise. It depicts a single comfortable social class (complete economic justice reigns) pampered in a mechanical utopia operating with the precision and grandeur of a Corliss steam engine. (Elegant machinery was that era's equivalent of today's computer wizardry.) In the book's utopia, everybody reports to gigantic automated public dining halls for every meal (mass public recreations and assemblies were the order of the day in the 1880s) and the population enjoys symphonic music performed by live orchestras magically broadcast throughout the city by a network of . . . speaking tubes! (Radio was unknown at the time.) And so on. One can't fail to notice how utopians believe that the future will be all about what is currently going on around them in their own time.

By the 1950s, of course, America's cities had begun their awful spiral into decay as populations decamped to the suburbs. There, the hyperindividualistic single-family house was replicated uniformly and relentlessly all over the landscape, a paradox that ever since has inspired cultural confusion about what constitutes a good place to live. In 1950 Beaux Arts neoclassicism was dead and had been replaced by the cartoon modernism of the highway strip. By 1950 the mass public leisure activities of the past had given way to consumerism, which kept families isolated at home with their televisions or in their cars. For Bellamy the future seemed to be modeled on life in the great resort hotels of his day. For futurists of the 1950s, it was all about tail fins on cars, space travel, and self-cleaning houses. For Kurzweil, it's all about the computer takeover of the universe, because computers happen to be the dominant phenomenon of Kurzweil's time. As it turned out, the twenty-first century is not about tail fins and not so much about space travel. Kurzweil's version of space travel is unlike anything previously dreamed up in the Tom Swift vein because it has nothing to do with mechanical conveyances to the stars and beyond. It is about a sudden, blinding chain reaction of algorithm-propelled hyperintelligence reaching out and infecting the cosmos. I'm not even persuaded that it *is* intelligence, rather than just numbers crunching. It doesn't involve human experience as we know it, in the sense that we are animals, and the references Kurzweil makes to sensation mediated by human bodies all seem to boil down to one thing: endless orgasm, which presents obvious conceptual problems already stated. Altogether, Kurzweil's singularity is a comprehensive vision but in a way strangely reminiscent of previous risible exercises in totalistic futurism, for instance, the vision of the French philosopher Charles Fourier (1772–1832), who was entranced not with computing but with architecture.

Fourier's ideas about the future were based wholly on an architectural arrangement of daily life in vast buildings he called *phalanstères*, a conceptual combination of a monastery, a factory, and boarding school and at the scale of the palace at Versailles, virtually a town under one roof. It was similar to a scheme advanced in the 1820s by the Welsh utopian Robert Owen but far more elaborate. In Fourier's heyday, science was preoccupied with taxonomy, the classification of things, and he wrote volumes attempting to construct a universal and complete taxonomy of social behavior, with the aim of eliminating poverty, idleness, economic injustice, and all the other woes of the human condition. His utopia of *phalanstères* is hopelessly diagrammatic, just as Kurzweil's is excessively computational. Fourier's writings seem quaint, even laughable now, though they were regarded earnestly in his own day and tried out in several prototypes. One Fourierist "phalanx" lasted thirteen years at Colts Neck, New Jersey, before it went broke, although architecturally it never got beyond a couple of linked farmhouses. Another, in Utopia, Ohio, failed repeatedly under multiple ownerships in a very few years and hardly a trace remains. The 1840s was a period of unusal spiritual ferment around the United States that saw the emergence of many secular utopian and religious groups including the Mormons, the Millerites, the Oneida Community, Brook Farm, Adventism, Transcendentalism, various occultisms, and numerous new fundamentalist Protestant sects.

Kurzweil is a product of a similar *saeculum*, an era that coincides with a certain generational mood, in this case a mood of spiritual seeking as represented in the upheavals of the 1960s.[3] I'm a product of the same generation. (So was Ted Kaczynski.) We baby boomers were swept up as young hippies in the counterculture, a reaction to the corporate conformity of our parents' era. The banality of TV consumer culture prompted many to seek deeper meaning in oriental mysticism, which dovetailed nicely with the use of consciousness-expanding drugs—a shocking development to our parents, who associated it with godlessness, communism, and criminality. For many of us who didn't go to the Vietnam War or the Ford assembly line, the period of 1965 to 1975 was one of prolonged adolescence, dreamy years of searching for nirvana.

It was also the boomers who brought about the computer revolution, nirvana in a box. Kurzweil recognized the consciousness-expanding aspect of the computer revolution and fashioned it into a compelling metaphysic. As an entrepreneur he was in on the action from the very start and succeeded fabulously before graduating from MIT. (He made a bundle writing a computer program for college admissions professionals in 1968, his sophomore year.) As it happened, many boomers in maturity abandoned spiritual seeking and embraced

3. See Neil Howe and William Strauss, *The Fourth Turning: An American Prophecy* (Broadway Books, 1996), in which they describe cycles of history and generational moods that attend them.

corporate enterprise with more zeal than our parents had. Kurzweil has excelled at building companies, and then selling them profitably. For all his business success his vision seems not at all cynical but as utopian as anything to the last limits of the imagination, and I mean the *last limits*.

It turns out the human technological experiment may have more limits in reality than Kurzweil can imagine, since it hinges lately on the question of available energy. Kurzweil has many critics in the advanced sciences, in which I don't pretend to be an expert—things such as neurobiology and quantum physics—but I believe he gives very short shrift to our predicament with fossil fuels. In *The Singularity Is Near*, he concludes that the nanobots will take care of the problem for us. "All technologies will essentially become information technologies, including energy," he writes.[4] This might seem to be the case seen from a worldview in which computation is everything, but I suspect it represents the notion that technology and energy are interchangeable, and that the second law of thermodynamics is absent from the scheme. I also suspect that if you fly into the wormhole of the universe as sheer computation, you are in a different universe, and it may be a universe that is just inside your head. If you hedge by asserting that you can be in all universes at the same time, then you are asserting, more or less, that you are God. Perhaps this cosmology admits infinite replications of God, so that everybody can get to be God. Intellectually, you are in a hall of mirrors. Infinity is a harsh mistress.

Back in the material realm, Kurzweil shows a weakness for the "abiogenic" oil theory (also called "abiotic"), the idea that the planet is a bonbon with a creamy nougat center of oil predating biologic life, as opposed to the geologic understanding of oil as the fossil remains of biological organisms associated with specific rock formations in certain

4. Ray Kurzweil, *The Singularity Is Near: When Humans Transcend Biology* (Penguin, 2005), 243.

places within a prescribed depth of the earth's crust. The abiogenic oil idea is a wishful hypothesis widely discredited. It includes the idea that oil fields replenish themselves from a colossal mother pool deep under the earth's crust. First, there is no evidence that any major oil field has ever replenished itself. Second, there is a phenomenon known as the "oil window," which means essentially that pressure and heat are too great below about 15,000 feet down for oil to exist in liquid form; it would necessarily break down into gases under those conditions and would not recombine into longer-chain hydrocarbon oil if the gases migrated up above 15,000 feet. There are such things as natural gas liquids, but these are just incidental accompaniments to gas fields, just as natural gas is often a by-product of oil production.

Otherwise, Kurzweil does not pay much respect to the specter of peak oil and its implications. Within the time frame of his singularity, which he sets for the 2030s, there would be oil in the ground around the world. But there is plenty of uncertainty about our access to it. One set of questions arises out of capital formation and economics. Peak oil, unsurprisingly, coincided with historic peak capital formation in the form of money available for loans; the ability to generate capital has everything to do with energy inputs in a given economy. In our growth-based financial system money is lent into existence. The world's energy industries run on borrowed money, business loans that have to be paid back. This revolving debt can work only when compound interest provides payback, and compound interest can work only when energy inputs to an economy increase.

Now that we have entered an era of declining available energy, available capital is bound to contract. Among other things, this will affect our ability to marshal investment (loans) for future oil projects. That suggests at least that we will not keep up with depletions. A related issue is net energy, that is, how much energy does it take to get energy resources out of the ground and then to refine and move it around to where it's needed. We are getting close to the point where that equation will not pencil out for a given oil or gas venture, in which case quite a bit of oil and gas will remain in the ground. The remaining oil is increasingly located in places that are difficult to work in—deepwater, up in the Arctic—or come in forms that are either poor quality or expensive to produce, for instance, sour heavy crudes, tar sands, oil shales. The light, sweet crudes found on dry land in places that are easy to work in are getting steadily scarcer. Exports are declining, which is problematic for a nation such as the United States, which imports more than two-thirds of its oil. These conditions point to the issue of catabolic economic collapse raised by the work of two authors, Dmitry Orlov and John Michael Greer.[5] By this they mean that economic feedback loops operate in a way that reinforces systemic failure, the bottom line being a more destabilizing "stair step" collapse of activities rather than a smooth glide path to a less complex system. I believe this is exactly the case for what I've called the long emergency.

Kurzweil is also sold on the prospect that we will be able to sequester carbon dioxide from burning coal, that is, to find some way to inject CO_2 into the earth so we can burn as much coal as we want without accelerating destructive changes in the composition of the earth's atmosphere. To date there is no effective process for doing this, and nothing workable on the horizon, despite much wishing that there might be. Meanwhile, time grows short for alternatives. Net available world energy is declining. Peak oil has already occurred (2006). Shale oil and shale gas are grossly overhyped, nuclear is in the doghouse following the Fukushima disaster, and so-called alternatives such as wind, solar, geothermal, biomass-to-liquid fuels, et cetera, represent only a tiny

5. John Michael Greer, *The Wealth of Nature: Economics as if Survival Mattered* (New Society Publishers, 2011); *The Ecotechnic Future: Envisioning a Post-Peak World* (New Society Publishers, 2009); and *The Long Descent: A User's Guide to the End of the Industrial Age* (New Society Publishers, 2008). Dmitry Orlov, *Reinventing Collapse: The Soviet Example and American Prospects* (New Society Publishers, 2011).

fraction of potential energy compared with current world demand, with poor prospects for amounting to a whole lot more.

In the fall of 2010 I was asked to appear in a TV program about the future, put together by the History Channel. It was recorded under the working title *The Futurists* but the network's suits changed it to the more sensationalistic *The Prophets of Doom* for the actual broadcast. Much of the program consisted of myself and five other guys with thoughts about the future sitting in a gloomy abandoned factory in Brooklyn yakking with one another.[6] (Ray Kurzweil was not among us, alas.) One of them, Hugo de Garis, an Australian-born artificial intelligence scientist, had been working in a Chinese AI lab for years and had come to the view that AI-enabled machines would eventually declare war on their creators, the human race, and perhaps succeed in exterminating us. He was quite serious, and his time frame for this was sooner rather than later. It was a chilling scenario, the dark side of Kurzweil's singularity.

In the course of things, we asked Hugo where he expected the power to come from for running those machines, given the onset of declines in global energy resources now under way. He was obviously a smart fellow but the question seemed to startle him, and his answer amounted to the admission that he hadn't really thought about it. He said a bit sheepishly that the question troubled him, now that we had brought it to his attention. Wherever he had done his work over the years, there had always been a plug in the wall. He didn't think about it anymore than he thought about whether there would be air to breathe in the lab. Apparently any sort of an AI singularity theory, sunny or dark, includes the assumption that the AI creatures will figure out the energy part for themselves. After all, they represent evolution to the nth degree and, whatever else you might say about it, they will be better

---

6. Myself, Nathan Hagens, Michael C. Ruppert, Robert Gleason, John Cronin, and Hugo de Garis.

equipped than we are to think of some way out of the energy box that we mortals perceive as limiting the explosive accelerating returns of computer technology. (We also asked Hugo why he continued to work in that particular Chinese computer lab if he had concluded it was a doomsday venture for the human race. He seemed to take it as a joke and evaded answering that question.)

When you get down to it, my notions about the future are pegged to the same time frame as Ray Kurzweil's. He maintains that the singularity of AI cosmic takeover will get going in the 2030s. I maintain that we'll be well into the long emergency around the same time. Kurzweil bases his ideas on the accelerating returns of technological evolution. My ideas are based on the diminishing returns of overinvestments in technology (with a nod to the anthropologist Joseph Tainter). I believe that by the 2030s we'll be shit out of luck with regard to fossil fuels, and that so-called renewables and alternatives will not begin to make up for our losses. At the least, I expect the progress toward Kurzweil's version of AI to be thwarted by the multiple reinforcing failures of all the systems we're currently running, including capital formation, electric power service, liquid transportation fuels, food production, and the ability of institutions to function within those failures. It is hard to imagine such conditions not being attended by sociopolitical disorder.

I've referred to the ensuing period of history as a "time-out" from technological progress. It's possible that Kurzweil's techno narcissistic reach for the stars could be engineered in something like a scientific monastery, a fortified outpost positioned over a gas well in farthest Saskatchewan, say, where scientists can work unmolested on AI while the rest of the world struggles to reset the terms of civilization. For my money, the singularity amounts to a deus ex machina fantasy based on the wish to escape our humanness and our tragic baggage of entropy, uncertainty, and death. Anyway, something with a gift for math already seems to be occupying the universe, and I'd rather continue the journey with it than with Ray's nanobots.

FIVE

THE FUTILITY OF
PARTY POLITICS IN
THE LONG EMERGENCY

In contrast to the celebrated, solemn brilliance of the U.S. Constitution, American politics as such — the rude theater of competing interests in the day-to-day world — has often trafficked in absurdities, superstitions, scapegoats, red herrings, sops to broad public ignorance, the bashing of straw men, the strenuous retailing of deliberate lies, and other efforts to evade the mandates of reality. Some incidents of political depravity in our history are worse than others, of course, as seen in any casual survey ranging from the paranoid Alien and Sedition Acts of John Adams, to the self-righteous defense of slavery in the mid-1800s, to the McCarthy-led persecutions of the 1950s, to the climate change deniers of our time, and lots more. The political mood in relation to a decent regard for truth follows a waveform pattern, up and down. Sometimes our politics are clearer, harder-headed, and more consistent with reality, for instance the progressivism of Theodore Roosevelt in the early 1900s and John F. Kennedy's exertions in the Jim Crow South.

I don't think there is any question that voters were by and large better informed in 1962 than they are in the early twenty-first century, despite the vaunted revolution in computerized connectedness. If anything, the digital age has made a wider range of the sore-beset middling masses stupider, more susceptible to unsound memes, as the diminishing returns of instant communications and multiplying media platforms drive out quality information for trivia, pornography, propaganda, and fantasy.

The present is a remarkable period of stupidity, even within the spectrum of what passes for extremes in our history. The challenges to the project of civilization have never been greater than in this moment of ecological overshoot, and the public conversation about what is happening to us and what we might do about it has never been so inadequate. Our aging two-party system gives off an odor of necrosis. Roughly dividing what we conceive to be the right and the left, both sides evince fabulous sweeps of cluelessness and dishonesty.

How the Democratic Party Became the Party of Nothing in Particular

What follows is the view of someone who has been a registered Democrat since 1972.

Many Americans now in the prime of life don't remember when Democratic liberalism represented the absolute mainstream of political sentiment in America. The high tide for this brand of politics was probably 1964, the year Lyndon B. Johnson buried conservative avatar Barry Goldwater in a landslide election. Goldwater's massive defeat happened the same year that the landmark public accommodations law (aka the Civil Rights Act) was passed. Despite the blow against the Jim Crow segregation system, only five states in the deepest Deep South voted for the Republican Goldwater—Louisiana, Mississippi, Alabama, Georgia, and South Carolina. Johnson, the liberal Democrat, carried Texas, Tennessee, Virginia, Florida, and North Carolina. Imagine that! Extreme conservatism, of the kind we associate with present-day Republicanism, had not yet attached itself symbiotically to the evangelical churches in terms of activist political operations. The so-called Solid South had known only one-party rule up until the election of 1964. Lyndon Johnson himself was a product of the Solid South. Republicanism was identified there with Abe Lincoln and everything that he inflicted on the region a hundred years earlier. That would change almost overnight.

Barry Goldwater, the presidential election loser of 1964, was widely regarded as a crazy person, portrayed in Johnson's campaign ads as a bug-eyed anticommunist zealot itching to press the nuclear button at a time when pop culture was vibrant with fear of accidental nuclear holocaust (e.g., note two of 1964's most popular movies: *Fail-Safe*, in which a radar malfunction almost unleashes nuclear apocalypse, and *Dr. Strangelove*, in which a paranoid air force general sets off World War III).

At the same time, there was tremendous sympathy for the civil rights movement, an awareness that the United States could not pose as the leader of the free world while 10 percent of its citizens were denied the use of public bathrooms, seats in restaurants, theaters, and buses and subject to other infringements on full citizenship. Hence, the corrective action of the Johnson administration was viewed as necessary, even by people who took it as harsh medicine, and it was not a small thing that President Johnson himself was a southerner, in effect making amends for the moral failure of his own people. The consensus was put to a test in the U.S. Congress and the result came out in favor of social justice. The Civil Rights Act of 1964 was followed and reinforced by the Voting Rights Act of 1965, which eliminated many barriers erected against black voters in the Jim Crow states such as poll taxes, onerous literacy tests, and official intimidation.

It turned out to be the victory lap for postwar Democratic liberalism. Everything went wrong for them after that, starting with the war in Vietnam. The year following the passage of the Voting Rights Act, 1966, began the ramp up of battle deaths in the war. It was no longer just a faraway brushfire. The years 1966 to 1968 produced more than half the war's entire death toll. By the 1968 presidential election the public was profoundly divided over the aims and justifications for the war. Democratic leadership as personified by the generation that had served in the Second World War—figures such as Defense Secretary Robert McNamara and his successor Clark Clifford—were discredited by Vietnam. The leadership style of the button-down cold warrior became tarnished. They were no longer "whiz kids" and "wonder boys" bringing a new birth of freedom to the world, as John Kennedy had put it. They'd morphed into warmongering bureaucratic baby killers. The glow from the civil rights triumphs faded and burned out. Lyndon Johnson himself went through a seemingly overnight transformation from moral avatar to moral monster.

The year 1968 marked the first significant urban riots of the era, provoked by the April murder of Dr. Martin Luther King Jr. Within the spectrum of the larger youth revolt of the late 1960s, black youth adopted a fiercely adversarial racially separatist stance that scared and confused working-class white people, who thought the old racial grievances had just been settled by all that landmark civil rights legislation. They took it very personally. The murder of Robert F. Kennedy a few months after King's death finished off much of the residual idealism that was left over from the years of the civil rights battles. Young voters especially were repelled by so-called establishment figures, such as 1968 Democratic Party presidential nominee Hubert Humphrey, once a progressive fire-eater now viewed as a pathetic shill for Johnson's war. By the election of 1968 the Democrats also had lost whatever remained of its old New Deal blue-collar political base to Richard Nixon and third-party candidate George Wallace, the Alabama governor who had personally blocked the door to the state university when it was ordered by the U.S. attorney general to accept and integrate black students.

The people who lined up for Nixon and Wallace couldn't understand why young people would not support the Vietnam War the way the older generation had pitched in for the war against Hitler and Japan and again for Korea. Meanwhile, the hippies' ongoing sex-and-drugs show, with the bizarre costumes, wild hairdos, and weird orientalism, drove the older folks nuts. A lot of these plain working people never came back to the party of Franklin Roosevelt. They wanted to punish the hippies for making them feel like sexually neutered beaten-down chumps who didn't know how to have a good time. Nixon was their chosen instrument of revenge, and when the president got in trouble with Watergate this "silent majority" shrank into the woodwork for a while.

Nixon's nauseating downfall, and the uninspired regency of Gerald Ford, made Jimmy Carter possible. Carter's Democratic Party was a hybrid of old Kennedy-Johnson types and up-and-coming boomers (many of them former hippies). Carter's soothing south Georgia manner and born-again Christian bonafides appealed to the voters in his home region, though he lacked the punitive animus, the urge to punish sinners and liberals, that was increasingly coloring southern politics as it merged with fundamentalism. Carter's U.S. Naval Academy background and obvious intellectualism appealed to the large new "yuppie" cohort of young urban professionals—boomers rising.

By the time Carter came along Vietnam was over and done with. The nation's attention was focused back on the homeland. The economy was still shuddering from an OPEC oil crisis in 1973. A second oil crisis in 1979, when the shah of Iran was toppled, brought another round of lines at gas stations while zooming oil prices amplified the damage to America's aging manufacturing sector. To conserve oil, the public went along with a federally mandated 55 miles-per-hour speed limit (an amazing instance of national self-discipline in the light of how we are now). Chronic trouble in the oil markets made the U.S. dollar wobble, along with the lagging effects of Nixon decoupling the dollar from gold back in 1971. The American standard of living had obviously stalled. It had become necessary for women to bring an additional paycheck home to keep households running at then current levels.

Carter's single term was the last time the Democratic Party leadership paid a decent respect to the reality of resource limits. Carter was vilified for saying that our energy predicament was the moral equivalent of war. The public didn't want to hear about war after the Vietnam debacle, even if the trope was strikingly apt. The public preferred disco and cocaine. Whatever else Mr. Carter represented, his standing was destroyed by the Iran hostage crisis, which monopolized the news for more than a year and obstructed the chance for a coherent national discussion of anything else in the public arena, in particular our energy problems. An ominous sense of futility gripped the political scene. It was answered by the election of Ronald Reagan, whose significance I will discuss in the section on the Republican Party.

Under Bill Clinton the Democratic Party made itself the abject captive of Wall Street. Offshoring what remained of the manufacturing economy was presented as a good thing, good for corporate profits and share prices especially. Ross Perot, the independent candidate in the 1992 election, talked up the "giant sucking sound" of jobs leaving the United States, but the voters did not seem that disturbed about it, and anyway Bill Clinton charmed the pants off them, whatever he stood for. When he won the election his appointees set about engineering a policy feedback loop that allowed the expansion of the financial sector of the economy from about 5 percent to roughly 40 percent, while the resultant ballooning profits in banking activities—many of them innovations that turned out to be pernicious swindles—were shoveled back to politicians working to dismantle financial regulation.

The systematic disassembly of the Glass-Steagall Act of 1933 and the removal of other effective controls on reckless behavior in banking—with no sense of consequence—set the stage for the financial woes of the twenty-first century, well before George W. Bush entered the scene. The manufacturing economy continued to elope overseas. The nation lied to itself that it was transitioning from an industrial economy to an information economy, or a service economy, or a consumer economy, when it was increasingly engaged in an economy of financial misconduct merged with out-of-control suburban sprawl building, aka the housing bubble, which fed impaired mortgages to the banks like logs into a fire. The self-reinforcing behavior ran a circuit between the government, a housebroken mass media, Wall Street, and a public too busy gorging on cheap credit to pay attention to national affairs. Societies give themselves permission to behave one way or another. While there were plenty of individual opportunists who benefited from the so-called neoliberal economy, it was something less than a conspiracy; rather, it was more a set of tragically cynical collective bad choices, as well as a systemically emergent, self-organizing phenomenon. Even some of the obvious villains, such as the Treasury secretaries Robert Rubin and Lawrence Summers, the Federal Reserve chairman Alan Greenspan, and Senator Phil Gramm, a principal architect of banking deregulation, plus many more technocrats, agency regulators, and politicians, probably thought of themselves as patriotic public servants, and none of them has been prosecuted for malfeasance, bribery, or other crimes of corruption (at this writing). But history is a merciless judge, and in hindsight they have a lot to regret. The net result was a political leadership that had set up the destruction of the U.S. economy with no consciousness of its moral foundering.

By the time Barack Obama came along, the Democratic Party had retained a loose coalition of baby boomer intellectual romantics, race-and-gender special pleaders, public employees, and transfer payment recipients, while its body of coherent ideas and aims had dwindled away to nothing. The party needed the votes of independents outside its base to swing the election of 2008. For decades, all the political ferment in the country had been on the right-wing scene. For progressives or liberals, there was practically no equivalent of talk radio on the order of what Rush Limbaugh, Michael Savage, and Glenn Beck served up to their fervid audiences. Public radio bent over backward to appear not to take sides, despite the threats against its government funding from conservatives in Congress. The old liberal think tanks such as the Brookings Institution were a shadow of the conservative Hoover Institution and Heritage Foundation. Few ideas came out of the Democratic power centers that were not reiterations of things already done, or overdone, some new disadvantaged group to valorize or bureaucratic gambit for sprinkling federal dollars around. The old print organs of liberalism, the *Nation*, the *Atlantic*, *Harpers*, had become virtually senile. Everything left of the political center seemed ideologically vacant, toothless, or AWOL.

In the minds of many Americans, where the borderline between dreams and reality had become squooshy, Barack Obama wouldn't even seem to be the first black president. That role had already been occupied by the actors Morgan Freeman, James Earl Jones, and others in movies that expressed the wish-fulfillment fantasies of Hollywood. The public was not mentally unprepared. Obama certainly had political charm and he milked the boomers' yearning for the moral victory of electing a black president, a kind of coda to the romantic idealism of their youth in the old civil rights marching days. Though Obama had written a couple of books, it was hard to discern a particular set of policy ideas he was passionate about apart from just treating other folks decently. From the voters' standpoint at that moment in history, it might have been enough that he was young, fit, emotionally self-possessed, and *not* George W. Bush.

The campaign that year took place against a background of financial collapse that was a fitting climax to eight years of accelerated wild west banking under Bush. The voters were terrified by the autumn 2008 stock market crash, which decimated retirement funds, and they were appalled by the fecklessness of the president who, when Lehman Brothers fell, obtusely remarked of the economy, "This sucker could go down." Around the same time, Senator John McCain made the mistake of declaring that the economy was just fine. All Obama had to do was say as little of substance as possible while McCain was left to defend his party's manifestly disgraceful recent record. If it hadn't been for residual racial animosity hidden in the political thickets, the Democratic candidate would have won by a wider margin.

Obama, the candidate of *change you can believe in*, governed as the custodian of the status quo, perhaps as its hostage, especially in matters financial. By New Year's Day 2012 the U.S. Department of Justice had issued no indictments for misconduct in the protracted set of disasters that had climaxed in the 2008 crash and continued, under Obama, in systematic securities fraud, chronic accounting irregularity and control fraud, failure to enforce standards, norms, and laws, and, of course, costly bailouts at taxpayer expense, a system sometimes called socialism for the rich in which profits are privatized while losses are socialized. Democratic Party ideology under Obama slumped into a spiritless propping up of every racket currently running both in and out of government. It wasn't exactly fascism, as it lacked the theatrical savoir faire of colorful costumes, parades, and overt jingoism, but it was the next best thing: a complete merging of corporate rapine with government assistance.

The Democratic Party's ideological essence under Obama was not entirely cynical. The Democrats, after all, were just human beings with weaknesses, at a moment in history when a fog of anxiety obscured all the landmarks and signposts of political necessity. Instead of offering leadership, they let the psychology of previous investment push them into a desperate defense of business as usual. To that end, the fatal element of Democratic thinking was the idea that the remedy for excessive complexity was . . . more complexity! Everything in America, every system, every activity that had been laboriously constructed over the decades, was suffering from grotesque layers of excessive complexity —from the way Americans got their food (global supply chains plus just-in-time supermarket inventories) to the way we did medicine (the utter clusterfuck of for-profit health insurance made worse by government bureaucracy). The Democrats proved incapable of simplifying, of managing contraction.

Even if massive intervention by self-interested parties and their lobbyists was the reason that Obama's health care reform came out the way it did—in nearly two thousand pages of incomprehensible law, counterlaw, cryptolaw, and irrelevant pork-barrel tag ons—the construction process was accepted as necessary by much of the rank and file and their interlocutors in the media. And, after all, the Democrats passed it in Congress and the president signed it with great fanfare. Of course, the lobbyists for the pharmaceutical companies and the for-profit hospitals and the insurance companies had to actually write critical parts of the legislation, for they were assumed to be the only ones competent to get the job done. Nobody else even remotely understood how the system actually worked, in particular elected politicians. How many people involved in the health care reform effort thought, deep down, that the system would implode under any circumstances is a mystery that may never be revealed. It's even possible, within the metareality of the collective zeitgeist, that the system needed to fail, because there was no salvaging it against the background of peak oil, the related crisis of capital, and the harrowing demographics of a nation growing old and obese. And perhaps nature's way of ensuring this outcome was to prompt American politicians to add more unendurable complexity to a system that was hopelessly hypercomplex. The exact same process was used to produce the Dodd-Frank financial regulation bill a year later, with the lobbyists for the banks left to virtually dictate new "reform" regulations for the Securities and Exchange Commission and all the other agencies charged with policing financial behavior. Facing a system that had become supernaturally incomprehensible, they made it even more opaque and elaborate.

Even if it was the natural weakness of smartypants policy wonks to craft ornate works of legislation for the sheer cosmic satisfaction of showing what feats their expensively educated minds were capable of, it still left the Democratic Party in a black hole of history, done in by the romance of too much magic.

The Official Party of Stupidity

It's not surprising that so much delusional thinking, whether in the form of denial or just plain ignorance, emanates from the political right wing, often melded with religious fundamentalism and located preponderantly in the Sunbelt. This warm region of the nation, half of it baking desert and the other half a steam bath much of the year, has completed a half century economic boom. I say "completed" because it is now headed back in the other direction: into economic contraction, perhaps even desolation, and I believe it can be stated categorically that the resulting hardships will come in exact proportion to the triumphs and pleasures its denizens enjoyed on the ride up. It is happening because the economic action that transformed places such as Atlanta, Houston, and Phoenix since 1960 came mostly in the form of suburban sprawl property development, the whole kit bag of tract housing with highway strip shopping, malls, business "parks," and interstate highways. Sprawl really *was* the Sunbelt's economy for fifty years. Other businesses sprang up there, or moved down there, and a lot of the ones that did, such as textile manufacturing poached from the old northern rust belt, ended up offshored soon enough in other countries where the labor was much cheaper.

Georgia, Alabama, Florida, Texas, Arizona—these were huge states with vast distances between things and where it was often painfully uncomfortable to be outdoors. The memory of those long hot days in fields and furrows was still vivid among broad classes of southerners, for whom the comforts of air-conditioned motoring seemed a kind of holy deliverance. They were increasingly joined by retired older people from elsewhere in the United States. Given the sprawled layout of these new surroundings, motoring became the natural response for people who preferred not to exert themselves in the heat. Driving around in cars became the defining, immersive medium of everyday life in the southern states. Everything was designed and assembled with the expectation that it would be hooked up by cars. NASCAR, the official sport of stock car racing, blossomed into a kind of secular religion, an adjunct to the region's aggressive Christian identity, along with Friday night football, party-boat drinking, and franchise fried food, which only made the population fatter, more physically ungainly, and less inclined to move from point A to point B without the assistance of powered locomotion.

The looming limits of peak oil spell the end of the South's dominant economic activity, sprawl building, and even the viability of sprawl as a habitat. Likewise, it suggests the end of certain omnipresent physical comforts now taken for granted, such as air-conditioned rides to the supermarket, and a return to direct experience with the punishing climate and austere economics that kept the Sunbelt backward for so long. One might suppose that a certain dread lurks there now: the fear of having to live like Grandpa and Grandma did in 1937, stuck out on the porch (if there is one) on a hot summer evening with a palmetto leaf fan, waiting for that cruel sun to finally go down, praying for a whisper of a breeze, listening to the dog pant, and fending off the blundering June bugs.

There seems to be next to zero conscious comprehension of what's in the cards for this region of America, but the population's collective unconscious churns in a vast psychic wilderness of angst about it. This mental discomfort expresses itself in persistent ethnocentrism, xenophobia, institutionalized ignorance, paranoia, and parochialism, which Karl Marx, for instance, identified as the conditions of "rural idiocy." The transition from a near feudal backwater to a place with the superficial trappings of modernity was so rapid in the American South that age-old cultural habits still exert a mighty influence over behavior, and these conditions were exploited maximally by the Republican Party during the rise of the "new" South.

It isn't coincidental that this part of the nation is also the hotbed of religious fundamentalism. It can be traced to the extreme poverty of the principal demographic groups that have inhabited the region side by side for so long: poor white "crackers" and African American slaves-turned-serfs. Note: there was scant piety among the planter gentry who ruled the South for a couple of centuries and dragged it into the Civil War. Many descended from royalist cavalier opponents to the Puritan Oliver Cromwell in the mid-1600s who fled England's civil wars to settle in the colonies. They had little taste for theocracy. The same class would produce figures such as Thomas Jefferson and James Madison, men not preoccupied with religion.

The poor agricultural peasants of the southern United States, however, resorted to religion because they led very hard lives, had low literacy rates, and knew few other ways of understanding their predicament besides the structured superstition of primitive Protestantism, transmitted orally. They prevailed on God incessantly for solace, succor, and release from their terrible toils and afflictions and, in addition, lacked other entertainments or social opportunities besides going to church. There they were subject to a relentless terror of hell as a means of social control, a way to keep the peace in isolated rural households and especially to rein in the rogue appetites of adult males. Some Protestant sects militated against social outlets that were common in other parts of the country. They inveighed against drinking alcohol, taverns, dancing, theaters, and card playing, which left little besides hymnody and prayer to mitigate the ordinary tensions of life.

The centrality of religion and church to the lives of poor country people in the South, once merely quaint regional behavior that mattered little in New York or Chicago, became problematic for the rest of the nation in the twentieth century. The radio gave country evangelists and moral crusaders a new platform for attempting social control beyond their own communities, while the automobile and rural electrification liberated them from the harsh isolation of farm life that had left little time for politics. City people of the early twentieth century, who had grown up on a high tide of scientific advancement and accepted its victories over superstition and ignorance as self-evident, were suddenly confronted by an aggressive new wave of anti-intellectualism, for instance the uproar about Darwin's theory of evolution that eventuated in the trial of small town Tennessee biology teacher John Scopes in 1925 for teaching the subject. Regular assaults on the authority of reason from a large, well-organized faction of inflamed simpletons became a chronic annoyance to a democratic polity founded on the idea that its participants could think rationally.

The projection of political power by pietistic southern country people helped push across the experiment of Prohibition (1920–33) and to this day dry counties exist from Georgia to Texas. Their influence was a major force in the 1928 presidential campaign when a reenergized Ku Klux Klan militated against the Democratic candidate, the governor of New York Alfred E. Smith, a Roman Catholic (a group disposed to favor barrooms). When Prohibition ended, in failure, the nation was bogged down in the Great Depression, which was especially severe in the South. The dust bowl and the boll weevil added to the money woes of a still mostly agricultural region. Franklin Roosevelt's Democratic Party lavished public works on the afflicted southern states. The huge Tennessee Valley Authority project (TVA) provided rural electric service and other benefits — e.g., fertilizer production — to seven states, preventing Republican inroads that might have countered rising Democratic liberalism in racial matters.

The Second World War began before the Depression was resolved. It temporarily unified the nation and focused its attention on a big external threat. Debate about whether the United States should enter the war ceased after the attack on Pearl Harbor. When the war concluded, the American South started to emerge from its long economic coma. The interstate highway program got under way in the following decade. Gasoline was super cheap. Much of America's oil supply was produced in southern states: Texas, Oklahoma, and Louisiana. The American southland was a vast rural region ripe for commercial exploitation, especially in property development, with new highways running everywhere and plenty of electric power to hook things up to, thanks to the TVA. Military bases were viewed as economic development engines. Southern states were awarded far more military bases and space centers proportionately than the northern states with their established industries and big cities. Southern congressmen and senators of the Democratic Solid South tended to hold their elected seats longer and enjoyed positions of seniority on the committees that handed out these plums.

The Cold War spurred a new iteration of military extremism in the states of old Dixie. Things military had long been romanticized in this part of the country. Southern culture venerated soldiering, warrior exploits, and brawling. An economy juiced on military spending out of Washington afforded the rise of a new middle class in a region that had formerly known only a few rich landed families lording it over masses of sharecroppers and other downtrodden country people. The rising middle class of the so-called postwar New South was therefore very much a military middle class. Lifting many southern families out of rural poverty for the first time, it inclined them, among other things, to self-conscious, flag-waving militant patriotism—ironic in a region that had tried to break away from the United States a century earlier.

The growing prosperity of the New South also expressed itself in burgeoning suburbia. The great highways were built rapidly—rationalized, in fact, as a national defense mobility network—and before long the predictable manifestations of car-centered real estate development followed. Wherever a set of on-and-off ramps was built, the housing subdivisions followed, and then the strip malls and the outparcel tilt-up commercial boxes sprang up. By the 1960s many a southern boy who'd grown up barefoot on a farm in the Great Depression had turned into a wealthy car dealer, owner of a real estate agency, production builder of tract houses, a paver and excavator, air-conditioning contractor, lumber dealer, strip mall magnate, or the lucky holder of multiple fast food franchises, all activities spun off by suburban sprawl. The economic transformation was very abrupt while cultural behaviors and beliefs lagged behind. The folks who had gone from rude shacks with no plumbing to country clubs and air-conditioned homes in a few decades still possessed the cultural programming of poor country people in their leisure pastimes (Grand Ole Opry), their religion (Jesus, hard and plain), and their prickly social relations with the other large class of people who shared their region: African Americans.

The New Dealers Become the Car Dealers

The Republicans' "southern strategy" of stoking white fears over the civil rights revolution, aimed at this new suburban middle class, evolved rapidly into a complete reversal of the old southern political order. The Democratic Party was virtually expelled from the region. After 1970 office holders switched parties in droves from Democrat to Republican. The Sunbelt suburbanites, the once but no longer poor, had very little sympathy for those who were still poor, especially poor blacks who had migrated north to work in factories just in time for the broad shut down of heavy industry in the places they'd moved to.

By the time Ronald Reagan came along the Republican Party dominated the South and took advantage of its growing connection with the political organizing apparatus of the evangelical and Pentecostal churches. TV evangelist Jerry Falwell had organized his Moral Majority in 1979, the year before Reagan's election. The group updated all the familiar elements of southern rural idiocy, with some new twists, such as "prosperity gospel," the idea that God rains money upon the favored. The evangelists themselves were swimming in money from their TV fund-raising rackets and were able to invest in public relations consultants adept at manipulating the public. These professionals joined with Republican political strategists to formulate new rhetorical codes for tapping voter discontent, especially for translating crude emotional impulses into slick political ideas, many of them riddled with contradictions. Hyperpatriotic pugnacious militarism became a strange bedfellow with the pro-life (anti-abortion) movement. Conservatives seemed to care little for the lives of civilians killed by the United States in our many foreign adventures, while pro-life advocates went as far as the assassination of doctors who performed abortions. The wholesale execution of convicts was also returning to favor after a period of judicial suspension in some of the most pious and conservative states.

Southern militarism had many origins, from rowdy cracker culture to the romanticism surrounding the "lost cause" of the Civil War to regional economic dependence on military spending and hatred of pacifist hippies who opposed it. The anti-abortion movement had as much to do with the sheer wish to punish educated liberal Democrats as with defending fetuses. The punitive instinct in southern conservatism trumped all of its ideological concerns. The simplicity of it was a good part of its appeal to simple minds, who wanted to discipline and punish groups of people who stepped out of line in any way—at the same time that it carried on about liberty. Sunbelt conservatism wanted the government to leave folks alone on matters of business regulation, land use law, and especially taxation. But it leaped at any opportunity to push people around on social issues: birth control (all kinds), government-sponsored prayer (in defiance of the U.S. Constitution), school curricula, family life (especially marriage between racial groups), and private sexual behavior between consenting adults. In these areas, such a political gang of audacious busybodies had never been seen before in the country. Finally, they seemed too stupid to comprehend their own obvious hypocrisy.

Of course, it wasn't about rational thinking. It was about raw emotion, grievance, resentment, hatred of people who prized intelligence and culture, the defense of foolish superstition, sentimental jingoism, and, uppermost, the fear of losing economic advantages that had seemed to arise out of nowhere, magically, in a region long suffering in premodern darkness, whose chief resource, the soil, had been so abused and depleted over the centuries as a result of ignorant tilling practices that even subsistence farming had become a losing proposition.

Reagan was the perfect figurehead for this new conservative movement, with his brown suits, his Rotary Club pompadour, and his aw-shucks boobery. Both he and his admirers benefited from the fact that he was not himself a southern native but rather a midwesterner transplanted to California. It made him appear to be a more national figure. Indeed, southern politics and culture were spreading all over the country by then. The politics of resentment found eager customers in the deindustrialized lumpenproles all over the rust belt. Paranoid conservatism was already well established in Southern California where an earlier generation of provincial economic losers had fled from the dust bowl. These people had established themselves as postwar American Dream avatars of car-and-real-estate-based suburban hucksterism and were now determined to devote their political energies to the rabid defense of that living arrangement. Similarly, commercial country music, churned out of Nashville very deliberately as a consumer product, was becoming the official soundtrack of aggrieved white people and flag-waving militarists. It appealed especially to men whose occupational reverses affected their sense of manhood.

Ronald Reagan's own formative sojourn in the Southern California industry of make-believe prepared him not only to play the role of president but to represent the emotions of successful businessmen, who like him had fled the Depression-era heartland to strike it rich, and their come-lately brethren in the new boomtowns of Atlanta and Houston and elsewhere. Republicanism before 1960 had been notably stringent. Under Reagan it converted into a sort of cargo cult—not unlike the prosperity gospel—in which the accumulation of riches eclipsed all other elements of the human condition, including such things as justice, beauty, or concern for the future.

The Republican-conservative nexus had an intellectual class, increasingly overshadowed, as it was, by the rural idiocy and money-grubbing factions. The leading light for decades was William F. Buckley, founding editor of the *National Review*, the conservatives' house organ. Buckley's views leaned toward internationalist with a slight paranoid tinge. The paranoia derived from the global conditions of Buckley's early adulthood after World War II: the sudden emergence of antagonistic relations with Soviet Russia, who had been our allies in defeating the odious Nazi regime. Instead of respite after that horrible ordeal, a few years, say, of global tranquillity, the Soviets turned around and came on with shocking truculence that included the theft of atomic secrets, the setting up of the iron curtain to seal off eastern Europe from the West, and the Berlin blockade. Their behavior made American conservatives extremely nervous and the mainstream political response was a series of virtual witch hunts for communists, including the thuggish misconduct of Senator Joseph McCarthy. Republicans lined up solidly behind the hunt for communists.

Some of the worst elements of this crowd joined under the banner of the John Birch Society, founded by the eccentric candy mogul (maker of Junior Mints and Sugar Daddies) Robert Welch. The John Birch Society went as far overboard as possible in its paranoid imaginings about communist subversion, along with a roster of other peculiar preoccupations and complaints, inveighing against the fluoridation of drinking water, denouncing the United Nations, inciting racist resistance to civil rights, and weaving conspiracy tales around international Jewish bankers and rogue brotherhoods such as the Freemasons, the Illuminati, and the Bilderbergers. The Birchers saw plots everywhere and by 1964, when Goldwater was running for president as an unvarnished ultra-conservative, they became an embarrassment to the Republican Party, making scurrilous accusations against the still-living former Republican president Dwight Eisenhower. Buckley worked hard behind the scenes to dissociate the party from the John Birchers and he helped keep them officially banned from campaign activities until his own death in 2008. They are back now with a new and improved extreme agenda.

Buckley also represented a conservative policy opposition to the Democrats in government money matters, against social engineering, expanding government, and the heaping up of complexities. It was this bundle of concerns that became the meat and potatoes of Republicanism from Reagan until George W. Bush. Much as Reagan affected to be the champion of conservative crusades for prayer in public schools and the reversal of *Roe v. Wade* (i.e., ending legal abortions), none of these aims was advanced in his tenure. He was inaugurated in a recession provoked by the oil crisis of 1979 and economics necessarily preoccupied him. When the economic situation improved further into the 1980s, it was because non-OPEC oil began coming out of Alaska and the North Sea and prices fell. The net effect of his administration's economic tinkering was to lower the marginal tax rates for wealthy people, increase military spending to levels not seen since the Vietnam War, and oversee the conversion of the United States from the world's leading creditor nation to a debtor nation, as foreign countries were enlisted to sop up U.S. Treasury debt paper.

While the Republican Party had long been the political ally of Wall Street, under Reagan it began to instigate the corporate takeover of the country by Wall Street, a program that continues to this day in an aggravated and increasingly unbearable manner — in effect, a leveraged buyout of the American government by large banks. Reagan's successor George H. W. Bush, a place-holder president, presided over the first fiasco of the new order in American finance, the savings and loan crisis, brought on by a combination of legislated deregulation (the Garn–St. Germain Act), poor oversight, insider trading, and fraud. The frauds were widespread, long-running, and arrant; 747 banks failed and 1,800 bankers were eventually convicted of felonies. Bush One, as he is sometimes called, also prosecuted the first Gulf War against Saddam Hussein's Iraq regime, which temporarily boosted his popularity. An internationalist by disposition, events allowed Bush One to ignore the Republican rural idiocy / family values agenda, much as Reagan had, by paying lip service to their rhetoric without actually doing anything. Though a WASP patrician Ivy League–educated son of a U.S. senator, he was widely ridiculed for his malapropisms and tortured language. Twelve years of Republican rule that included the stock market crash of 1987, the Iran-Contra scandal, and the savings and loan crisis climaxed in an economic recession. Bush lost in 1992 to the baby boomer Bill Clinton.

Clinton's roguish personality was enough to drive the Republicans to extremes again, though he aggressively continued the systematic dismantling of banking regulations, which conservatives favored. Sunbelt conservatism had spread far and wide through the United States by the 1990s. Even the movement's supposed liberal adversaries, the two Democratic presidents Carter and Clinton (nickname: Bubba), were products of the Sunbelt's dominance. The spread of a punitive, puritanical conservatism correlated with stagnant wages through the middle and lower-middle classes all across the nation, beginning in the 1970s, and with the victims' growing sense of powerlessness, humiliation, and grievance. The descendants of well-paid factory workers watched their prospects tumble, along with their literacy rates. In short, many of the struggling people outside the Sunbelt were becoming more like southern crackers. They were increasingly induced by Republican spinmeisters to vote against their own economic interests and easily manipulated on emotional issues, the syndrome so well described in Thomas Frank's book *What's the Matter with Kansas?*

During the Clinton years the Republicans' own baby boomer intellectuals tried to give respectability to all the retrograde religious bullying that bubbled in the background. It was an attempt to put across an impression that the Republican Party was unified and coherent, from the megachurch mobs of Dixieland to the Wall Street bankers, when, instead, it was clearly divided between big city corporate interests and "flyover" yahoos with an ax to grind. The party used right-wing agitprop organs such as the *Weekly Standard* and the American

Enterprise Institute to retail rationales for the anti-abortion and school prayer crusades. Corporations, especially banks, benefited hugely from the support of people they would ultimately defraud. No small part in the political dynamic was played by the insidious spread of a suburban sprawl living arrangement and the consequent destruction of community that left the alienated ordinary people little besides TV, talk radio, and fundamentalist churches for a social armature.

After the 1994 midterm election the Republican Party turned yet more conservative. The remnants of the old secular conservatives, moderates such as John Chafee of Rhode Island, William Cohen of Maine, and Mark Hatfield of Oregon, would disappear as a type, replaced by extremists the likes of James Inhofe of Oklahoma, the leading climate change denier, and Rick Santorum of Pennsylvania, an avid anti-evolutionist. Yet they still could not deliver on any of the family values issues, or perhaps didn't dare try, especially where abortion and organized women voters were concerned. In their frustration, they engineered the ridiculous impeachment prosecution of Clinton for his romance with the intern Monica Lewinsky. In the process, Republican Speaker of the House designate Bob Livingston of Louisiana had to resign due to imminent disclosures of extramarital affairs on his own part.

Both Bush One and Two and Bill Clinton presided over the run-up to the global oil peak. The last great discoveries of the oil age had allowed a final exuberant expansion of human activities and population. The price of oil sank to $11 a barrel as production increased in Alaska and the North Sea. Americans partied *like it was 1999*, accelerating the run-up of household debt as boomers entered their prime earning years and leveraged themselves into new suburban McMansions with fleets of sport utility vehicles. The Federal Reserve's Chairman Greenspan coined the phrase "irrational exuberance" to describe the effect of all this on markets. Then the "Maestro," as he was called, embraced it wholeheartedly to set the conditions for serial Internet stock and housing price bubbles. The 9/11 attacks on the World Trade Center announced the replacement for the Soviet Union as the United States' archenemy: militant Islam. Contrary to historian Francis Fukuyama's 1992 pronouncement about "the end of history," history came back onstage after 9/11 with a vengeance.

The Current Situation

It wasn't a coincidence that the blowup of the banking system in 2007–8 followed directly on the heels of the global oil production peak. It demonstrated, among many other things, that there was a direct relationship between net energy available to the economy (usable energy after the costs of getting it) and the operations of capital (accumulated wealth as represented by money). It also turned out that finance was the most fragile of all the complex systems that the industrial economies had constructed over the decades. It was probably the most fragile because it was the most abstract, the most removed from the direct material reality of the world. Unlike farming or mining or the manufacture of plastic products, finance was based on symbols, certificates, and eventually by mere digital keystrokes. Under George W. Bush the mischief begun by Reagan ("voodoo economics"), and then logrolled by Clinton (the repeal of the Glass-Steagall Act and more), culminated in the crash of trillions of dollars represented in securities.

By the fall of 2008 Bush Two stood by helplessly as the days of his second term dwindled and the U.S. economy hemorrhaged wealth and jobs. The public, always more sensitive to personal economic standing than to ideology, rejected John McCain, the Republican nominee that year. In the fall home stretch of the campaign McCain had made the mistake of saying that the economy was sound, when it was obviously falling on its ass. All the strenuous, fast-paced bailout arrangements being shoved through Congress by Treasury Secretary

Henry Paulson that season made the voters very nervous and gave off an odor of fraud, especially the rescue of AIG, the insurance giant, and the fishy doings inside the government-sponsored enterprises Fannie Mae and Freddie Mac, the giant mortgage guarantors, which had to be nationalized. The result was the election victory by the paragon of "change," Barack Obama.

In the aftermath of George W. Bush, the Republican Party had not stood in such disrepute since the Watergate days. Bush Two started two wars and had nearly destroyed the economy. He'd run up the national debt at a rate never seen before. He'd made conservatism look ridiculous, and not even on the grounds of its worst elements — its hypocritical puritanism — but on the basis of things that conservatives were supposed to be good at, namely, the prudent management of money. For a while after the national election of 2008, the Republican Party looked like it would go the way of the Whigs back in the 1850s, flushed down history's memory hole.

What nobody imagined at the outset of his presidency was that Barack Obama would not only continue the bailout policies begun under his predecessor but also do nothing to arrest the more worrisome takeover of the government by banks and other corporations, including the flagrant intervention in financial markets by the Federal Reserve (a consortium of private banks, despite its name). Finally, President Obama's Department of Justice did nothing to hold banking officials or negligent government regulators responsible for their frauds, swindles, and failures. Entering Obama's reelection bid, no executives of the too-big-to-fail banks or officials of federal oversight agencies had been prosecuted in a federal court of law.

This failure to reestablish the rule of law in money matters, or to begin to shrink the pathological gigantism of the financial sector and rein in or modulate its swindling operations, demoralized a sore-beset public even more. Of course, in the congressional debates and impasses of spring 2011, the Republican Party did not show any greater eagerness than Obama's party to prosecute financial crime, to discipline banks, or to address the failures of regulation. In fact, they avoided any mention of it and moved to new extremes of cultivating the rural idiocy themes that had worked so well for them in the past. Disillusion with Obama did not spur the Republican opposition to reform. In the early run-up to the 2012 election, Republicans indulged the celebrity exploits of former vice presidential candidate Sarah Palin, the American exceptionalism of congresswoman Michele Bachman, and the absurd crusade by New York City real estate billionaire and TV performer Donald Trump to agitate the public over Barack Obama's birth certificate. When the public grew bored with them, John Boehner's House majority and Mitch McConnell's Senate posse resorted to any tactic that would make the economy worse, so as to stoke voter animus against the incumbent Obama. By the same token, Obama made little more than lame gestures for stimulus programs he knew were doomed. American economic life skated through the end of the year on little more than cooked unemployment numbers, stewed GDP statistics, and ever more accounting fakery.

Heading toward the 2012 elections, both parties now vie for irrelevancy and, more perilously, loss of legitimacy, which could lead to political upheaval as faith in governance per se evaporates. Neither party is interested in disentangling corporate interests from public interests. No effort has been made to limit lobbying activities or to close down the revolving door that allows government regulators to go on the payroll of those they have regulated, and vice versa. No effort has been made to explicitly redefine in law what a corporation is in terms of its supposed "personhood" for the purpose of limiting corporate campaign contributions. After all, corporations do not have duties, obligations, or responsibilities to the common good as citizens are presumed to have. Rather, corporations are by definition responsible only for increasing shareholder value and for answering to a board of directors acting on behalf of those shareholders. To hold that citizenship and corporate personhood are identical, as a bare 5-4 majority in the Supreme Court did in the 2010 *Citizens United v. Federal Election Commission* case, is an act of the most extreme and reckless relativism, the unwillingness to make distinctions or set boundaries. Though the court majority might characterize itself as conservative, the decision is the most radical outcome imaginable, an invitation to sell government lock, stock, and barrel. Democracies are typically subject to corruption and this decision guarantees it.

Political parties don't last forever, nor do governments. Ours are facing an epochal bottleneck of human events. Democracy itself may not be up to the task of managing contraction. The fights over shrinking capital and resources are too paralyzing, nothing is being resolved, and things just fall apart.

SIX

GOING BROKE THE HARD WAY: THE END OF WALL STREET

By the time you read this the empire in question may be a smoldering ruin. Things were really wobbling at the end of 2011 when I was finishing this book.

It so happened in the course of things, with the arrival of peak oil, that the banking system was the first of our major activities to run down, probably because it had become the most abstract of the major complex systems we rely on, the one most grounded on fantasy and sheer confidence, and therefore the most vulnerable when confidence turned to uncertainty. Reality is a harsh mistress.

The banking system as we know it in so-called advanced industrial economies originally evolved to be a service for productive activity, to provide these economies with the means to expand, do more, produce more, and sell more. The means usually came in the form of money, which can be thought of as claims on future work. (That's not all money is but we'll get to the rest shortly.) If you have money, you can pay for people to do things for you: make things, get things, move things, and attend to things. You can also buy materials for them to accomplish it with. Money, as we know it, is loaned into existence by extending credit (allowing someone to take on debt).[1] The continual generation

---

1. See Chris Martenson, *The Crash Course: The Unsustainable Future of Our Economy, Energy, and Environment* (Wiley, 2011).

of debt is possible because, for a long time, a consensus has reigned that productive activity is certain to generally expand. Growth, as we call it for short, allows for waves of expansion and contraction within a generally upward-tilted channel lifting ever higher into the future. Cumulative growth thus becomes progress. When you believe this, you believe that wealth will naturally increase and accumulate and be available for use as capital, that is, money to invest in new or expanded activity. So individuals seeking earnings, profits, dividends, and yields are eager to get in the game. They will allow other people to use their money in order to make more money. Invested money may produce handsome returns in shares of a venture, such as digging a copper mine. Of course you do have to carefully pick and choose the ventures you invest in, since not all will succeed. Some ventures are even deliberate swindles, designed merely to part someone from his money.

A more abstract spinoff of this process involves interest paid on some form of IOU, a bond, a bank deposit, a mortgage, some instrument designed to let money work, to increase itself via a set fee (the interest rate) paid over a set period of time (or term). This is also made possible by the assumption that aggregate capital will generally increase, even allowing for some IOUs that are never paid back—in normal times a small and predictable proportion of all IOUs aren't repaid. This assumption of continual increase has been with us since the Renaissance, and the developed world has received a lot of reinforcement for the reality of it, despite countless horrible wars, depressions, and other setbacks. This has been due largely to another assumption that basic resources are inexhaustible, if you can go to the trouble and expense of getting them. This has seemed to be the case for an awfully long time anyway. Just when Europe was beginning to seem cramped, and resources such as timber, ores, and good farmland were growing scarce, along came the new world. That really amped up the increase of wealth for Western cultures. The introduction of industrial methods of production accelerated it even more.

Now, though, that consensus assumption about the limitless increase of wealth has run into some troubling signs that limits exist, namely peak oil and just about all other essential material resources. Many of the people who work with money don't believe it, but enough of them are beginning to wonder whether something is amiss, and this is shaking the markets and banks where capital performs its magical operations. To keep the wealth increasing we'd need another new world, this time in the form of a whole new planet earth, not just a couple of extra continents, and we've pretty much given up our efforts to get to Mars, which is less hospitable than Antarctica and presents some transportation problems.

Is it possible that we can't expect to increase the human population a whole lot more and then also lift the standard of living for everybody? Have we reached some kind of limit to the supposed perpetual increase in wealth? It begins to look that way. The cornucopian followers of the late Julian Simon thought that human ingenuity was so fantastic it was the true primary resource, much more important than oil, iron, farmland, and water. Wall Streeters certainly thought so, just as the peak resource issue popped up, and that is how they cleverly engineered financial instruments that promised to increase their own profits from no productive activity whatsoever.

Money Matters

It's useful to separate your beliefs about the world from the reality of how things work in the world. Capital is not ideological.

The idea of perpetual, limitless wealth increase in connection with limitless human population growth is merely a belief, even a wish, and the production of goods and wealth is and has been a fact—even if I very much question just how things might be produced in the future and what kinds of additional wealth can accumulate. We call the nexus of goods production with money "capitalism." I don't mean to suggest that all the complex workings of capital in themselves amount to an "ism," a set of beliefs, since beliefs can be renounced, opted out of, unlike the mechanisms of reality, which you're just stuck with. You can't renounce the Second Law of Thermodynamics (entropy) just because you don't want your coffee to cool off. In money matters, you can't get something for nothing, even if it seems that way for a little while. Eventually, reality will step in and cause your gains to vanish, if not for every individual then for a complex society trying to defy reality. When something seems too good to be true it generally *is*.

Capital requires the rule of law to function optimally, a clear set of rights, obligations, and limits regarding the ownership of property, including land, personal possessions (chattel), and money itself. If anyone can take your property away from you capriciously, or if ownership of something cannot be clearly established, then people will be very reluctant to hold on to it or go to the trouble of making it do productive things. The ownership of property must be provable, and instruments of the law called titles, deeds, bills of sale, and other documentary procedures that follow agreed-upon protocols accomplish this. Societies that do a poor job of establishing property laws, or fail to enforce them in a publicly transparent, fair way, generally end up with money problems, a lack of productive activity, and poverty.

Capitalism as I am using the term refers to a set of reality-based laws governing the behavior of surplus wealth or capital in a society. Property laws are not identical to the laws governing capital, though one consequence of industry's disruptive character is that some of the world's political leaders believed that if you could abolish the ownership of property, you could better control society's accumulated wealth. That notion didn't work out so well when it was tried in the Soviet Union.[2] Capital functions according to its own laws whether you are ideologically on the left or on the right. Using these laws, we have constructed many ways for storing wealth,

2. The motto of Soviet workers: "We pretend to work and they pretend to pay us."

for multiplying it, and for deploying it as investment for productive enterprise, especially within the context of industry. These storage mechanisms have evolved from the barter of goods such as grains and other useful commodities to gold and silver tokens, which can both represent claims on goods and have commodity value of their own, and paper certificates and electronic entries in computer ledgers that represent claims on work and goods but have no inherent value of their own.

All in one way or another are promises of something owed to somebody. In the course of things, as the paper certificates gained credibility, they became tradable. You could buy and sell them. Some of them paid interest and dividends or went up and down in value, creating incentives for speculation in their rises and falls. These tradable instruments are called currencies, stocks, bonds, debentures, and the like. Human societies have gone through several cycles of money in alternating notional and hard forms. Claims on future work or future stuff probably originated in oral promises to trade before coinage appeared on the scene. *I will give you fifty head of cattle for the contents of granary X in Nineveh at the end of the harvest season.* Eventually they were recorded on clay or paper or represented by tokens. Promises like this could become exchangeable between secondary parties, and so the complex trade in promises began.

Coinage came on the scene later — about twenty-five hundred years ago — as a convenience of kingdoms and empires, especially as a way of paying soldiers in a medium that was freely accepted by vendors of commodities. So a Roman legionnaire could take his pay and go buy some wine and a bauble for his sweetheart. Discontented soldiers make for very bad politics. Coin likewise became convenient for the general civilian public in complex economies where many specialized trades and forms of commerce existed. Paper money came along about a thousand years ago in China. Other representations of wealth, such as the things traded in stock exchanges, are much more recent. There is an argument that notional and hard currencies come and go in cycles.

Classical Greece and Rome used coinage. Coins became scarce during the dark ages, when verbal promises and barter trade dominated, and then came back in the Renaissance, especially when the discovery of the new world flooded Europe with gold and silver. Hard currency has diminished in our time as nations unpeg their money from a gold standard, and more people now use plastic promises to pay digital money. As the hypercomplex matrix of promises destabilizes, we may see a return to harder ideas of what money is as 1) a medium of exchange or 2) a store of value or 3) an index of account for establishing prices. These are all very useful practical functions that must have a role in civilized life, despite calls for the abolition of money by moralizing cranks.

During the two hundred or so years of the industrial adventure, the procedures for trading paper have become highly systematized and tend to operate within comprehensible cycles of business activity, like the pulses of a giant living organism. These cycles became known as booms and busts, periods of expansion and periods of recession (contraction). In fact they became ever more regularized, and more complicated, with the steady rise and rational distribution of energy resources in recent time. In the early decades of the industrial era the cycles swung wildly with nothing to buffer the system from collective social moods ranging from ebullient greed to fearful despair. Things were built up, things were overbuilt, fortunes made and lost, winners and losers sorted it out in fits and starts. The busts especially were severe, sharp, and painful. Psychologists have demonstrated that, in money matters, human beings are affected emotionally more so by losses than by gains. When human emotions tangle with the laws governing capital strange things happen.

Strange Days at the High Tide

At the high tide of American industrialism in the twentieth century, economists sought ways to try and flatten out these booms and busts, to overcome the emotional components of the cycles and subject them to rational management. The belief in rational management was never higher than the moment in history when global politics was plunging into an era of murderous insanity. At the time, the expansion of wealth seemed ensured by fossil fuels and other abundant resources, so growth per se wasn't the issue. The objective was to find some golden equilibrium in which the good times might not be so delirious but the bad times would be less severe, with less chance of the kind of political upheaval that could disrupt a whole society. The creation in 1913 of the Federal Reserve System was intended to be the primary vehicle for this.[3]

The Fed is called America's central bank but it is actually a consortium or network of twelve regional Federal Reserve banks and many private banks. America's official central bank has circumscribed but potent legal powers operating under a board of governors nominated by the president and confirmed in Congress. It can make decisions without the consent of the president, Congress, or other official agencies, though Congress can call Federal Reserve officers to report and testify and the U.S. General Accounting Office has some limited audit powers over it.

The Fed's job when first chartered was to manage the money supply and act as lender of the last resort so that the nation would not have to turn to private rich individuals, such as J. P. Morgan, which is what had happened in the 1907 financial crisis when mischief in the stock market set in motion a daisy chain of bank runs. At that time America

3. The Federal Reserve is often demonized these days and its origins are adumbrated in legend and superstition. Coteries of the extreme right wing often refer to it as a conspiracy along the lines of the John Birch Society's occult fantasies about the Rockefellers and other wealthy families trying to corner all the world's wealth and impose a "new world order" planetary government. I regard all that as nonsense. While I believe a banking oligarchy exists, I think it was far too incompetent and competitive to have set up the Fed strictly as a looting operation. Rather, I believe it was created out of a sincere intention to rationally manage the financial part of the economy after a series of devastating post–Civil War booms and busts. Its current hapless role as handmaiden to the big banks is more a consequence of many bad political choices than it is a conspiracy of any sort.

was generating massive quantities of new wealth and there was little regulation of its movement, nor of the quality of the instruments that it moved in as represented in stocks and other paper traded on antiquated, unruly exchanges. When investors and depositors lost confidence in any part of these operations—the stock markets, the paper itself, the banks—panic ensued, parties would not trust each other, depositors would line up to yank their money out of banks, banks would not lend to one another, and available money in the form of credit (liquidity) suddenly dried up so that trade could not operate normally. It was very bad for business.

The Fed's first challenge came in the depression of 1920–21, which should not be confused with the crash of 1929 and the Great Depression that followed. This lesser-known event came on the heels of World War I, which ended an earlier edition of the global economy that ran from about 1870 to 1914. England nearly bankrupted itself in the First World War. France was badly weakened. The colonial system had begun to unravel. And Germany was both a political and financial basket case. The economic disruptions that followed the war required major readjustments in trade, manufacturing, markets, and international banking. In the face of that, the American economy shuddered for eighteen months. The new Federal Reserve did little besides raise interest rates, which aggravated the situation because it made credit expensive. The government under Warren G. Harding deployed a few committees looking into unemployment and not much else. But when all was said and done, the United States was in a very favorable position vis-à-vis the other advanced nations, with a strong internal economy of well-paid workers who could buy new technological wonder products such as cars, radios, toasters, hair curlers, washing machines, and so on. And, of course, we had the world's most well developed oil industry, the lifeblood of twentieth-century enterprise. So the depression of 1920–21, now almost forgotten, resolved itself quickly, with little attempt at intervention. What developed next, though, was another harsh lesson in emergent economic systems.

The Great Depression, a Reality Failure

The American scene changed hugely in the 1920s. Modernity transformed everything from women's clothing to the human imprint on the landscape. The car liberated rural America and began cluttering up the cities. The first tractors started a revolution on the farm.[4] Muscular American industry outinvented and outproduced all competitors around the world. Foreigners watched our movies and learned to play jazz. A sense of intoxication ran through Wall Street, prompting excessive risk taking and wild speculation in any novelty, the participation of easily snookered, inexperienced investors buying stocks with borrowed money ("on margin"), unregulated investment pools that behaved like hedge funds do today, "bucket shops" that amounted to betting parlors, and a great deal of insider banking misconduct around financial markets that were hardly policed at all. After it all crashed in October 1929 the loss of confidence was epic. Decades later, scholars still puzzle over the cause of the Great Depression. It was a reality failure. The things that people believed in proved spectacularly unreliable, especially in the realm of money and other abstract paper extensions of it.

When the reality of the boom vanished, money vanished. The country had everything it needed for an economy—oil, coal, ores, grain, livestock, railroads, manpower, millions of machines in good running order, industrial infrastructure, new cities—but no money. Money drained out of the system in bankruptcies and forced liquidation of assets (selling whatever you have on hand, usually at a loss, to raise cash). Numerous bank failures in which ordinary people lost all their savings destroyed faith in institutions that had clothed themselves in the trappings of rectitude. After 1931 both banks and markets stood in disrepute. There were no other systems for capital formation, so capital

4. Farmers produced so lavishly that grain prices collapsed in the mid-1920s, causing a farm depression that preceded the Wall Street crash and then led to the epidemic of farm foreclosures in the 1930s.

became unavailable. The Federal Reserve blinked and did not act as the lender of last resort. The catastrophic precedent of the German monetary inflation of 1921–23 made American officials extremely wary of money printing (what today might be called "quantitative easing"), and the recovery from the earlier 1920 slump led them to suppose the markets would self-correct in short order. The Fed did not bail out failed banks and companies that ran out of money. There were too many of them and the deflationary contraction was too massive. The death spiral of falling money supply, falling prices, and falling wages became a self-reinforcing feedback loop. The failure of the system left the public shell-shocked. It translated into loss of faith in the future and the mechanisms that were supposed to deliver it. The previous reality had shattered and there was no constructed set of narratives to account for it or replace it.

Plenty of other reality-based problems had been festering in the background of the roaring 1920s to undermine the boom in finance. The rapid mechanization of farming brought on overproduction of crops and prices collapsed, leaving many farmers indebted and ruined. Global trade was a shadow of what it had been before the First World War. New tariffs just made that worse as nations retaliated with trade barriers of their own. Domestic markets for cars, radios, and other such products became saturated—after a while everyone in America who could have bought these things had done so—and you couldn't sell them in lands with no decent roads and no electric grid. In the faith-based world of finance, however, a consensus slowly emerged that confidence in capital formation could not resume without reform and policing of markets. Congress dawdled with toothless committee hearings until 1933 when, by a fluke, a young New York assistant district attorney named Ferdinand Pecora, hired to write the committee report, got permission to add some extra hearings to clarify the issues. Once the Pecora commission hearings got under way the politicians could not rein him in. He subpoenaed a who's who of Wall Street's most glittering figures and made them reveal a netherworld of corruption, swindling, fraud, double-dealing, cons, and dodges that reinforced the public's view of the financial world as a contemptible systematic looting exercise. A number of prominent bankers and stock market players went to jail. The revelations led to substantial reform. The 1933 Glass-Steagall Act mandated the separation of banks by their type: it separated investment banks, which underwrote stock issuance and engaged in high-risk lending activities, from commercial banks, which accepted deposits. No longer could bankers play fast and loose with other people's money. Commercial banking was made very boring but safe. Conflicts of interest between investment banks, the things they invested in, and the clients they advised were strictly circumscribed. Firewalls were eventually extended between banking and insurance activities. The government, via the new Federal Deposit Insurance Corporation (FDIC), took on the role of insuring retail bank deposits in the case of bank failures. Since the government assumed enormous risk in backstopping the whole deposit system, it strictly limited what such banks could do. Another reform was the founding of the Securities and Exchange Commission (SEC) to regulate stock issuance and trading. The SEC could bring civil suits against companies engaged in fraud or insider trading and had the power to recommend and assist in criminal prosecution with the U.S. Department of Justice through district courts and the U.S. attorney general's office. The SEC required public companies to issue regular reports and supervised the registration of stocks listed for sale on exchanges.

In all, these new acts and agencies were intended to modernize the movements of capital in markets and punish misconduct where greed lurked, which was everywhere around money. The hope and expectation was that with these new rules in place capital would begin to flow again and revive business. The new laws did not accomplish that in and of themselves. World markets were still impaired for the kind of world-class products America made and the domestic market could not make up for it. It took the Second World War to resolve the contradictions of the stalled global economy, and they resolved brutally by leaving the United States in sole control, for a while, of the world's industrial capacity and markets.

Oh Happy Golden Boomer Morning!

The postwar moment, when all the other supposedly advanced nations limped and staggered back to peaceful normality, was a golden time for triumphant America. For a while, it appeared that we ruled the world—at least those parts worth ruling—and we aimed to do it fair and square as a way of emphasizing our moral victory over the crazed, murderous war machines of our defeated enemies. We dispensed with punishing reparations, since those had crippled Germany after the First World War and served only to set the stage for Hitler. No cruel treatment or territorial grabs. Being the plain-dealing people we liked to think we were, we aimed to get them on their feet and turn them back into trading partners, putting that whole awful two-decade-long intermezzo of Depression and war behind us. Of course, the United States yearned for normality as much as any nation.

In the 1950s, the Eisenhower years, the years that spawned most of the baby boom generation, banking was as dull as a gray suit. Commercial banking, where people kept savings and checking accounts, now heavily regulated, became based on the simple 3-6-3 formula: borrow at 3 percent, lend at 6 percent, and get out to the golf course around 3 o'clock. Retail bankers did not make what we would consider big bucks. They were ridiculously middle class. Their big thrill was being able to join the local country club. They made most of their money on mortgage loans to people who lived in the same town, and only after rigorously qualifying them to borrow. Or else they made loans to local businesses, generally at short term. And that was about the size of it. In the rare event of default, the collateral (say, a house) was easily located, foreclosed on, and disposed of. The returns of around 3 percent were unspectacular but very dependable. Wall Street investment banks, in those days, were private partnerships, meaning the officers of the firm risked their own money in whatever they invested in. They were personally liable for bad choices, lawsuits, and other catastrophes of business. There were no shareholders to pawn risk off on. It all promoted a culture of prudence that today seems quaint.

The America of those years made most of the goods that the world bought. For a while we had the situation all to ourselves. All the other countries that even knew about industrial manufacturing were out of the game. We lent them money at modest interest to buy our goods. We had most of the oil production in the world, and other nominally advanced countries didn't use much because their citizens were too broke and dazed by war to buy cars, while a good percentage of the United Nations members—the ones we call "developing" nations now—barely had what we would call roads. It was a fabulous situation for the United States and the reality that took shape had a peculiar rhetoric all its own: America, the heroic and powerful leader of the free world. America, the beacon of freedom, the world capital of fair play and progress. That was the narrative, anyway. We had become an empire and we had no idea what kind of empire we had become.

This was the cultural climate that the baby boomers grew up in. Because human beings are perverse, it had its dark underside. The staggering prosperity of the United States in the two decades after the Second World War needed the counterpoint of the Soviet Union, and the paranoia it inspired, as a foil. Memories of the Great Depression and the horrors of war were so vivid that Americans almost couldn't believe their good fortune to find themselves suddenly in a remade nation of interstate highways, brand-new houses in the country, and all the Betty Crocker cake mixes they could ever want. The Soviet menace was constantly at hand as a reminder of how societies could go wrong and how fragile world peace was after half a century of war. But altogether these were years of stupendous prosperity and stability when anyone who wanted to work could find a job, pay grades were not supernaturally different from the executive suites down to the factory floor, and Wall Street minded its manners.

That reality began to crumble in the mid-1960s. The assassination of President John F. Kennedy (and other public murders that followed), the tragic insanity of Vietnam, and the tumultuous adolescence of the baby boomers took the nation through what felt like a bad trip. It woke up in the 1970s to an economy in disorder. U.S. peak oil arrived stealthily in 1970 but wasn't recognized until 1973, when you could look back at the production numbers and actually see the trend line. Other nations that we didn't get along with had developed very substantial oil reserves of their own (with the help of American oil companies) and then nationalized them. All of a sudden, it seemed, they controlled the worldwide price of the stuff that everybody needed to run a modern economy. In 1971 President Nixon took the U.S. dollar off what remained of the gold standard when France showed up at the Treasury window one day and demanded redemption in gold for the American paper it held. That ended the Bretton Woods system of currency management and left the U.S. dollar the world reserve currency, only with phantom value, based solely on the faith that the U.S. economy was sound and its finances in order, which was not altogether so certain anymore. Most of all, though, the manufacturing nations that were ruined in the war resumed making many of the same things that we were selling. Some, such as the Japanese carmakers, did a much better job. On a level global playing field America turned out to be not as special as it liked to think.

For the nation's psychology, the 1970s can be boiled down to one word: *demoralizing*. Watergate, two oil crises, the shocking decline of our industry, President Carter's humiliation over the Iran hostage incident, persistent price inflation, high unemployment, and the decline of major cities eroded what was left of the collective identity from the good years. The baby boomers' parents' generation, especially, dreaded the passing of that golden time and feared what was coming. It was a decisive moment. Would America opt for a profoundly different new economy, some kind of low-speed, retrograde Foxfire handicraft and granola idea of life? Where had all the pizzazz of the space age gone? Did we face a future of buying gasoline based on whether your license plate ended in an odd or an even number and wearing cardigan sweaters in cold houses?

Indeed, in response to these traumas of the day, many economic and cultural changes in the "small is beautiful" mode did bubble up at the margins and the grass roots. Now-maturing boomers entered craft trades, started organic farms and businesses, rediscovered small-scale hydroelectricity, explored passive solar building techniques, and acted on the recognition that we'd felt the first tremors of a population over-shoot / resource scarcity crunch as laid out in the 1972 neo-Malthusian manifesto *The Limits to Growth*. But that movement was effectively killed by politics when voters elected Ronald Reagan. The genial actor reminded the older-than-boomer generations of that earlier golden period and he made the most of it, dedicating his two terms to national self-esteem boosting, reclaiming the mantle of greatness, whether it was for real anymore or just acting. It would be "morning in America" as long as he was on the scene, Reagan promised. Advertising triumphed over reality. To rub it in, Reagan even removed the solar panels that Jimmy Carter had installed on the White House roof. Now even the former hippie boomers began to lose their Foxfire mojo. Meanwhile, the next-in-line youth generation became known not for its idealistic zeal but for slacker indifference.

The financial sector had gone from dead boring in the 1950s and '60s to frightening in the early 1980s. The price inflation of goods and services associated with suddenly high oil prices was especially disorienting. It thundered through the economy, changed the equation for doing business, and made voters very angry. Federal Reserve chairman Paul Volcker used the central bank's powers aggressively to beat down inflation that was making lending impossible and choking business, though farmers and the construction industry were clobbered in the process. The public was barely cognizant of where things stood inside the international oil industry. It just seemed vaguely unfair and incomprehensible that a coterie of third world countries in OPEC could mess with America's economic security.[5]

To the great good fortune of Reagan, however, and also Margaret Thatcher in Britain, some of the last great oil discoveries in the non-OPEC world went into production just as they entered office, began to come onto the oil market, and took the price pressure off their economies. Prudhoe Bay, Alaska, and the North Sea made Thatcher and Reagan look like economic geniuses when they were just lucky beneficiaries of a resource bonanza that allowed so many of the illusions of the cheap energy age to extend two more decades. By the mid-1980s so much oil was flooding the market from these new fields, plus the new Cantarell field in Mexico and Siberian discoveries from a Soviet Union desperate for hard currency, that the worldwide price of oil crashed. It stayed supernaturally low until 2000, buying time for a U.S. economy that still had not resolved the problem of declining manufacturing. Baby boomer president Bill Clinton, the computer revolution, and Wall Street would figure a way around it that compromised just about everything the nation still claimed in the way of the legitimacy of its institutions.

Prelude in a Minor Key

The decline of heavy industry had a big upside for Wall Street. Finance could be positioned as one of the few remaining profit centers for

---

5. OPEC, the Organization of the Petroleum Exporting Countries, is an international organization made up of Saudi Arabia, Iran, Iraq, Kuwait, Libya, Nigeria, Angola, Ecuador, Algeria, Qatar, the United Arab Emirates, and Venezuela.

the U.S. economy, something even the government would eventually come to see as advantageous. Banking, and especially the venturesome precincts of investment, became sexy again. A new breed of leveraged buyout artists, many of them boomers of the nongranola stripe, discovered that they could acquire controlling interests in aging, tired American companies, using the "innovation" of high-risk junk bonds to fund the takeovers. Then they could sell off many of the assets or divisions of the companies—deconstruct them in such a way that the discarded parts added up to more than the sum of the whole—and neatly dispose of the remaining husk of the original company, dust off their hands, and go do it again. The last thing they were interested in was the making and marketing of goods. It was a scavenging operation, expressly devoted to asset stripping. Hostile takeovers became a popular way to take advantage of wheezing, old-line companies that didn't want to cooperate in a buyout. Boomers were beginning to grasp what kind of miracles could be performed with debt, ideally leveraged (amplified in power) with other people's money. American industry might be dying a slow death, but the landscape of finance looked like a bountiful savannah of juicy fresh meat to the new packs of Wall Street jackals, hyenas, and vultures.

A few people engaged in the junk bond / takeover / buyout / arbitrage fiesta of the 1980s were prosecuted for fraud and racketeering—famously, for example, Michael Milken of Drexel Burnham Lambert (which firm went out of business as a result). Milken went to prison for nearly two years, paid out roughly $1.2 billion in fines, and was banned from the securities business for life. Ivan Boesky, another colorful figure of the day, who had informed on Milken, likewise paid for his insider trading and other misdeeds in fines and jail time. But Wall Street was hardly chastened. In fact, too many young people were inspired by the new alchemy of getting something for nothing. As profits shifted from the old heavy iron economy to finance, the salaries and bonuses of the young new masters of the universe shot way up. Banking was no longer about driving a Cadillac and joining the country club; it was about living in a house that was the size of a country club.

Around the same period, the savings and loan debacle was slowly metastasizing in the background. This tragicomedy was recounted in detail in *The Long Emergency*, and I won't belabor it here, except to say that the S&L crisis was the first instance where the housing industry presented itself as economically problematic, a harbinger of the destructive consequences of the suburban sprawl dynamic. Compared to what would happen twenty years later, the S&L crisis was relatively small-time grift by a lot of greedy local individuals rather than the systematic racketeering operations that would characterize too-big-to-fail banks, which we will get to presently. The earlier crisis also represented the first major failure of banking deregulation. Barriers on risk taking had been removed by Congress so bank executives took advantage of playing fast and loose with deposits (an end run around the Glass-Steagall Act), which happened to be covered by federal deposit insurance. You could loot a Phoenix, Arizona, bank in a set of cockamamie real estate development deals and collect all sorts of points and kickbacks for doing the deal, and if it fell apart you'd keep all that side money while the U.S. government would pay back the depositors. A lot of bank executives thought they could walk neatly away from their spavined small-time, off-the-radar strip-mall banks and nobody would notice. It may be hard to believe now but regulators actually looked into these shenanigans and issued warrants; 1,852 bank officials were prosecuted and 1,072 landed in jail. From 1986 to 1995 the government performed resolutions on more than fifteen hundred impaired S&Ls. Of that number, 747 of them failed altogether. It eventually cost the taxpayers about $124 billion, which was small change, though, compared to what would come in 2008.

The Housing Fiasco

Another profit center for the supposed post–heavy manufacturing new economy was the construction industry, especially houses. It was something that could occupy the demographic of brawny men who did not go to college, liked to work with their hands and power tools, or who used to work in the factories that had closed. As the price of oil went down in the early 1990s all the fears of gas station lines and shortages were forgotten. The hottest state economies were in various parts of the Sunbelt, big states with lots of room for suburban sprawl to do its thing. In these places, building stuff any other way than sprawl was unthinkable, even in Virginia and the Carolinas, where there was some residue of pre-automobile America. Out in the western states, of course, sprawl was the *only* template. But across the Sunbelt it was all about staying out of the heat at all costs, which meant remaining in your car or some other air-conditioned place whenever you weren't at home. There were few geographic spots in the Sunbelt that were considered too far-flung to put up a housing development and some strip malls. And people were flocking from other parts of the country to live in states that didn't get snow.

By the late twentieth century the U.S. government was so deep into subsidizing the house-selling industry that it took a stupefying effort to sort out all the agencies that guaranteed mortgages, helped folks get mortgages, and routed mortgages into trusts, bonds, pools, and tax-free conduits. Without government intervention, the housing market could never have grown into the monster that it did. At the same time, the financial industry, also expanding, wanted to generate more business in new ways using new kinds of securities that went beyond the tired old stocks and bonds that were the meat and potatoes of investing. Mortgages seemed pretty boring, too, but a new generation of financial whizzes discovered that you could subject them to alchemy and turn them into gold. The more easily banks and, increasingly, nonbank "mortgage originators," such as the infamous Countrywide Financial, could unload loans they made by the bale, the more new loans they could crank out, and so on, in a sort of perpetual motion system. The system was sold to the public and to elected representatives (and to the news media) as a way of spreading out risk in lending so that more and more people could join in the American Dream of owning their own home.

It seemed to be the kind of fair and square deal that was part of our generous, welcoming national character. It turned into an international catastrophe that wrecked whole national economies and may even bring down the entire modern system for managing money. It also added a huge amount of additional suburban development to the landscape, trapping more people in a psychology of previous investment that will never allow them to imagine living differently, even when their way of life is failing.

The Up Ramp to Disaster

The Federal National Mortgage Association (aka Fannie Mae) is an ambiguous government-sponsored enterprise, originally chartered during the New Deal to help stimulate the then moribund construction trades.[6] The purpose of Fannie Mae was to make home loans more freely available by guaranteeing mortgages (backstopping them in the event home owners quit paying) and buying up existing mortgages from local banks, thus freeing them up to issue new mortgage loans and ensuring a perpetual stream of financing for house building (and home ownership) all over the country. The agency also enjoyed a monopoly on securitizing mortgages. This was done by bundling them into bonds that could be bought by institutional investors such as pension funds and insurance

6. To avoid confusion, I'll just leave out Fannie Mae's later subdivision Ginnie Mae and its sibling GSE Freddie Mac from the discussion, since the mechanisms of their operations and current difficulties are similar.

companies to provide streams of interest payments. In 1968 President Lyndon Johnson pushed Fannie Mae to go public, i.e., sell shares. It was essentially an accounting trick to get Fannie Mae's obligations off the government's books and to make the nation's debt look smaller at a time when the country was fighting both a war on poverty and a war in Vietnam. It also made Fannie Mae's status more ambiguous. Though government sponsored, the government did not explicitly backstop its holdings, that is, until the financial crisis of 2008, when mammoth losses prompted an official rescue by the Treasury Department.

Through the Bush One, Clinton, and Bush Two years, numerous iterations of the Community Reinvestment Act pushed Fannie Mae to open the mortgage market to more low-income Americans, people with less secure prospects for keeping up with their payments. The idea was to make up for earlier decades of discrimination (redlining, or refusing loans to whole neighborhoods) and to engineer an improved class of less well-off citizens by making them vested property owners. These would become known as nonconforming loans. In the years ahead, they would become grotesquely "creative."

There were many flaws in the mission to make property owners of the poor, but the main one was probably the fact that the old neighborhoods politicians sought to rescue, in cities such as Cleveland and Detroit, were in the remorseless grip of postindustrial entropy and new houses outside the cities in the sprawl zones just cost more than used houses, so it was hard for poor people to buy them without bending the rules of lending. But cheap old houses typically incurred higher repair costs, which poor people couldn't afford on top of mortgage payments. So, predictably, poor people fell behind on their payments while the quality of the collateral (the house) deteriorated.

In any case, for a decade or so Fannie Mae used accounting legerdemain to conceal the unsoundness of its trade in mortgages and was able to ignore its own mounting portfolio losses while generating ever more business on top of the paper they sat on until they entered the twenty-first century holding trillions of dollars worth of mortgage paper of deteriorating quality. Among the company's notable achievements was paying gigantic salaries and bonuses to its executives. Because of its quasi–public / private GSE status, its books were protected from scrutiny. So nobody from the outside fully knew what was going on inside it.

In the background, other forces were gathering to produce a slow-burning banking disaster. One was the militant opposition of Bill Clinton's Treasury secretary Robert Rubin and Fed chief Alan Greenspan to the oversight of derivatives under the Commodity Futures Trading Commission (CFTC), chaired at the time by the lawyer Brooksley Born.[7] The episode became notorious for the brutal treatment Born was subject to when top Clinton administration officials ganged up to stop her. She was particularly concerned about the trading of esoteric derivatives called swaps, which were unregulated, nontransparent, and had no set clearing procedures—meaning any old player could traffic in them, there was no control over conflicts of interest or reserve requirements that would ensure payments by counterparties (buyers and sellers of swaps), and there was no established mechanism for processing payouts in an orderly way. It was just assumed that they would work out. In short, swaps were extremely risky instruments, wholly unregulated. Neither

7. Derivatives: abstract investment vehicles based on bets on the performance of other investments. They started out as contracts for future delivery on commodities. A cocoa trader might take a position on cocoa beans, betting that the price in November would be higher or lower than the price in June. Betting correctly could boost profits for middlemen and end users (i.e., chocolate bar manufacturers) in the business. Ditto corn, soybeans, pork bellies, copper, and many other useful things. In the 1990s derivatives betting started to include things like the direction of interest rates, the soundness (or not) of certain bonds, currencies, you name it. Eventually it was sold as a form of insurance against failure, allowing players (investors) to hedge the risky plays they made in one thing or another, so in case a particular play went bad (say, a risky bond purchase) losses were covered. It was a nice theory but it left room for all sorts of mischief in practice.

Rubin, nor Greenspan, nor White House adviser Lawrence Summers wanted to impede Wall Street from profiting off financial so-called innovation. Nor did they and others in the Clinton administration want to do anything that would prevent the financial sector of the economy from occupying the vacuum left behind by dying manufacturing. In a few years the amount of bets being placed in over-the-counter derivatives such as credit default swaps (CDS) would become so large that it dwarfed the money produced annually by the global economy. A great many CDS contracts were tied into mortgage-backed securities and the Frankensteinian investment vehicles spun off of them. This "shadow banking" system would become a huge and dire threat to the system.

Another big factor in the gathering storm was the repeal of the most important elements of the Depression-era Glass-Steagall Act. With the 1999 Gramm–Leach–Bliley Act, the division between investment banks and banks that accepted deposits was dissolved, making it possible for bankers once again to play fast and loose with depositors' money, just as they had in the 1920s. The weird case of Citicorp illustrated the erosion of the rule of law in this period. Citi had gobbled up the giant Travelers Insurance company in 1998 to form the colossal Citigroup in blatant violation of Glass-Steagall. But Citi was excused from discipline on the grounds that Gramm–Leach–Bliley was under discussion in Congress, meaning that the law might soon change in Citi's favor, *so don't bother enforcing the current regulations.* The process was greatly assisted by the growing influence of bank industry lobbyists, since banking was becoming so supernaturally complex that lawmakers could barely understand what they were being paid to do (via campaign contributions). In fact, it was becoming routine practice for lobbyists and their lawyers to actually provide the content for legislation.

During the Bush Two years, the action in the housing sector grew red hot. House prices zoomed as "flippers" profited on quick sales. Ordinary people all over the country cashed out on the putative increased value of their house by taking out additional loans and a home equity line of credit (HELOC). It was classic mania. At the same time, Wall Street banks and hedge funds shoved aside stodgy Fannie Mae—with its pain-in-the-ass underwriting standards—and got into the act of packaging creative mortgage-backed investments on a furious basis. These mortgages were churned out by unscrupulous nonbank companies such as Angelo Mozilo's Countrywide, which sold them to Wall Street banks for repackaging into securitized investments. The variety of strange new mortgage arrangements was impressive. Adjustable rates had been around for a while but a new menu of payment dodges was added to give borrowers the impression that they could get something for nothing. These included zero down-payment mortgages, interest only mortgages, payment option mortgages (in which the borrower could pay less than the monthly rate, with the difference loaded onto the back end of what was owed, compounding the total interest and principal due further). And of course qualification standards had decayed utterly, so any parking valet could get the green light to buy a half-million-dollar house with no money down.

Anatomy of a Swindle

Wall Street was prepared now to go much further into a wonderland of profits with another strain of genetically modified investment instruments: collateralized debt obligations (CDOs). As discussed earlier, these were bundles of mortgage-backed securities (which were already bundles of mortgages), so they were bundles of bundles of bundles of debts, at least in their most plain vanilla form. There were plenty of other flavors. There were "synthetic" CDOs that were bundles of CDSs, that is, bundles of bets that other assorted investments would fail, and CDOs "squared," which were bundles or pools of other CDOs. The innovation was endless, until it all ended. CDOs could be sorted out (sliced and diced) into various quality levels of bundles (tranches) that supposedly carried more or less risk, so investors could balance revenue streams against the hazard that something would go wrong. But this sorting process was compromised by the wish to make CDOs as incomprehensible as possible, so that potential buyers would not have a clue as to what they were actually buying. The mischief that this process opened the door to is now legendary. The exemplars were the Magnetar CDO deals and Goldman Sachs' activities in its Abacus and Timberwolf CDOs, the latter being the "shitty deal" at the center of Senator Levin's April 2010 Senate subcommittee hearings.

Magnetar Capital was a Chicago hedge fund that, around 2005, pioneered a procedure for creating CDOs designed to fail in order to make side bets to profit from these failures.[8] This was sometimes called short-selling ("shorting") the investment (though the classic form of shorting is to bet that a stock will go down). In the case of Magnetar, the device, or hedge, for shorting was credit default swaps, since a CDO was basically a very complex type of bond and the failure of a CDO would be the inability of a bond to produce the revenue stream it promised to pay: a default. So if the poor schlubs at the bottom of this feeding chain of credit who held the mortgages in the bundles of bundles of things—these poor idiots who had bought overpriced Las Vegas McHouses with no-money-down, adjustable-rate, payment-option mortgages—stopped paying anything at all for a few months, well, each one of those "nonperforming" mortgages was like a bit of gangrene in a body infected with rot. The Magnetar executives made sure that in the slicing and dicing process certain tranches, or layers, of a given CDO would be guaranteed to be rotten. Other tranches would be infected too, just not necessarily as badly, but they would fail eventually as well. Securities law required an independent CDO

8. In nature, a *magnetar* is an imploding star in its death throes. Financiers clearly do not lack a sense of humor the way they have lacked a sense of ethics.

manager be brought into the process to act as a sort of quality control agent in selecting the bundles of mortgages that would go into a CDO. This so-called manager collected a commission or fee for so doing. Of course, this CDO manager had a glaring conflict of interest insofar as an incentive existed to please the client (Magnetar) so as to be hired again to collect more commissions. This perhaps explains how Magnetar seemed to exercise occult influence in getting its CDO managers to cherry-pick exactly the mortgage bundles that Magnetar wanted.

In creating a given CDO, Magnetar would have to find a buyer for the riskiest tranche or slice. This buyer was called the CDO sponsor. The whole CDO could not be constructed and sold without such a sponsor. One might assume such a buyer would be a prime patsy, the worst sort of chump, stuck with the dodgiest part of the investment. But Magnetar itself chose to be the sponsor, retaining the riskiest tranches of its own CDOs. The rest could be sold off to insurance companies and pension funds. The beautiful part was that even the riskiest tranche produced a trickle of payment flows, and Magnetar used that revenue to pay for credit default swaps on the better (less bad) tranches. So when the better tranches became impaired, Magnetar collected "insurance" on the CDS. The cost of being the sponsor (buying the lowest tranches) was a lot less than the whopping payoff from the CDS, plus Magnetar had collected commissions and fees for generating the CDO in the first place. The institutional investors who were stuck with the other parts of the CDO suffered losses, but Magnetar was unconcerned with their fate and never had to account for it, except to deny press reports that there was anything wrong with their activities.[9] The company was involved in thirty CDO deals altogether between 2006

---

9. The Magnetar scam was widely reported on by National Public Radio, by the independent investigative Web site ProPublica.org, and by the NakedCapitalism.com Web site, whose principal writer, Yves Smith, also covered it in her book *EConned: How Unenlightened Self Interest Undermined Democracy and Corrupted Capitalism,* (Palgrave Macmillan, 2010). Michael Lewis discussed elements of it in his book *The Big Short: Inside the Doomsday Machine* (W.W. Norton, 2010).

and 2007, just as the housing bubble was bursting. By 2009, 96 percent of the Magnetar CDO deals had defaulted (and triggered CDS insurance payouts). Big banks that marketed Magnetar CDOs—including JP Morgan, Citigroup, Royal Bank of Scotland (RBS), and Merrill Lynch—had trouble unloading them on investors and ended up stuck with them in their own deteriorating portfolios. No one at Magnetar was ever prosecuted for the fund's CDO activities.

"One Shitty Deal"

"This is one shitty deal!" Senator Carl Levin (D–Michigan), chairman of the Permanent Subcommittee on Investigations, repeated at least a dozen times in televised hearings in the spring of 2010, just to make sure that nobody in the C-SPAN audience missed his point.[10] He was quoting directly from an internal e-mail between Goldman Sachs executives. The shitty deal referred to was a Goldman Sachs–engineered CDO. The executives sat in a long row at tables facing the committee members, affecting looks of guilelessness. In the course of a long day's testimony, they artfully denied that a *shitty deal* was the bank's consensus view of the investment product they had created and were selling to the same sort of institutional investors who bought Magnetar's CDOs. Goldman Sachs, with its legendary attention to detail, had also engineered itself a fall guy, a thirty-one-year-old bond salesman named Fabrice Tourre (aka "Fabulous Fab"), hung out to dry for the company's sins. Tourre's job had been to find buyers for whatever the Goldman Sachs mad scientist CDO creators sent through the pipeline for marketing. Tourre was only one of many such young CDO salesmen selling all kinds of freaky gourmet bonds, but he happened to be the one who

---

10. Contained in an e-mail from Thomas Montag, Goldman Sachs' former head of sales and trading, to Daniel Sparks, then head of Goldman's mortgage desk.

sold the particular shitty deal in question, the CDO called Timberwolf. As the Senate hearing proceeded, Goldman's chief, Lloyd Blankfein, and the executives who reported directly to him played dumb. They appeared blissfully unaware and unconcerned about the securities at the heart of their operations during the housing collapse.

The Timberwolf CDO was issued in March 2007 and immediately hemorrhaged value as Goldman aggressively sold it into the market. Meanwhile, Goldman had shorted 36 percent of Timberwolf's tranches, so as the CDO's value collapsed, Goldman profited. In the construction of the Abacus CDO, Goldman allowed hedge fund operator John Paulson to pay a fee for the privilege of advising the Abacus independent CDO manager to cherry-pick the worst possible junk to fill out the CDO's portfolio—three million subprime loans, many of the no-down-payment variety—which allowed Paulson, in turn, to confidently short the CDO, knowing exactly the dreck it contained. Paulson made $3.4 billion on the deal. Regulators never identified Paulson's participation in the CDO as a form of insider trading. Goldman never informed its other clients, the buyers of the Abacus CDO, that Paulson helped engineer a booby-trapped security he could bet against, a deliberate omission of material fact in the firm's sales pitches and, from the legal point of view, the prospectus.

A civil lawsuit brought against Goldman Sachs in the Timberwolf matter was dismissed on a technicality: that the paperwork for the deal, hence the deal itself, occurred outside U.S. jurisdiction in the offshore money-laundering center of the Cayman Islands. The report by Senator Levin's committee accused Goldman Sachs of systematic fraud and referred the case to the Securities and Exchange Commission. In the case of the Abacus CDO, the SEC decided on a civil action against the banking firm rather than a referral to the Justice Department for criminal charges. The matter was settled out of court, so the conflicts of interests and omissions of material facts to clients were never publicly aired. Goldman Sachs paid a $550 million fine but was not required to admit guilt in the matter. We will get to the question presently as to why there were no criminal prosecutions in these misdeeds, or anybody else's transgressions, in the years that followed.

Welcome to Zombie Island

Then, as a result of shenanigans like the traffic in booby-trapped CDOs on a wholesale basis throughout the Wall Street scene, as well as a multitudinous variety of other ingenious frauds, cons, grifts, scams, swindles, and shady sideshows, the financial collapse of 2008 ensued. It actually began in an official sort of way a year earlier, in August 2007, when two hedge funds contained within the nearly century-old investment bank Bear Stearns choked to death on mortgage-backed securities that it had not been clever enough to hedge against in the manner of Goldman Sachs. For eight months, Bear Stearns stumbled around Wall Street zombie-like, pretending it was a going concern, desperately seeking a merger deal, and working the media in an attempt to prop up its share price, which fell off a cliff at about $85 in February of 2008. One month later, in the first of many such bailout deals to follow, the Federal Reserve Bank of New York issued $30 billion in rescue loans in order to persuade JP Morgan to buy Bear Stearns for $10 a share (up dramatically from the initially offered $2). This transaction also commenced the process of the Federal Reserve vacuuming up the "toxic assets" (i.e., loans that would never be repaid and derivative securities of such loans) that Bear Stearns' vaults had been stuffed with and which lay rotting in scores of other financial companies. These were stashed in the Fed's now infamous Maiden Lane portfolios.[11]

---

11. There were eventually three Maiden Lane companies formed by the Fed specifically to warehouse massive quantities of devalued securities in order to get them off the balance sheets of the remaining too-big-to-fail banks. The Fed ended up with ownership and even responsibility for an inventory of property ranging from a bankrupt Hilton Garden Inn in Panama City, Florida, to the Crossroads Mall in Oklahoma City.

Developments were escalating quickly now. Around the same time that Bear Stearns died, Bank of America bought the remnants of Countrywide Financial. Countrywide's CEO, Angelo Mozilo, managed to cash out $141 million in his company's stock options just prior to its collapse and sale, still touting its soundness.[12] As the housing crash steepened, and securities derived from mortgages imploded, two of the principal companies that had issued insurance on CDOs, Ambac (American Municipal Bond Assurance Corporation) and MBIA (Municipal Bond Insurance Association), went down. In June 2008 Senate Banking Committee chairman Christopher Dodd proposed a bailout for subprime mortgage holders; simultaneously, press reports revealed that Dodd had received campaign contributions and special real estate loans from Countrywide Financial (as did many other "friends of Angelo" in public office and especially over at Fannie Mae). But the swirl of events was such that the public barely noticed. Congressman Barney Frank told the news media that Fannie Mae and its sibling GSEs had a "solid" future. About a month later, on September 7, 2008, the U.S. government effectively nationalized Fannie and its sibs, backstopping their obligations explicitly for the first time and putting taxpayers on the hook for the entire mortgage meltdown. The companies owned or guaranteed about $12 trillion in mortgages altogether. Nothing the government did resolved any of the nation's housing bubble–related dynamics. The value of houses on the real estate market still had a long way to fall.

In this epochal moment of financial history, the nation was distracted by the presidential campaign between Barack Obama and John McCain, on top of the fact that only a microscopic fraction of the public could have even comprehended what these arcane events in

---

12. In October 2010 Angelo Mozilo settled civil fraud and insider trading charges brought by the SEC for $67.5 million in fines and penalties. Mozilo paid only $22 million himself because his employment contract indemnified him against such actions. His personal fortune at the time amounted to more than $600 million.

the financial sector were about or wrapped their minds around the associated gigantic dollar figures zinging across all the media. After all, a trillion dollars is a thousand times a thousand million dollars. If you piled it on pallets in bundles of $100 bills it would occupy the equivalent of a football field six feet high. A week after the U.S. government backstopped (and rescued) Fannie Mae, Lehman Brothers, a company that went back to an Alabama cotton brokerage started in 1850 by three Bavarian immigrant brothers and had become the fourth largest investment bank in the country, filed for bankruptcy. No attempt was made to rescue it. Lehman had been up to its ears in subprime mortgages and derivatives of them. Lehman's senior management had been too dumb to see the housing bust coming and apply hedges Goldman-style. It ignored advice from, and then fired, its own employees who had pushed to short the mortgage market. Then, as its own portfolios went south, it had used accounting tricks to shuffle assets (losses) off the balance sheet from one quarter to the next to conceal its condition, but mounting losses through 2008 could no longer be stuffed under the repo rug.[13] Over the summer of 2008 Lehman famously tried (and failed) to sell itself to a Korean bank. Its stock price washed away like a sand castle in hurricane surf. Most conspicuously, the then Treasury secretary Henry Paulson, former CEO of Goldman Sachs, did nothing to arrest the failure of Lehman Brothers, a major competitor to his former employer. As Lehman shut down, the stock markets shuddered and lending seized up, especially the kind of short-term lending that big institutions depended on to keep the blood of the financial system flowing. The result was a kind of global banking heart attack.

Within hours, Paulson, Federal Reserve chairman Ben Bernanke, New York Federal Reserve Bank president Timothy Geithner, and a team of crisis management subalterns were at work hammering together

---

13. Repos: repurchasing agreements that allow companies to take securities off their books and park them elsewhere temporarily as a sort of short-term loan. The gimmick makes it possible to cook quarterly reports more favorably.

a giant rescue package to present to Congress, which had to approve any comprehensive, mammoth bailout that proposed handing public money over to scores of private companies. So many simultaneous frightening developments were taking place so rapidly in the background that leading participants, including the presidential candidates, couldn't stay ahead of developments.[14] Low-risk money market funds were suffering such deep redemptions (customers pulling cash out) that the funds "broke the buck"—i.e., fell below a $1 net asset value. More ominously, the failure of Lehman bonds started a bond panic that triggered credit default swaps, which, as described above, traded in utterly nontransparent, unregulated markets that no one could see into so that the counterparties to these CDS deals were not known. All that was known was that they included many of the major banks, perhaps all of them in one way or another, and so the panic in CDS further stiffened the global paralysis in moneylending—a liquidity crisis. All the big banks suspected one another of imminent failure. If the movement of money were not restored in fairly short order the life of the financial system would terminate, just as a human body cannot continue to exist without the flow of blood. After some initial resistance, Paulson, Bernanke, and company buffaloed Congress into approving the bailouts. President George W. Bush had made himself largely irrelevant by that time, the lamest of lame ducks, whose only contribution to the crisis was the pithy observation, worth repeating, "This sucker could go down."

The autumn of 2008 was such an enormous, multifaceted clusterfuck that even a casual rehearsal of the particulars would require a whole book in itself, and indeed there are already many such popular histories of the event. Suffice it here to summarize that financial relations in the United States underwent a tectonic shift, and yet one

---

14. Senator John McCain "suspended" his election campaign, but then unsuspended it a day later.

shockingly devoid of effective reform and change for the better. The greatest shift, of course, was that consequences of misbehavior in banking were shifted from the managing executives of giant companies to the taxpayers. Half a dozen banks were declared, infamously, "too big to fail," while the taxpayers entered a perdition of financial insecurity with lost jobs, lost retirement accounts, lost homes, lost middle-class status, and a lost future. JP Morgan, Goldman Sachs, Bank of America, Morgan Stanley, et al. were reorganized into bank holding companies, which, theoretically, exposed them to more regulation but actually was done to give them legal access to the Federal Reserve's lending window. It enabled these limping giants to run more money-grubbing rackets, for instance, borrowing money at near-zero interest rates from the Fed, then turning around and investing it in bonds that paid a few more interest points—an arbitrage called a "carry trade," which, when done with tens of billions of dollars, yielded a very tidy and regular revenue stream. This kind of public / private partnership was intended to "help the economy," but it did nothing to affect the swelling unemployment rolls or the foreclosure rate, while near-zero percent interest rates punished retired people who counted on old-fashioned interest yields from savings to pay their bills. Senior executives at big banks continued to receive jumbo bonuses even as one acronymic TARP, TALF, and FSP bailout program after another funneled astronomical sums of public money into their vaults, like fattening the livers of so many Strasbourg geese.[15] The triggering of credit default swaps did bring down the insurance giant AIG (American International Group) and the U.S. Treasury had to stuff $85 billion into its zombified husk

---

15. In the fall of 2011 it was discovered via an FOIA suit brought by the Bloomberg News Service that total aggregate bailouts through the Federal Reserves loan window following the crash of 2008–9 had actually amounted to more than $7.77 trillion—not the $700 billion approved by Congress. A substantial amount went to foreign banks including Barclays, Banco Santander, Credit Suisse, Deutsche Bank, BNP Paribas, and the Royal Bank of Scotland.

to pay off CDS bets with too-big-to-fail counterparties. Quite a few beneficiaries of the federal monies were foreign banks designated as primary dealers by the Federal Reserve.[16] Goldman Sachs managed to walk away with $14 billion of the slops from the AIG bailout.

Surely most demoralizing of all to the nation as a whole in the years since 2008 was the complete failure of the new president, Barack Obama, to reintroduce the rule of law into the financial system. Bailouts and stimulus programs are not regulatory measures or law enforcement. Not only did Mr. Obama omit to apply any of his advertised *change* to the deliberate inaction of the Bush Two Department of Justice, he managed to find an even more inert attorney general in Eric Holder. He brought into the White House inner circle a cast of characters—Robert Rubin, Lawrence Summers, Timothy Geithner, and others—who played major roles in the string of failures that had just occurred. And Goldman Sachs happened to be Mr. Obama's top source of corporate campaign contributions in the 2008 election, with Citigroup and JP Morgan not far behind. It hadn't been necessary for Mr. Obama to propose and ram through Congress a groaning bill of regulatory reforms to rein in the behavior of bankers. All he had to do was appoint people to the existing regulatory bodies who would enforce laws already on the books. Instead, he appointed people who did nothing.

The Aftermath that Keeps on Giving

As I write, the financial meltdown of 2008 is ongoing more than three years later. Nothing has been resolved. No important distortions or perversions of the system have been rectified. And most of all not one senior executive of a major bank has been subjected to so much as

16. Banks that trade in (i.e., "make a market for") government-issued securities. They are a conveyer belt between the Treasury and the central bank (the Federal Reserve) and receive premium payments for acting as such.

an official investigation. The arrest of the lone wolf Ponzi fraudster Bernard Madoff by the FBI in December 2008—after the election melodrama and all the histrionics of the initial stock market crash that fall—was a rogue event in a pattern of official lawlessness, a tiny cherry on top of a monumental cake of criminality. The $50 billion or so Madoff winkled out of his clients was spare change compared to the untold trillions that the financial system lost through wholesale financial racketeering during the bubble era. The 2008 crisis emanated from the biggest systematic control fraud in world history.[17] Networks of people in privileged positions violated the trust vested in their authority and subverted legitimate enterprise, clouding the boundary between business and crime, right and wrong. They have been covering it up in plain sight since, both in banking and in government—for instance, the 2009 Financial Accounting Standards Board ruling that made "extend and pretend" accounting possible.[18] The extended crisis has shredded confidence in authority in general and faith that we are capable of governing the most critical of our collective responsibilities: running complex systems that actually work. The resounding question is: where were the agents of regulation and enforcement, both before and after? Who was looking out for the American people?

The principal agencies overseeing financial market affairs in our country are the Securities and Exchange Commission and the U.S. Department of Justice (headed by the attorney general and including the FBI). These institutions failed miserably. The Federal Reserve, apart from its chartered mission of running our currency supply and managing select base interest rates, also had regulatory authority over standards

17. Control fraud: when bank executives use their authority and position to extract personal gain from the legitimate enterprise they work for, usually involving accounting misbehavior.
18. FASB Rule 157 (the fair value rule), revised in 2009 to allow "mark-to-fantasy" as opposed to reality-based mark-to-market value of assets, that is, a price on securities based on what they would realistically sell for in a market.

for home loans and could have at any time after 1994 disallowed the kind of innovation that led to widespread "liar loans" and deliberate negligence in underwriting (verifying borrowers' qualifications). Many other government agencies had parallel roles in investigating irregular behavior and responsibility to make referrals for criminal prosecution.[19] Referrals are absolutely crucial for making cases, according to William K. Black, the University of Missouri economics professor who secured over a thousand felony convictions in his earlier role overseeing the resolution of the savings and loan crisis.[20] Black called referrals the "heavy lifting" of criminal prosecution. They are road maps for government attorneys, providing detailed explanations for how frauds work and identifying key witnesses and documents needed to make a case. Such legal grunt work is absolutely crucial in cases involving super-rich white-collar criminals who can hire teams of the most expensive defense attorneys in the land with endless resources for depositions and obstructive filings. In fact, many an elite white-collar criminal defense attorney worked previously at a regulatory agency and knew their procedures intimately.

As it happened, however, referrals to the Department of Justice were practically nonexistent during the George W. Bush years and through the first three years of Barack Obama's administration. After 2001, the SEC slid into a policy known as "deferred prosecution agreements." The commission allowed banks suspected of misconduct to

---

19. Other bodies that have a role in the proper, legal functioning of the system include the CFTC (Commodity Futures Trading Commission), the FINRA (Financial Industry Regulatory Authority), the OCC (Office of the Comptroller of the Currency), the FDIC (Federal Deposit Insurance Corporation), the FTC (Federal Trade Commission), the FHFA (Federal Housing Finance Agency), the OTS (Office of Thrift Supervision), HUD (the U.S. Department of Housing and Urban Development), and both houses of Congress (particularly in their committee hearing process).

20. Black is also author of *The Best Way to Rob a Bank Is to Own One* (University of Texas Press, 2005). He was interviewed on the *Financial Sense Network* (FinancialSense.com), September 14, 2011.

police themselves, permitting the banks' own attorneys to run investigations. Even in cases of transparent wrongdoing, the SEC regularly let off banks if they promised not to misbehave in the same way again.[21] As for the FBI, President Bush had shifted the bulk of the bureau's white-collar crime division to the Homeland Security detail because of their skills for "following the money" in cases of suspected terrorism. After 2001 there were only about 120 FBI white-collar crime specialists deployed around the entire United States pursuing an overwhelming number of banking and mortgage frauds. By comparison, during the S&L crisis, the FBI had assigned more than a thousand agents to banking cases. Bush's third attorney general, Michael B. Mukasey, who served through the height of the financial crash, alluded to banking frauds as mere "street crime," as though it were too trivial to investigate. Indeed, directives came down from the top levels of the Justice Department to avoid being too aggressive with the floundering big banks, such was the fear that the whole system would collapse. A similar order to avoid making referrals went from the Federal Reserve to the SEC. It was like a page from the annals of an eighteenth-century Spanish colonial viceroy of Mexico, whose motto for administration was "Do little, and do it slowly."

The SEC refused to make criminal referrals in the case of Angelo Mozilo of the "liar loan" factory Countrywide Financial, despite being in possession of e-mails (which they used in their civil case against him) in which Mozilo disclosed that he knew his company was making junk mortgages and that, at the same time, he omitted to tell investors he was selling his own stock in the company hand over fist. In another mortgage fraud case handled by the U.S. attorney's office in New York, Deutsche Bank was accused of lying about loans and yet none of the bank's officers involved in the action were named as personally culpable,

---

21. Louise Story, *New York Times* reporter, transcript of interview with Terri Gross on NPR's *Fresh Air*: "Why Prosecutors Don't Go After Wall Street," July 13, 2011.

just the bank as a corporate "person." In a glaringly exceptional case, ten officers of a Georgia bank, Taylor, Bean & Whitaker Mortgage, were prosecuted and convicted only after being caught defrauding the TARP bailout fund in 2009; as far back as the year 2000, Fannie Mae had cited them as fraudsters but refused to make a referral because they wanted to dump tainted securities that included Taylor, Bean & Whitaker's mortgages and did not wish to alert the markets.

In 2011, an SEC whistleblower named Darcy Flynn told the Senate Judiciary Committee that his agency had for years systematically destroyed the records of some eighteen thousand "matters under investigation" (MUIs), including cases of insider trading and financial fraud against Lehman Brothers and two involving Bernard Madoff.[22] MUIs are a key tool for identifying patterns of repeated lawbreaking and hence in making referrals for prosecution to the Department of Justice. The eighteen thousand–plus MUIs existed in computer files that were dumped down history's memory hole. If duplicates or backups exist anywhere, on some lost laptop or forgotten server, their whereabouts are unknown. Because of the destruction of these records, the extent of abuse on Wall Street during this period may never be known.

The revolving door of employment between SEC senior enforcement positions and jobs in the Wall Street banks, or in law firms that serve Wall Street banks, is blatant and notorious. Often, SEC officers jump onto the payrolls of banks they were regulating within a few weeks. This indecency is replicated, of course, at the highest levels of government, with Wall Street executives such as Robert Rubin, Lawrence Summers, and Henry Paulson rotating in and out of Goldman Sachs, Citigroup, and assorted hedge funds in between various governmental appointments. The Wall Street revolving door is matched by another turnstile that takes former regulators to the K Street lobbying

---

22. The SEC ignored complaints about Bernard Madoff's Ponzi operations, including the repeated detailed letters of forensic accountant Harry Markopolos beginning in the year 2000.

corridor. Bank lobbyists are now de facto in charge of writing banking regulations.

This was certainly the outcome of the Dodd-Frank financial regulation bill (that's former senator Christopher Dodd, recipient of multiple favors from Angelo Mozilo). The Dodd-Frank law, passed in 2010, provided very little in the way of clear regulation. Rather it called for additional new bureaus in existing regulatory agencies with rules for their operation to be supplied at a later date. Hardly any rule changes were specified in the more than two thousand pages of the completed "Fin-Reg" legislation. Since passage, the new regulatory language has been workshopped by congressional staff aided by banking lobbyists, with no operational results so far. In the meantime, congressional Republicans are doing everything possible to retract the few key provisions of Dodd-Frank, so the entire exercise is likely to end in futility with the rule of law left on the roadside as just another casualty in America's war against its own future.

Where's Waldo's Mortgage?

Adding to the immense difficulty as to how any of these banking crimes, blunders, and turpitudes might be unwound is the confusion about who actually holds the mortgages on the millions of pieces of real estate that amount to the collateral on the original loans stuffed into derivative securities. In many foreclosure cases the documents can't be located. In numerous cases, the documents appear to have been fraudulently processed, with false signatures of people who were not actually bank officers but merely minimum-wage shills hired to sit in rooms and sign reams of paper. Titles to properties could not be found in the local registries of deeds of localities where the houses stood. Mortgages were resold and repackaged into so many esoteric bonds (MBS, CDOs et al.) that their ownership has vanished down a chain of securitization.

The loan on a house in suburban Stockton, California, may reside in the toxic investment of a Norwegian pension fund. There is evidence that some mortgages were inserted into bonds multiple times. To get around this confusion of responsibility, banks repackaging mortgages would arrange for "servicing companies," sometimes owned by the big banks themselves, to collect the monthly payments. But dealing with the millions of mortgages in default was an overwhelming task, and the banks had incentives to do nothing to resolve properties in default.

Court decisions subsequent to the crisis of 2008 held that foreclosures could not proceed if the title documents to a property did not exist in the registry of deeds in that jurisdiction. The problem, which was greatly complicated by the so-called MERS system (Mortgage Electronic Registration Systems, Inc., a private company), had several interesting ramifications. One was that people ended up staying in their houses, some for years, without making any mortgage payments, in clear default, because there was no legal way to evict them. Banks that did not pursue foreclosures could just hide the defaulted mortgages in their vaults and not have to declare losses on their quarterly reports. This was classic "extend and pretend" at the micro level, one mortgage at a time. Declared losses would have sent up a red flag to FDIC bank examiners and the Federal Reserve, which could then compel the banks to increase their reserves against losses and even shut the bank down.

Even where home foreclosures did go forward, they sometimes did so under massively suspect conditions, for instance, the notorious Florida foreclosure mills in which retired judges were hired to set up courts in empty office park conference rooms or vacant shopping mall stores where hearings were conducted on a mass production basis, in concert with law firms dedicated to streamlined cut-rate bulk filings for as little as $1,200 per property. The system worked well if the foreclosee did not contest the action, and especially if they did not show up at the hearing, which happened more often than not since their situations were generally hopeless anyway. If the foreclosee did happen to contest the action and sue to prevent it, the case was "back burnered," postponed and consigned to a stack of cases deemed not worth the trouble to pursue.

Legal fallout from all these shenanigans is mounting uncontrollably as foreclosures, bankruptcies, and retirement fund wipeouts. In the years after the crash of 2008 mountains of lawsuits against the big banks had accumulated from investors punch drunk with losses in mortgage-backed securities. In these suits by private individuals, pension funds, and insurance companies, the object has been to get the big banks to pay back the money swindled. Good luck. The cases will take years and years to resolve if they ever *can* be resolved, which is far from certain given the complexity of the bonds at issue and the tenacity of the lavishly paid law firms defending the banks. In the fall of 2011, the Federal Housing Finance Agency (FHFA), which is essentially the appointed conservator of nationalized Fannie Mae and its siblings, filed a lawsuit against JP Morgan, Deutsche Bank, Goldman Sachs, Bank of America, and several other too-big-to-fail banks for misrepresenting the quality of the mortgage-backed securities they packaged, seeking to recover $30 billion in losses suffered by the GSEs. Good luck with that too. Sadly, of course, the mischief in Fannie Mae at any point along the line was certainly as bad as the banks' misdeeds.

As of this writing an inept, bizarre, desperate deal was also floundering whereby a consortium of the individual state's attorneys general, in concert with several federal regulators, would accept a $20 billion payout from too-big-to-fail banks in exchange for limiting exposure to liabilities for improper practices such as "robo-signing" documents. New York's state attorney general Eric Schneiderman explicitly refused to sign on to the deal and the AGs of Massachusetts, Delaware, Nevada, and Minnesota had expressed reservations. The $20 billion is chump change compared to the liabilities at issue in lawsuits already filed around the country, which amount to hundreds of billions. The banks were trying to get off easy.

All this was happening while Europe was caught in an agony of a sovereign debt unwind, the pending default of the national bonds of Greece, Italy, and, lagging only slightly behind, Spain, Portugal, Ireland, and Belgium. The biggest European banks sat on bales upon bales of bonds from these countries and were wobbling on the rim of insolvency. The European Central Bank (ECB) and the governments of Germany, France, and the Netherlands had, through the spring and summer, tried every extend-and-pretend trick possible. None of them had worked and there was imminent expectation of yet another lending freeze and credit default swap meltdown.

The failure, around Halloween 2011, of the commodities hedge fund MF Global, fronted by CEO Jon Corzine, a former U.S. senator and New Jersey governor, as well as past CEO of Goldman Sachs, may turn out to be the spark that sets off the final conflagration of contemporary finance. The failure of MF Global resulted in the evaporation of an estimated $1.2 billion in segregated accounts of more than forty thousand clients, many of them ordinary wage earners, retirees, and farmers (MF Global was involved in the trade of agricultural commodities, including grain and cattle futures). The hedge fund also placed enormous bets leveraged at 100 to 1 on European sovereign bonds. When the bets went bad, the company faced a monumental margin call (the requirement to fork over collateral) and appears to have raided its clients segregated accounts in the process. By New Year's Day 2012, the missing money was still unaccounted for, despite a series of three congressional hearings held in the late fall of 2011.

The great danger posed by the MF Global affair grew out of the failure of the Chicago Mercantile Exchange (CME), which handled the bankruptcy, and the Commodity Futures Trading Commission (CFTC) to protect the holders of segregated accounts. This seemingly esoteric point has far-reaching implications as it suggests that no segregated client accounts in any investment company are safe any longer, with the further implication that massive redemptions and withdrawals will follow. The message to retail investors now is that the system has surrendered its last residues of trustworthiness. This has very grave portents for the future of capital formation as we have known it. Entering the winter of 2011–12 the global financial system stood in nearly complete disarray, so that if you are reading this you may be doing it in the smoldering ruins of modernity.

Immense predicaments loomed on the margins of the global financial meltdown that exerted pressure on the world's ability to carry on in the system that had been set up after the Second World War. In fact, the endless financial crisis could be viewed as an extension of peak oil, climate change, and population overshoot. These predicaments were coinciding with cycles of history that suggested a convulsion of change. The millennial generation was rising, as expressed in the Arab Spring movement, the London riots of August 2011, and the Occupy Wall Street movement that went viral in cities all over America. The great contraction that comprised an epochal debt deflation and resource-constrained limits to conventional growth was about to drag the developed nations kicking and screaming into a convulsive reset of everyday life. Nobody wanted to leave modernity behind. It had been such a great party.

Postscript

How the rule of law was defeated in money matters will remain one of the abiding puzzles for historians to dissect around the campfires of the future. The origin of its banishment seems to have occurred in the United States, with Europe part victim and part copycat of depredations that began here. The United States became the economic engine of the developed world in the past century not just because of its abundance of mineral wealth, its amber waves of grain, and its fantastic endowment of oil, but largely because the rule of law was so firmly established here that people knew where they stood with things they'd worked for all their lives. Property and contract law in the United States unambiguously spelled out what they owned free and clear, how they could dispose of these things, and what their obligations were. These rights and responsibilities were enforced with more than the usual rigor found in other parts of the world. They enabled business to be conducted freely and mostly fairly. The confidence that people all over the world felt for the rule of law in American financial matters was expressed in their respect for our money and the moneylike instruments issued by our companies and banks, the stocks and bonds, et cetera. We threw it all away: our honor, our faith in ourselves, our credibility with others, and the legitimacy of our institutions.

Fair dealing in a bounteous land was apparently not enough even for us, who had established it and cultivated it. We became greedy and craven and decided that lying to ourselves incessantly was the same as telling the truth. And all the wreckage that remains to be sorted out is testimony to that tragic change of heart.

SEVEN

THE ENERGY SPECTER: OIL AND GAS, ALTERNATIVE ENERGY, AND WAITING FOR SANTA CLAUS

Events since *The Long Emergency* was published in 2005 have borne out the proposition that peak oil is for real. The basic outlines of the story haven't changed but some interesting new twists and turns in the plot have emerged. Few can fail to notice, for instance, the disarray in the global economy over the past several years, especially in banking, and I maintain there is a direct relation between peak oil and the behavior of capital in economies, a linkage our leaders refuse to acknowledge.

Something happened around the turn of 2005–6. Worldwide production of conventional crude oil hit a ceiling at roughly 74 million barrels a day and has jostled around that figure since.[1] By conventional oil I mean the stuff that comes out of the ground through a pipe in liquid form, the kind most familiar to the general public, represented by a common drilling rig on a scrubby landscape. This oil was the

---

1. 2006: 73,427,901; 2007: 72,985,231; 2008: 73,669,877; 2009: 72,281,594; 2010: 74,048,670. U.S. Department of Energy, Energy Information Agency. In the spring of 2011 the U.S. DOE EIA announced that it would no longer collect information on oil production outside the United States due to "budget cuts."

low-hanging fruit of the industry, the stuff that was easiest to get at, of the lightest and "sweetest" quality that yielded the most gasoline and contained the fewest impurities, the stuff found in the easiest locations to work in, that had the highest return on what you invested in terms of money and energy to get it out of the ground. Back in the early days, the energy return on energy invested (EROEI) was something like 100 to 1 in Texas and Oklahoma. And it was similar in Saudi Arabia and other foreign lands back then. The world was used to cheap, abundant oil. It needed it just to keep things running the way they were set up to run.

The peak of conventional crude oil had been widely and loudly heralded, first by legendary geologist M. King Hubbert back in the 1950s, and then by later generations of scientists, who began to speak and write more openly about it when they retired from their jobs in the industry. They all saw it occurring early in the twenty-first century. One of them, a former student of Hubbert's, Kenneth Deffeyes, later in life a professor at Princeton University, cheekily predicted that global peak production would occur precisely on Thanksgiving Day 2005. Deffeyes admitted it was partly a gag, but monthly production figures later eerily showed that he had called it pretty much to the day. Deffeyes's figure held for several months. Then production inched up slightly further and there was a second slightly higher top (not by much) in July 2006. Ever since, the production figures have followed a downward trend line.

Okay, that was conventional crude oil. Meanwhile, other forms of petroleum could be produced to keep total world production growing by tiny increments after 2006. This was so-called unconventional oil — tar sands, shale oils, biodiesel, natural gas liquids. Natural gas liquids had long been a significant part of the total production picture, about 10 percent in recent years. This was an oily residue that dribbled out of gas wells, just as natural gas was often a by-product of oil wells. Tar sands were also well known and ignored for years by the industry as not worth the trouble to process, that is, until oil prices moved higher around 2003 and intimations that peak oil might be for real forced the issue. Tar sands also presented frightful environmental pollution problems. But there was a lot of it, strewn over the subarctic prairie of Canada's western provinces, and the risks of massive investment in mining and processing infrastructure paid off as it coincided with the first tremors of peak conventional oil.

Shale oil had been a marginal resource before 2005 but went into a boom afterward due to refinements in horizontal drilling and hydraulic rock fracturing ("fracking") that allowed oil to be liberated from "tight" rock formations previously undevelopable. High hopes were invested in shale oil and I shall discuss it in detail presently. Both tar sands and shale oils were more difficult and costly to get at than the old light-and-sweet crude had been, with much lower returns on investment. Biodiesel, like its cousin ethanol made from various seed crops, arguably took more energy to produce than it gave back, at least at the current stage of development. (Hopes were raised in alternative energy circles that bioengineered algae could eventually generate sizable supplies of instant biopetroleum, but this was as yet at the science-project stage of R&D.) Altogether these various additional oil substances kept the world total oil supply barely even with rising world demand between 2006 and the end of 2010, up around 86 million barrels per day (mm/b/d). As I write, world demand now marginally exceeds world production by about 1 mm/b/d, an ominous note.

With world oil production ranging narrowly in the mid to high 80 mm/b/d since 2005 the picture conformed to the image of the "bumpy plateau" I wrote about in *The Long Emergency*, a period when global oil production, flow rates, and market mechanisms would stall in a range of nervous volatility before entering permanent decline. This was the Wile E. Coyote moment of the fossil fuel economy. The bumpy plateau itself generated some weird behavior in economies and markets. One was an episode of extreme oil price volatility in 2008, where the price of oil shot up to $147 a barrel and crashed back to $32 six months later, spooking the entire global economic system. The aftereffects included a sharp recession that led to "demand destruction" as businesses shuttered or pared back operations and ordinary people had less money for gasoline. It was in the nature of this demand destruction feature of the bumpy plateau that eventually businesses and ordinary people (I refuse to call them "consumers") would respond to once-again-lower oil prices by using more oil, though the reset of around 19.5 mm/b/d in late 2010 fell short of the previous average high of around 20.5 mm/b/d prior to the 2008 financial meltdown. Then, in the spring of 2011, oil use in the United States went down again when the benchmark West Texas Intermediate crude price flitted above three digits for the first time since 2008. The trend line of the bumpy plateau was turning down in the United States (though in China consumption was up 10 percent in 2010).

Meanwhile, it became obvious by the end of the decade that previous rosy projections of oil supply punching through the 100 mm/b/d mark, issued by America's official data-gathering agencies such as the U.S. Geological Survey, the U.S. Department of Energy's Energy Information Agency (EIA), and the oil industry's own go-to public relations shop, Cambridge Energy Research Associates, fell short.[2] By the spring of 2011, with global demand for oil hovering above total oil production (conventional and nonconventional both), the world had entered the fat part of a crisis.

Then there was the Paris-based International Energy Agency, the IEA, which was the European version of the U.S. EIA. (IEA, EIA? Confused yet? Sorry.) The IEA (Europe) had, for years, issued the rosiest of rosy projections for endlessly increasing oil production well into the twenty-first century. Observers on the peak oil beat—the same cohort of retired oil industry geologists and insiders who first brought the issue to public attention—considered the IEA reports laughably

2. IHS CERA, originally founded by Daniel Yergin, Pulitzer Prize–winning author of *The Prize* (1992), a history of the oil industry, was later absorbed into IHS, Inc., a contractor to the military and the aerospace industry.

optimistic over the years.[3] To the surprise of many, in the fall of 2010 the IEA's chief economist, Fatih Birol (a Turkish national), came out with a rather extravagant acknowledgment of peak oil. "It is definitely depressing," Birol told the BBC program *One Planet*, "more than depressing, I would say alarming, which is what we try to do, to alarm the governments." This was a startling turnaround. The IEA's acknowledgment of peak oil was reiterated in its 2010 end-of-year *World Energy Outlook* report.

If top political leaders remained mum about peak oil, a slew of other significant reports in 2010 came unexpectedly from a diverse group of worldwide authorities ranging through Lloyd's of London, the U.S. Joint Forces Command, the German Defense Ministry, the New Zealand Parliament, the UK Industry Taskforce on Peak Oil and Energy Security (ITPOES), Oxford University's Smith School of Enterprise and the Environment, the University of Kuwait, and the Shell Oil Company. They uniformly presented peak oil as a problem of the utmost urgency. But these alarms too, failed to provoke politicians to speak out and did not register on a general public that was beaten down and preoccupied by the financial side effects of the problem.

Peak Oil, Peak Economy

It was not a coincidence that the global financial system wobbled and crashed in mid-2008, the same moment that oil shot up to $147 a barrel. Underlying the price event was a growing recognition by buyers, users, and traders in oil that oil had reached an inflection point, which was, of course, peak oil. Among this group were airlines, chemical and plastics makers, big agriculture, trucking companies, heating oil

---

3. Colin J. Campbell, Jean Laherrère, Chris Srebowski, Robert Hirsch, Ken Deffeyes, Matthew Simmons, Kjell Aleklett, et. al.

distributors, and electric power utilities. The public might have been asleep at the wheel but these industrial-scale oil buyers ran gigantic enterprises and rising prices had been playing havoc with their business formulas for several years.

Since 2002, for instance, Delta and United Airlines had been operating in bankruptcy, until they merged, respectively, with Northwest and Continental. Japan Airlines went bankrupt in 2010. In the fall of 2011 American Airlines entered bankruptcy. They all had to worry continuously about securing large amounts of oil-based jet fuel, which rose from between 10 and 20 percent of their total operating costs in the 1990s to between 30 and 50 percent in 2008. All big buyers of oil in the OECD countries also found themselves bidding increasingly into the market against China and India (Chindia!), which were seeing economic growth rates around 10 percent in recent years. Fear and greed drove the oil markets in the spring and summer of 2008, egged on by speculators, including Wall Street banks and investment firms, who took advantage of the anxious mood. In turn, oil prices ramping above $100, then $120, then $140 in July very decisively crushed economic activity. It wasn't long before these troubles moved to the heart of the economy, with job losses mounting and mortgages going bad at a frightening rate.

In September of 2008, Lehman Brothers gazed into an abyss of leveraged real estate holdings and fell in. No other bank wanted to acquire the firm's assets—which were hardly assets at all but just bales of loans that would never be paid back. Peak oil and peak credit had led to peak banking. The banks that survived went on government life support and liquidated what they could, including a lot of forward-dated oil contracts. As jobs and incomes vanished, the price of oil began its descent down to the eventual $32 mark, creating more havoc among investors.

The so-called housing bubble was about way more than overpriced houses and lending fraud. Suburbia had peaked precisely with peak oil. The correlation was uncanny but could have been easily predicted by any casual observer. For twenty years, the nation had been drunk on the final blowout of cheap oil, which commenced as the Alaskan and North Sea oil fields got into full production in the mid 1980s. It had climaxed around 1999 with oil at $11 a barrel. But where suburbia was concerned, a giant toxic sickness was burning through the system, and inertia would keep it going until its poisons seeped into every cell of the economy. The building of ever more suburban houses had morphed into a dreadful racket that had sucked all the participants—everyone from individual house buyers to production home builders to mortgage originators to giant banks to government-sponsored enterprises (GSEs) Fannie Mae and Freddie Mac to federal regulators—into a monstrous matrix of dishonesty in which everybody lied and defrauded other parties or turned a blind eye to criminal activities. It never would have happened if the suburban living arrangement had been viewed for the insanity that it was, a system absolutely dependent on cheap oil, with no future. You can't use something for collateral on debt that has no future.

None of it would have happened this way if Americans had seen that there was a connection between the end of cheap oil and the risks of far-flung suburban development. It also happened because of the flow of cheap credit—*peak* credit!—promoted by either direct government policy (e.g., federal officials leaning on banks to give money to sketchy borrowers) or de facto government policy (Fed chairman Alan Greenspan touting adjustable rate mortgages as he did in 2005). The construction industry had become a huge part of the economy, around 40 percent of new jobs created after the year 2000, yet there was no public conversation about the value of what they were so busy building. It was just assumed to be a good thing. By the early twenty-first century most Americans did not know any other way to live. They had invested their life savings in it and government had gone into hock outfitting the infrastructure. Politicians didn't want to rock the suburban boat (or rock the vote in the wrong direction).

Though world peak oil happened in 2006, few realized that it was also world peak economy, even after 2008 when the systemic feedback loops started the slow-motion train wreck of the long emergency in earnest. Ever since then the U.S. financial system has been barely kept going on additional reckless borrowing, accounting fraud, and market manipulations. These machinations are fundamentally not wealth-generating activities. They all just add up to a Polish blanket trick where the guy wants to make his blanket longer by cutting six inches off the top and sewing it onto the bottom (and, in the process, loses four inches just in the hemming).

Similar tricks are reaching the endgame for other advanced industrial nations as the volatile oil market weakens their economies. They may not have as much suburban sprawl to contend with as the United States does, but they are headed into a compressive contraction, too, with massive debt issues. And, except for Norway and Russia, they have next to no oil of their own. China's economy got even more intoxicated on the final blowout of cheap oil than any of the OECD countries did, and its banking system is arguably a worse form of racketeering than the West's. The Chinese got into the industrial development game late and they will hit the wall of peak economy just as surely as every other industrial nation. Japan, following the manifold Fukushima disaster of 2011 and twenty years of zombie banking, is hitting the wall so hard that I believe the country may sooner or later just return to something like a seventeenth-century traditional culture. The only big remaining questions are whether this sort of compressive contraction can be called collapse and what happens afterward.

The Flavors of Collapse

There is plenty of disagreement even among those of us who followed the oil story for ten years about where this is all leading. One way you can subdivide the range of opinions is between those who think we are in for a slow, predictable, mitigated, perhaps even orderly decline of our oil supplies and economic arrangements (a gentle slope on a graph) and those of us who think it will take the form of a more rapid, disorderly collapse (falling off a cliff). John Michael Greer, the author of *The Wealth of Nature* and other books, uses the term "catabolic" collapse to describe an organic destructive process that quickly decomplexifies modern life and resets the terms of modernity at smaller scales within a matter of a decade. Dmitry Orlov, author of *Reinventing Collapse*, having witnessed the effects of the Soviet collapse, also sees the oil production system and everything dependent on it coming to grief shockingly soon for all of industrial society (including, all over again, the new Russia of oligarch capitalism). Richard Heinberg, author of *The End of Growth* and many other books, seems to reluctantly agree. My own view is consistent with theirs, and here is why.

A major dynamic in the larger picture of all this is the relationship between oil production and available capital going forward. I have already tried to make the case that a direct feedback loop operates between capital (or money) and energy. Just as ever increasing energy inputs to the global economy expanded the total amount of money and credit available since the mid-1800s, so will a declining base of energy inputs contract the amount of money and credit available—most critically, money and credit to finance exploration for future oil discovery and production to keep up with even declining existing oil resources. Every year from now on there will be fewer total exploration efforts, less money for drilling rigs and for the necessary steel, copper, and other basic resources to make them, less money to pay for technicians and scientists or even to educate new ones to replace the ones who are getting too old. Each step-bump down in recessionary response to peak oil, or scarcer oil, or volatility in oil markets will result in ever more scarce capital for future oil. We are bumping up against the idea not just that resources are finite but that the side effects in capital formation lead to deeper scarcities.

Among the additional side effects will be the breakdown of oil markets themselves, the mechanisms that allow oil currently produced to be allocated among customers in a dependable way. And bear in mind that giant, integrated industrial economies do not work well when supplies of vital resources are not predictable. These side effects can be seen clearly in the oil export dilemma. Dallas geologist Jeffrey Brown has depicted this in his Export Land Model, which states that exporting nations with declining yearly production and growing domestic consumption of their own oil will necessarily see their export rates fall dramatically in the years ahead. Many of these exporting nations — Saudi Arabia, Iran, Venezuela, Mexico et al. — have very fast growing populations. They run more cars every year and subsidize the price of gasoline to their own citizens. In Venezuela gasoline was selling for 12 cents a gallon in the spring of 2011.

Mexico is the poster child for America's import problem. For years that export land was our number three source of imported oil. At current rates of domestic consumption and rapid depletion, Mexico will be out of the oil export business completely before 2015. All of their oil production will go to satisfy their own needs and America will get nothing. There is no discussion of this dilemma in the American news media or the political arena. The net effect of the worldwide export crisis will be less total oil available to all the importing nations. The United States, Germany, Japan, Great Britain, France, China, India, and many other import lands have a big problem.

Adding to the problem, as the world price of oil goes up due to growing scarcity, those countries still exporting oil will make more money, leading to even more consumption of their own oil with less available to sell elsewhere. Even if oil production in some export lands were to remain flat, their export rates would still decline with accelerating rates over time. As all this occurs, friction is liable to increase among nations vying for imports, with great potential for conflict. One can easily see, too, the probability of other geopolitical complications, including internal strife in the export lands themselves, already under way in 2011 across North Africa and the Middle East. The revolt in Libya shut in that country's exports and the world oil market lost 1.3 mm/b/d. So on top of an inexorable feedback loop affecting finite supplies of the developed world's primary resource, you have other layers of political and market disorders that can only exacerbate the export problem.

This oil export crisis has a disturbingly close horizon. Under the Export Land Model net exports from all the oil export lands will reach zero in nine years as, one by one, the export lands cannibalize their own export capacity. Note: the United Kingdom went from being an oil exporter (from the North Sea fields) to becoming an oil importer in only six years. The United States imports 12 mm/b/d, more than two-thirds of our total consumption. We will not be able to compensate for our losses of conventional crude from any combination of tar sands, shale oils, or other unconventional (more expensive) resources, as I'll discuss below. Conventional thinking in business, government, and the major media would have the public believe in infinite increases in finite resources. Jeffrey Brown said, "In my opinion, we will see an epic collision between the conventional wisdom expectations of a continued exponential rate of increase in net oil exports, versus the rapidly developing new reality of an exponential decline in net oil exports."

Wishing for Miracles, Part 1: Shale Oil

Lately, not a week goes by when I don't receive mail from some anxious stranger asking my opinion of the latest game changer in America's awful struggle to remain energy-positive, to fend off any threats to our vaunted way of life. These inquiries generally involve some element of fantasy or wishful thinking. Someone e-mails me saying that an article in *Forbes* magazine states America has more oil than Saudi Arabia! Isn't that great news? Could it be true? Another report somewhere else says that we have enough shale gas to last for three hundred years. Wow! A guy in a Salt Lake City garage has invented an engine that runs on water! Hooray! We live in a very delusional nation these days. Americans desperately want to believe that we can keep running all the things we've invested our collective life savings in, and we're bargaining for miracles along the emotional gradient of Elisabeth Kübler-Ross (author of *On Death and Dying*).[4]

Naturally, the most desperate wishing swirls around the petroleum question, because if we could just get our mitts on more of it we could keep all our stuff running—the cars, the suburbs, Disney World, Walmart, the whole kit that is engineered to run that way. We wouldn't have to change anything we do and our investments would be safe. And so it happened that just around the very moment that the world inched past peak oil—2005 and 2006—great hopes were suddenly raised around a resource called shale oil. It is found distributed over wide areas of the United States, especially in the western parts of the country. The deposits had been well known for decades but were thought to be uneconomical to produce, so few people bothered with them. By mid-decade, though, with the price of oil rising, companies went in and took another look. Pretty soon the media were saying there was at least a hundred-year supply out there, surely enough to serve as a bridge to the also wished for nirvana called *the renewable energy future*. What was the reality of shale oil?

There are two distinct types of so-called shale oil. The catch is that one is not oil. The stuff found in the Williston Basin, for instance, which overlaps North Dakota, Montana, and on into Canada, is real oil. The stuff in the Green River Basin straddling Wyoming, Utah, and Colorado is not oil, it's a substance called kerogen, organic matter that is a chemical precursor to actual oil. So let's just get it out of the way.

4. The stages of grief: denial, anger, bargaining, depression, acceptance.

Kerogen is the chemical residue of the fossil organisms that become oil when cooked underground in the "oil window"—between, say, 2,500 to 16,000 feet down—where heat and pressure over time are sufficient to break down kerogen into petroleum hydrocarbons. By geologic accident, however, some rocks containing kerogen have never been folded or thrust down low enough to enter the oil window, so the stuff never got cooked. That is the case with many of the touted deposits in Wyoming, Utah, and Colorado; they remain uncooked. If you want to make oil out of this you have to cook it yourself. That takes quite a bit of additional energy and investment in equipment, some of it rather elaborate (depending on whether you want to cook the kerogen in situ, where it sits down in the rock, or mine it and put it into some kind of a heating vessel after that). Pretty soon you're talking a lot more money to produce the stuff.

For years, the Shell Oil Company made noises about developing Green River Basin shale oil. They ramped up some science project–size demonstrations but never got commercial production going (there still isn't any) for the simple reason that it didn't scale up or pencil out. For one thing, there isn't much electricity out there. Among the infrastructure you'd have to invest in is new generating plants, probably with rail lines to transport the coal to them. Some trial balloons were sent up about building a nuclear reactor out in the Green River Basin but the costs of that were out of sight, not to mention the permitting difficulties, and, well, after the Fukushima disaster of 2011 the proposal was stone dead. Making oil out of kerogen also requires a lot of water to process the material and the Utah, Colorado, Wyoming region is very dry. There is barely enough now for the sparse population to drink and bathe with. Lately, Shell affects to complain that environmentalists are preventing them from going forward with their hypothetical kerogen recovery-and-conversion operations. But it was probably not much more than a public relations dodge all along, an attempt to make Shell look patriotic and "pro-active" in the face of our oil import problems (incidentally casting environmentalists as unpatriotic negativists) and most of all to buff up the company's share value. For additional reasons I'll get to presently, it will never be economical to work this play, as geographical resource sites are called. So we'll lay aside the Green River Basin part of the story.

The oil in the Williston Basin, also known as the Bakken formation, is actual oil. The U.S. Geological Survey estimates that the formation holds about 4 billion barrels of recoverable oil, about one-fifth of the Prudhoe Bay, Alaska, conventional crude fields. Bakken shale oil is characteristically found sandwiched in thin rock strata, 10 to 50 feet thick and 4,500 to 12,000 feet underground. This stuff is called "tight" rock, meaning it has low porosity, low permeability. The oil doesn't flow out of it. Rather, it's trapped in the rock. Conventional oil will seep or migrate out of source rocks over centuries and pool into oil fields in high-porosity strata such as sandstones under salt domes and other underground capping formations. You can thrust a vertical pipe into the ground like a soda straw and get oil out. In the early days of the oil era, when the deposits were new and fresh, oil gushed out under its own pressure.

In Bakken shale and formations like it, the oil doesn't seep out of the source rock over time and collect in concentrated underground fields. It stays trapped in place. This is one reason that the shale plays are touted to be so geographically large, with sweet spots here and there amid a matrix of source rocks from which concentrated fields have never formed. When you sink a plain old pipe into a shale layer from a drilling rig nothing comes out. It's one thing to say that there's a lot of oil in the Bakken play, and it's another to understand the difficulties associated with getting enough of it out of any given drill site to be worth the effort.

The technological refinements of recent decades made it seem at least economically practicable to try. Horizontal drilling was one nifty trick that had been around for a while. But it was hard to keep a lateral pipe in the very narrow 10- to 50-foot range of the shale layer. Then seismic imaging and computerization of the controls over the business end of the drill bit combined to make the drilling process extremely precise. You could go 5,000 feet down vertically, and then drill another mile laterally, and keep the drill bit right in that thin oil-bearing shale layer. However, the oil still would not flow out of the tight rock, even with pipe driven through it. So one more procedure was added: fracturing, or "fracking." This involved pumping down a fluid cocktail under high pressure that contained, among other things, tiny sand particles (lately manufactured ceramics) that would get down into the fractures and hold them open like tiny doorstops. Explosives were also used to help the process along. When you pumped the fracking fluid back out, oil liberated from the shattered rock collected in the fractures.

It does work. You can get oil out of the ground that way, but it is hard and costly. The average deepwater conventional oil well in the Thunder Horse formation in the Gulf of Mexico produces 40,000 barrels a day, which might justify the billions spent on giant platforms built to get at it. The average Bakken well produces around 52 barrels a day, which may not justify the thousands of truck trips and other operations needed to get it. Think of it as like comparing a fire hose to wringing out a sponge. For the moment Bakken gives the appearance of working economically, though I argue that the so-called shale oil bonanza is running on the fumes of hype and financial leverage in order to goose money out of investors' pockets on the front end of the play, no matter what happens in the Bakken later on. From the broader perspective, whatever else the fracking process might be — techno wizardy, human genius, a financial scam — it seems to be a way of getting oil to migrate artificially out of source rock, a process that ordinarily happens over eons of geological time. It's very expensive to try to shortcut geological time. And not all that effective.

When you go to the trouble of fracking these shales the oil moves only into the fractures. It doesn't form extensive underground pools or fields, even when you set off charges and force tiny granules into the fractures to hold them open. The oil that collects in the fractures drains quickly and the fractures do not refill within any meaningful period of time because the rock matrix is not permeable. No more oil will seep out into the fracture. Generally "recompletions"—as fracking the same hole again is termed—do not increase production much, and it is expensive. To get more production, you have to drill another hole and run another fracking operation. Ultimately, you have to drill an awful lot of holes to keep production up in any particular area of the play. It requires a lot of drilling rigs, a lot of steel pipe, a lot of fracking fluid trucked to the site, and a lot of capital to complete a well, as they say.[5] The oil companies have gotten better at extending the lateral pipes. At first, the limit was about 500 feet with one explosive charge. Now a mile-long lateral, with a dozen or more charges, can be run. But then a mile-long hole will take a lot more fracking fluid to work, and the Williston Basin is a comparatively dry part of North America. Consider how many thousands of tanker truckloads of water it will take to run these fracking operations, and how much diesel fuel each trip will consume. Also note, fracking operations fall off steeply every winter in the harsh climate of North Dakota and Montana where the Bakken shale fields are located.

The Eagle Ford play in Texas is currently the other shale oil hot prospect. It presents more opportunity for year-round fracking than the Bakken. Eagle Ford shale is distributed in a band across south-central Texas. The population is sparse, which removes a lot of pain-in-the-ass costs associated with battling environmental law enforcement if citizens complain. On the other hand, south-central Texas is arid, so tens of thousands of tanker truckloads of water will be required to carry on fracking activities there. Of sixteen initial wells completed between December 2005 and November 2009, nine are no longer producing. Of the seven remaining wells from that group still producing, the best

---

5. Shale oil recovery, using lateral drilling, uses four times as much steel pipe as conventional oil drilling.

(Burlington #3 Kunde) was averaging 16 barrels of oil a day in the spring of 2011. That's barely better than the volume you'd get from a stripper well, which is where the last drops of a regular old played-out oil well are wrung. By 2011 well over one hundred wells were working the oil play at Eagle Ford (with more wells in place for gas).

The Bakken play was producing about 350,000 barrels of oil a day in the spring of 2011 and Eagle Ford under 40,000. The hype has claimed that full production of U.S. shale oil might reach 2 million barrels a day. It sounds good, but it is the most extreme high-end forecast and, remember, America burns through about 20 million barrels a day. Whatever the production high for shale oil might turn out to be, it is not likely to be sustained, given the rapidity of shale oil well depletion. It will also not make up for the one-two punch of America's conventional oil depletion and the certainty of steeply declining imports. For instance, the flow in the Alaska pipeline has fallen from 2.1 mm/b/d at its high in the 1980s to about 0.5 million now. The oil used to make the eight-hundred-mile journey in four and a half days. Now the rate of flow is down so significantly that it takes two weeks, during which the oil cools so much the water residues flowing with it can freeze and cause major problems. If the flow rate falls much lower the pipeline will have to either be reengineered at great cost (there's talk of heating it) or just go out of business, leaving Alaska's North Slope oil stranded. The additional problems with imports are inevitable and largely beyond our control. Even the rosiest forecasts for all shale oil would not compensate for our prospective import losses.

Oil has always been a boom-and-bust business. The shale oil boom is under way now because America is desperate for oil, and all the activity downstream from that, including the finances, is driven by utter desperation. This is another place where dangerous feedback loops between oil and capital meet. The United States is already reeling economically from the peak oil predicament. The nation has never recovered from the crash of 2008, despite the Federal Reserve's legerdemain and the coddling of too-big-to-fail corporations. At best, the economy seemed to stabilize for a couple of years at a lower real GDP level, which included some demand destruction for oil. In the spring of 2011 oil demand in the United States had picked up some but was still shy of its former peak, and the price of oil rose into the $100+ per barrel range for a while. Predictably, the economy tanked again, in May 2011. We'll progressively use less oil going forward but there will also be less economic activity in the country, especially that pegged to oil, which is just about everything. You can call this involuntary conservation.

If global demand goes down, the price of oil will fall from the $100+ range, perhaps very low, if the contraction under way reaches Great Depression levels. If that happens there will be a lot less capital (money) available for oil companies to explore for oil, drill for it, and complete new oil wells, especially in places like the Bakken, when it is acknowledged how quickly these shale plays peter out. If the price of oil goes below $50 per barrel, shale oil will not be worth producing. I'd assert that this is exactly what is about to happen. The oil out there may hypothetically amount to 150 billion barrels, but it is not sufficiently concentrated to make sustained recovery economically viable. The luster will quickly wear off the hype. The result will be even less oil available to the U.S. economy as a whole and you begin to see a spiral of remorselessly declining economic activity, oil production, wealth, and capital. Long before that spiral reaches the bottom America will run into huge problems with regard to its vital infrastructure. In the meantime, we're doing almost nothing to rearrange our manner of living.

Wishing for Miracles, Part 2: Shale Gas

Shale gas was the other big rescue remedy for an energy-strapped nation. The basic fantasy was that we could make up for our declining oil supplies by swapping in proportionally more natural gas to run all our stuff, and do so in an orderly way that would not entail any economic disruption.

Just to be clear: natural gas is methane (CH_4). It is not the same as gasoline, which is, of course, a liquid. Natural gas is geologically associated with oil. It forms in the earth similarly and comes out of drilled wells. It burns more cleanly than coal, oil, or gasoline, that is, it produces less carbon dioxide waste, but it is still a hydrocarbon fossil fuel with climate implications. We use it for home heating, cooking, and about 23 percent of our electric power generation. Mostly we have to rely on the gas found on our own continent, North America, where it runs through a very elaborate network of pipelines from the wells to the customers. Importing gas from overseas requires expensive processes of liquefaction and compression, transport by highly specialized tanker ships, and offloading to terminals, all of which makes it much more expensive. We do import gas from Canada but it gets here in pipelines. We also export some gas to Mexico.

As with oil, there is conventional natural gas and unconventional gas. The latter includes shale gas and coal-bed methane (i.e., gas associated with coal deposits, a tiny part of the whole picture). Conventional natural gas migrates out of permeable source rocks into underground fields under a layer of capstone. You run a vertical pipe through the capstone and gas comes out under its own pressure until the pressure stops, and then the gas stops coming out. Shale gas works differently. Like shale oil, it is trapped in tight rock—low-porosity, low-permeability source rock. It can't migrate out of this rock into concentrated fields. You have to fracture the source rock and collect the gas from the fractures.

Conventional natural gas reached peak production in the United States in 1973. (U.S. peak oil was 1970.) Production declined accordingly. New offshore gas came online in the 1980s and the decline flattened out below the level of the 1973 peak. In the late 1990s the number of drilling rigs started to steeply increase. Even so, the average productivity of individual gas wells decreased just as steeply. Overall, production remained flat. By 2005 we were drilling three times as many new wells every year—up from ten thousand to thirty thousand—just to get the same amount of gas. This was the Red Queen syndrome (from *Alice in Wonderland*) in which you run faster and faster just to stay where you are. By the early twenty-first century there was a lot of talk about having to import liquefied natural gas from overseas and the need to build receiving terminals for the shipments, which nobody wanted anywhere near them because of the potential for catastrophic explosions (multiplied by the threat of terrorist attack after 2001).

Natural gas is priced in units of a thousand cubic feet (mcf). The price moved up sharply from about $2 mcf in 1999 to above $14 in late 2005, fell to $4 in mid-2006, spiked back up above $13 in mid-2008, and crashed again to its current price at this writing in the $2 range. This was rather extreme volatility, only partly explained by the seasonality of gas consumption (a lot of it is used for home heating). Large quantities are routinely injected into old salt caverns in an annual storage cycle, but the capacity has limits. Storing it in liquid form requires temperatures around −260 degrees Fahrenheit, plus high compression steel tanks, making this form of stockpiling an expensive issue. One of the major industrial users of gas, the fertilizer industry, virtually shut down in the United States around 2005 in response to rising prices. So we started importing fertilizer made in Trinidad, Tobago, and Qatar, with the further implication of making the United States dependent on a Middle East country for yet another vital resource.

By 2005, just as with oil, horizontal drilling and fracking opened up new possibilities for getting gas out of tight shale rock, and for getting capital out of investors. The price of natural gas was reaching new highs that year, over $10 mcf. Initial high production rates in the new shale plays inspired massive hype about "recoverable reserves"— the amount that these plays would supposedly yield in the long run, assuming there was a long run, which was a big assumption. But Wall

Street was swimming in money, nervous about rumors of this kooky new theory called peak oil (which so many barely understood), and credulous about anything that sounded like a solution to it. Shale gas sure *smelled* like money.

Texas oil billionaire T. Boone Pickens jump-started the idea that natural gas could be America's energy savior with a gala TV advertising campaign that proposed taking the gas that had been allocated to electric power plants and shifting it to running trucks, then putting up wind turbine farms on the blustery Texas plains to generate electricity and incidentally gin up an electric automobile fleet. In the process, Pickens said, we could reduce the amount of oil we had to import from unfriendly foreigners. He repeated the pitch in an appeal before a U.S. Senate committee. It was not immaterial that Pickens had investment interests in the new shale gas plays, though I believe his motives were based on a sincere concern about the nation's well-being.[6] The so-called Pickens plan attracted a lot of attention, mainly because he was the only leader in either politics or big business who stepped up to the plate with any plan whatsoever for America's energy predicament.

I viewed the Pickens plan with skepticism from the outset because it did not address what I regarded to be the deeper problem of America's extreme car and truck dependency. It merely proposed shifting fuels around. In fact, part of its appeal was the idea that Americans would not have to change any of their habits or living arrangements. But the Pickens plan also assumed a substantial increase in America's natural gas resource base. This was, of course, predicated on the development of the new shale gas plays, which were just then exciting so much intoxication among the oil companies and Wall Street. A classic boom was under way. Perhaps even a bubble. Between 2005 and 2008 the money

6. Pickens cited my work to the Senate Homeland Security and Government Affairs Committee in April 2008. He had turned up for a lecture I gave at Southern Methodist University in Dallas in 2007, where I met him. As it happened, I had no further correspondence with him.

side of the game was all about the gas drilling companies inflating perceptions of fantastic returns on investment, just as had happened in the housing boom. It was not a coincidence that the air was coming into the shale gas bubble at exactly the same moment that it was going out of the housing bubble. Big money was looking for someplace else that would yield similar returns.

The early shale gas action was in the Barnett play around Dallas and Fort Worth, the Haynesville play straddling the Texas–Louisiana border, and the Fayetteville play in Arkansas. Then there was the Marcellus play, which covered a seemingly vast area of Pennsylvania, New York, West Virginia, and Ohio. Development of the Marcellus started a little later than the others but the prospects wowed investors, as well as news media pundits and politicians looking for "green shoots" in an otherwise bleak economic picture. The Marcellus was next door to the New York–DC–Philadelphia–Boston population belt, right in among a mammoth customer base. As word spread from the industry about the miracle of the shale, a meme entered popular circulation to the effect that America had a hundred-year supply of natural gas. Almost all the information about the shale gas plays, especially production forecasts, came directly from the companies involved who would benefit from positive reports, or from industry PR touts such as Cambridge Energy Research Associates (CERA). The boosters were shouting that our energy worries were over. Aubrey McClendon, CEO of the Chesapeake Energy company, a major player, told reporter Lesley Stahl on 60 Minutes that America had "two Saudi Arabias worth" of natural gas.

The shale gas plays were for real, to a point, but a point that would not exactly converge with a lot of people's hopes and wishes about it. A report by the gas industry's appointed group the Potential Gas Committee estimated that there were 650 trillion cubic feet of resources in the shale plays. Independent analysts such as Houston-based Arthur Berman and Bill Powers of the *Powers Energy Investor* newsletter, looked more closely at the production figures between 2005 and 2011 and concluded that a more reasonable figure was 100 tcf, when all was said and done, which represented perhaps five or so years of U.S. consumption at current rates of around 19 tcf a year. That was apart from the conventional gas, which amounted to perhaps a ten-year supply on top of that—hardly a one-hundred-year supply or two Saudi Arabias worth.

Beyond the stupendous drilling rig counts needed just to keep the flow rate steady, there were other limiting problems or conditions, and they were all pretty severe. Foremost was the relatively rapid depletion of the wells. Shale gas wells declined at a rate of between 63 and 85 percent in the first year. (Conventional natural gas wells typically fall off between 25 and 40 percent in year one of production.) The gas drilling companies had equations that suggested the wells would have long, productive lives—thirty, forty years—but their method for projecting "hyperbolic" (increasingly flattened) decline rates was easily manipulated by slyly changing a factor or two in the calculations on the right side of a decimal point. The forecasts were designed mainly to impress the bankers, who were unlikely to examine the abstruse math. It turned out that very high initial production rates in shale plays belied the starker reality: shale gas wells were very short-lived, more like five or six years for some of the best. Plus, there were plenty of dry holes, where nothing came out. It was also soon discovered that the productive action in the seemingly massive geographical areas of the various plays turned out to be quite modest in terms of sweet spots.

These resolving realities made the shale gas bonanza a bit sketchier when combined with erratic prices, high capital spending requirements, an economy that would soon shudder from the effects of peak oil, a housing sector bust, manifold banking woes, and zero real economic growth (when you winnowed out all the hedonic bullshit and statistical gaming that had become routine in official reporting). U.S. natural gas prices spiked and fell four times between 2000 and 2009. Overall, the volatility reflected the long-standing inability to adjust the gas supply at will. Many companies, large and small, were competing in the plays, and they were all going for as much initial production as possible to attract investment. And there were major elements of the demand that weren't very elastic, namely electricity production and home heating. You had to keep the electric grid operating and stay warm.

The companies going into the shale spent huge amounts of their up-front borrowed money obtaining drilling leases from thousands of individual property owners. The leases required the companies to get to drilling within a set term or the leases would be canceled, because many property owners had a stake in royalties on any gas produced and they didn't want a company just sitting on it. So the companies were in a use-it-or-lose-it situation and had to get these leases into production. Even so, in the mad rush of activity after 2005, the industry could not get beyond the 1973 annual production peak of 21.73 trillion cubic feet, no matter how many holes they drilled in the ground.

The price spikes did not mitigate the cost of adding the additional twenty thousand drilling rigs over a ten-year period. Each shale gas well cost between $3 million and $10 million to drill and complete (i.e., frack). Then there was the economy's response to the decade-long oscillating differential in gas prices between $2 and $13. At under $8 companies couldn't make a profit off the new shale gas plays. Above $8 ordinary householders couldn't afford to heat their houses. Throw in a black swan event such as the successive hurricanes Katrina and Rita—which in 2005 caused a lot of damage to offshore conventional gas drilling platforms, pipelines, and refineries around the Gulf of Mexico—and you had another factor in the volatile prices. Considering the yo-yoing price picture against all the debt tied up in it shale gas was looking marginally commercial at best.

The price spike of 2008 was associated with the crack-up boom that brought on the Wall Street crash, when peak oil caught up with peak credit. By 2008 the shale gas plays were in full production mode. The number of drilling rigs was at its height from Texas up into

Pennsylvania. They were producing too much gas. Large initial flows along with recession and demand destruction led to a gas glut that quickly drove prices back to the $4 range by early 2009, where they have remained. The worst part about it for the industry was the lack of a dependable, predictable price that would have allowed them to make rational plans. Hence, the plans the industry did make were not rational but crazy, especially in terms of capital financing.

In the permanent contraction that characterized the new economy of scarcity capital was among the things getting scarce. The equation between unpredictable prices, nearly flat overall gas production (despite new shale), vastly increased drilling activities, and rapid well depletion suggested that the initial shale gas boom would crash spectacularly on vanishing prospects and a shortage of capital sometime before 2015. Among the first victims of this dynamic was Chesapeake Energy and its CEO Aubrey McClendon, the fellow who had touted shale gas on 60 Minutes. When gas prices crashed with the Wall Street debacle of 2008, Chesapeake's stock fell from $66 a share to $11. McClendon personally lost about $2 billion in his own stock interests. He had drunk too much of his own Kool-Aid. That same year he sold a 32.5 percent interest in his company's Marcellus gas leases to Norway's Statoil national petroleum company.

The Fear Factor

In April of 2011 one of Chesapeake's shale gas wells in rural Pennsylvania spilled fracking fluid into a nearby creek. It was among the more dramatic such incidents highlighting the dark side of the shale gas miracle: the problems with water and fears of pollution from the sinister fracking fluid.

As shale oil and gas production took off in a big way after 2005, suspicions developed among people living near the field operations that the fracking fluids could contaminate the water table and pose serious long-term health hazards. There was also some question of natural gas seeping up through rock layers disturbed by the fracking and getting into people's homes. The fear was so great that the state of New York imposed a moratorium on shale gas fracking in the summer of 2010 and extended it an additional year in May 2011. The award-winning documentary *Gasland*, made by Josh Fox and released in 2010, showed home owners in the Marcellus shale region of Pennsylvania who had so much methane coming out of their kitchen faucets they were able to ignite a jet of flame. Fugitive gas leaks in Pennsylvania have long been associated with coal mining there, so the incident was inconclusive. But there were plenty of reasons to worry about the chemicals used in the shale plays.

Up until about 2010 the contents of the fracking fluid remained shrouded in mystery. The gas drilling companies claimed they were working with proprietary formulas that amounted to trade secrets and so couldn't be revealed. The Energy Policy Act of 2005 exempted hydraulic fracturing from federal regulation under the Safe Drinking Water Act (and many other antipollution regulations), so companies were not compelled to disclose their secrets, but the information eventually got out.[7] There were many different recipes for fracking fluid, depending on the exact character of the shale and whether the resource was gas or oil. It was generally composed of 99 percent water and 1 percent other stuff. Each component of the *other stuff* had an engineered purpose. Often there was more than one chemical that could be employed for a given purpose. Here are some of them.

Potassium chloride made the fracking fluid more slick, reducing friction as it flowed down the well bore under high pressure to

7. Prior to the presidential election campaign of 2000 Vice President Dick Cheney had been the CEO of Halliburton, leading developer of advanced hydrofracking technology used in the new shale plays. Thus, the provision in the 2005 legislation that exempted fracking operations from EPA scrutiny is known as the Halliburton loophole.

hit harder. (Among the other common uses of potassium chloride: as fertilizer and as one of three chemicals used in lethal injections for executions.) Ethylene glycol antifreeze went down the well bore to prevent ice from forming. Hydrochloric acid helped dissolve some drilling debris that might clog pipes. Various chemical poisons (e.g., glutaraldehyde) were used to prevent algae from growing in the fractures. Corrosion inhibitors went down to protect pipes and valves against rust. When fracturing had been accomplished, a gelling agent was added to the fluid to suspend the sand or ceramic particles designed to hold the fractures open. When it was time to pump the fluid back out again, a breaker chemical went down the hole to turn the gel back into a liquid, sometimes benzene, a proven carcinogen, sometimes methanol, an industrial poison.

A horizontal shale gas well can require 6 million gallons of water in a completion. Much of the time, it has to be delivered to the well pads in tanker trucks, involving more than a thousand individual truck trips per well. With wells in the Pennsylvania Marcellus region spaced in forty-acre units, running to a thousand wells in some townships, that represents a lot of rural truck traffic. The noise is an issue for opponents of shale gas drilling, and the wear and tear to county highways and back roads is a cost that must be borne by municipal governments. Additional noise comes from the drilling and fracturing operations themselves and pipeline compressor stations.

Between 30 and 70 percent of the fracking fluid eventually comes back out of the ground, most of it in the initial months of development. In addition to the fracking chemicals, the flowback contains heavy metals and sometimes radioactive material (radium, uranium ore). In the western shale plays, the wastewater is often disposed of by injecting it back into the ground. The geology of the Marcellus in the Northeast makes that more difficult so the used fracking fluid is removed from the well pad in tanker trucks (more diesel fuel, noise, damage to roads) and taken to wastewater treatment plants. The treated water ends up being released back into the watershed. There is scant evidence that fracking operations conducted 5,000 feet or more underground has contaminated water tables under 1,000 feet down that home owners drill their wells into, but water can migrate underground and nobody knows at this point how fracking operations on a massive scale might affect existing faults and fractures in strata above it over the long run. The behavior of methane gas itself contaminating wells was a totally separate matter. Of more concern vis-à-vis frack flowback was the fact that the drilling companies subcontracted the wastewater hauling to outfits who were not above dumping their loads on woodsy back roads under cover of night to avoid the tipping fees or else taking the stuff to treatment plants that were not equipped to process industrial-strength wastewater.

One of the arguments used to promote shale gas at the outset of the boom was the idea that it produces about half the volume of CO_2 as coal so theoretically we could reduce damage to the atmosphere by using proportionately more gas and less coal. More recent information from the U.S. Environmental Protection Agency suggests that "fugitive" methane leaking out of wells in the drilling and completion process is substantial (4.2 percent of production during the years 2006 to 2008). Methane is a much more potent greenhouse gas than carbon dioxide. The EPA study did not include the emissions of those trucks delivering and taking away all that water.

It's worth noting that the United States is hardly the only region in the world where shale gas exists in theoretically commercial quantities. There is a significant formation under the city of Paris, France, and its environs, and an even larger one in Poland, which is now being explored and developed. For many years, Europe has had to rely on Russia and Libya for pipeline imports as well as liquefied gas from countries in the Middle East. European gas prices are uniformly higher than in North America and thus much hope has been invested in these new shale plays. According to EPA maps there is an enormous shale basin extending from Brazil into Argentina and including virtually all of Paraguay. Similar geological and financial constraints are liable to apply to all these plays, even if environmental protection is weak.

To me, the shale gas and shale oil booms mostly signify how desperate we are in the industrial economies to keep the fossil fuels coming, and how many other resources (steel, investment capital) we are prepared to throw at anything that offers a possible extension of our comforts. Based on what I've learned, I have to conclude that these shale resources will founder on the capital investment side of the equation. They were economically dubious enterprises at the start, and initially everything possible was done to make them appear to suit our wishes. These are resources that require investments in energy and capital beyond the comprehension of folks tuned in to the CNBC money shows. Certainly a lot of people got rich off shale for a few years. By the time you read this the bonanza may be over.

Waiting for Santa Claus

By now the remaining people in the United States of sound mind probably understand that our oil, gas, and even coal will not last forever, even if there is a range of views as to how long they will last. But the hopes of many about the lives of their children and grandchildren are vested in the bundle of things we call "alternatives" and "renewables." This includes solar and wind, hydroelectric, biodiesel, algae-generated hydrocarbon fuels, hydrogen (fuel cells still hanging in there), nuclear fission (and its new stepchild thorium fission), atomic fusion, and so on, into the murkier realms of theories about dark matter and powers as yet unknown lurking in the interstices of the universe.

Right off, there are two fundamental principles that need to be hauled out in the light of day and clarified.

First, whatever we do in the future to generate heat, electricity, and mechanical power beyond the economically recoverable supplies of fossil fuels, we must be prepared to live very differently. We are not going to run the familiar infrastructures of modernity on any combinations of wind, solar, et cetera. We will probably have to say good-bye to continent-scaled electric grids, the interstate highways, suburbia, air travel, Walmart, Disney World, the U.S. military in its current form, and many other giant systems. Unfortunately, the baseline expectation of most people in America is that all we have to do is switch from one energy system to another to keep everything going, and that the new replacement systems will appear magically as a result of the amazing synergies of creative innovation leading to *new technology*. If that fantasy doesn't work out, the disappointment is sure to be fierce, and it would be very dangerous to underestimate the impact of it on our ability to make new arrangements. It could provoke all kinds of animosity, conflict, grievance, and turmoil that would thwart a reset to more realistic modes of living and make things much worse. I hope we can get over the emotional reaction to the discovery that a simple switchover just won't happen. I'm confident that we will use alternative and renewable energy systems of some sort, but whatever way we end up employing them the human imprint on this planet is going to get smaller.

The second principle requires an understanding that although the sources of solar, wind, hydro, and other known or proposed alt.energy systems may be renewable, the equipment needed to harness them will not be—and it may be difficult, eventually, to replace the equipment we start out with. Just because we can manufacture photovoltaic hardware and wind turbines now, with all the complex systems of our fossil fuel economy to assist us, does not mean we will be able to manufacture them in the future, when fossil fuels are scarce, expensive, and possibly unavailable. Today's hardware will wear out. And I wouldn't be so sure that the means for making new hardware can be shifted to alternative and renewable energy systems themselves.

Both of these principles should inform us that we will use alternative and renewable systems on a smaller, more modest, and more local scale than many people currently suppose, and perhaps for only a limited period of time in the high tech sense. We probably won't construct many of the giant solar thermal or photovoltaic arrays being proposed for, say, the Mojave desert, or gigantic wind farms using Godzilla-sized turbines. True, we've already got some big wind farms up and running, but I doubt we will build a whole lot more or be able to fully service the existing ones a decade or so from now. Instead, we'd be much better off focusing our efforts on whatever alternative and renewable systems we can rig up on a community and household basis, taking care to keep it as simple as possible and using nature as directly as possible with the fewest technological interventions. For instance, we can construct houses, and retrofit older ones, to use solar gain from sunlight to keep warm and to heat water. We can rig up relatively simple household windmills out of salvaged metal parts and wood and hook them up to old automobile alternators, of which there are tens of millions sitting in junked cars around this country.[8] We can use wind to pump well water too—something that was very common in America before rural electrification and quite rare now. We can rig up small hydroelectric systems on a community basis. In and around the upper Hudson Valley, where I live, there are many decommissioned local hydro sites that once served small towns. The big power companies were not interested in maintaining them and shut them down, often breaching the existing dams. What a waste!

The biggest deal killer against our ability to do alt and renewable energy on the grand scale is Liebig's Law of the Minimum and its implications for the marshaling of resources. Liebig's Law basically says that the development of something is restricted by the scarcest input. In the case of a major shift to alternative and renewable energy, we face the coming scarcity of not just fossil fuels but its knock-on

8. John Michael Greer has discussed this in his writings at the archdruidreport. com.

effect diminished capital. Without investment capital to pay for these new systems (materials and labor) the only other methods for getting them up and running—at the grand scale—would be war, slavery, and authoritarian government. In war, you take other people's resources by force, with slavery you get cut-rate labor, and with authoritarianism you can make the first two happen. And even if that gets you a collection of giant wind farms and deserts paved with solar cells you're still eventually stuck with long-term maintenance and replacement issues.

They Say Malthus Was too Malthusian

Now, obviously the whole point of alt.energy and renewables is to *not* need fossil fuels but alts and renewables don't come close to what fossil fuels provide in the way of power, and without that massive ability to do work we will not be able to generate the massive amounts of capital needed for massive projects. This is crucial because capital is the lifeblood of all the other activities necessary to run a complex industrial economy. Without capital—deployable surplus wealth—in large quantities, we are not going to have the kind of mining operations, or refining, or the global-scale gathering of scarce materials such as the ores and rare earths needed to make advanced electronics. In fact, without the continued growth of economies and capital, much of what we've come to know as the global system won't work anymore—the resource allocation networks and markets associated with them, the networked manufacturing infrastructures, the transportation networks, and even the banking system itself, without which whatever capital you have (or thought you had) can't be managed.

The idea that technological innovation trumps Liebig's Law and its knock-on effects is perhaps comforting intellectually but doesn't comport with reality. It is the basis of views like the cornucopian vision of the late Julian Simon that human ingenuity is the ultimate resource and that there is no shortage of it. He apparently didn't think there were limits to it, either, and in fact for years he battled Paul Ehrlich, author of *The Population Bomb*, on whether the planet earth could or could not support so many billions of us and ever more to come. Simon believed that technology invariably overcomes any resource scarcity, and that when high prices signal a problem with any given resource human ingenuity invariably works around it to invent new technology. He and his followers called this the Law of Substitutability.

In fact, the observable manifestations of this putative law have been known only in the industrial era and only in a few certain instances that may amount to a sequence of events, but not one that is repeatable indefinitely. It is true that the developing nations provoked a scarcity of whale oil by commercially overhunting whales by the 1850s and that within the decade the human race learned how to recover "rock oil" (petroleum) in quantity to light our parlor lamps. It is true that the same developing societies used wood, coal, oil, natural gas, and nuclear fission in sequence to do their societies' work. This sequence is largely what informs our understanding of what progress *is*, in a way that is, unfortunately self-reinforcing, so that we simply cannot imagine any other outcome of our current situation besides the guaranteed automatic appearance on the scene of a technological rescue remedy. It leads up a blind alley where too many people ought to know better. Julian Simon's view equates technology with energy, assuming that one is substitutable for the other. When you run up against a scarcity of energy just plug in new technology. This is the essence of too much magic.

The human race has had some experience with resource shortages before and these instances generally end in the collapse of a complex society, one way or another. We know plenty about this and how such resource scarcity has historically prompted societies to solve their problems with quixotic efforts to double down on whatever mode of doing things they are already invested in or are most used to. The environmental anthropologist Joseph Tainter summarized this tragic tendency neatly in his phrase *overinvestments in complexity with diminishing returns*. What Simon and his fellow cornucopians refer to as ever increasing innovation is just another term for that process minus any recognition of the consequences. In general, the only thing that complex societies have not been able to do is contract, to become smaller and less complex, and to do it in a programmatic way that reduces the pain of transition.

What we also know for the moment is that, despite years of wishing and asserting fallacious ideas such as Simon's Law of Substitutability, our vaunted ingenuity has not produced a revolutionary energy resource to replace the cheap fossil fuel that modernity absolutely requires in colossal amounts. The time for such a savior technology to arrive is now past the moment when it should have been here. As we enter the long emergency, our systems are already wobbling badly, especially global banking, where the capital dwells. We're now past peak cheap oil. Where is the energy messiah?

Down and Dirty

I discussed the weaknesses of alt and renewable energy in my 2005 book *The Long Emergency* and, again, I don't want to belabor the details here, but I will remind you of a few particulars and mention some things that have changed. What has not changed is my contention that our current thinking is unrealistic about what these technologies can do for us.

Wind power now amounts to 1.25 percent of electricity generated in the United States and solar (photovoltaic and thermal combined) is less than one-tenth of a percent.[9] The price of photovoltaic solar cells has come down a bit in five years and the efficiency has gone up a little. Photovoltaic materials that double as roofing materials can

9. Solar thermal is a process that uses mirrors to concentrate sunlight and produce heat, which is then used to generate electricity. Photovoltaic solar cells turn sunlight directly into electric current.

now be manufactured so your shingles can generate electricity. There is even talk of developing a photovoltaic material than can be applied on metal surfaces like a coat of enamel. These represent refinements but they are not revolutionary leaps. Solar electricity is still expensive. Meanwhile, American incomes are going down while home foreclosures mount (symptoms of increasing capital scarcity). Solar panel makers consume about 11 percent of the world's supply of silver. The price of silver has gone up from about $4 an ounce to over $40 in less than a decade. If the world doubled its solar cell production, the silver required would be either unaffordable or unavailable. Thin solar panels are now being made with tellurium (cadmium telluride). However, tellurium is an extremely rare element and it may not be possible to scale up the production of thin panels to the wished-for volumes, a case of the law of receding horizons.

The tale is similar with regard to batteries needed to store energy generated by solar cells for stand-alone solar electric systems not connected to the grid. Some kinds of batteries are getting better, for instance, more powerful, lighter lithium-based batteries for electric cars (which will never become a mass-market phenomenon anyway, and bring with them added problems involving the world's limited lithium resources). Home-scale solar electric systems still rely on the classic lead-acid format that is not substantially different from a 1932 car battery. Talk of a solar electric revolution is premature and may remain so indefinitely. Solar is still a relative luxury for individuals and very probably a net energy sink at the utility scale, even though demonstration projects are up and running.[10] Virtually all alternative and renewable technologies represent a lot of *embodied energy*, that is, energy required to fabricate the equipment, mine the ores, transport the units, and more, which can't be ignored by reality-based adults.

10. The U.S. military is investing in solar installations as a precaution to keep bases in operation under adverse conditions. EROEI issues do not concern them.

If we could quintuple our solar and wind capacity—a long shot, given the resource and capital issues—they would still amount to less than 7 percent of our current electric consumption. Overall, considering depletions in natural gas and the certain shutdown of aging nuke plants, we will surely have less electric power overall in decades to come than we do now. The United States does not have a coherent energy policy and we've run out of time. Other nations have had energy policies in place but there is only so much they can do. Germany gets over 6 percent of its electricity from wind and 0.7 percent from solar (it's a cloudy region and, due to its high latitude, winter days are very short). Denmark, a tiny nation of 5.5 million (about the same population as Maryland), gets around 20 percent of its electric power from wind, which sounds fabulous, and is, for now. But it will have to reckon with future replacement costs in a post-oil economy. Sunny Spain is getting 0.8 percent for solar. Japan is at 0.2 percent. China has become a leader in manufacturing the equipment but still gets less than a percent of its electricity from it. Note: these nations embarked on their alt.energy programs when they were flush with money early in this century, before the global banking system began to destabilize and capital grew scarce. All nations will encounter the same problems with parts replacement issues and capital shortages.

An additional problem for solar- and wind-power hardware involves the so-called rare earths they require—the exotic minerals found in low concentrations that are difficult to refine. Dysprosium, praseodymium, neodymium, terbium, europium, yttrium, and indium are used in electronics, permanent magnets, and metallurgy. A big wind farm turbine requires some seven hundred pounds of rare earths to fabricate. The mining process for rare earths is associated with radioactive wastes and other pollution problems. Over the years, China has ended up with a virtual monopoly on rare earth production because the Chinese could mine the stuff cheaply with lax regard for pollution and paying near slave wages. America's leading rare earths producer, the

Mountain Pass company in California's Mojave Desert, shut down its less competitive operations in 1998. Then, in late 2011, China slapped a 25 percent export tax on rare earths. Concern rose that China intended to hog the world's available rare earth resources and thus control production of wind and solar devices as well as cell phones, televisions, and other ubiquitous electronics. Molycorp, of which Goldman Sachs is a primary owner, eventually bought the Mountain Pass company. Molycorp then received a $3 million earmark from Congress in 2009 to encourage the restart of mining operations. For the moment, China still controls the bulk of the world's commerce in rare earths.

Squabbles like this presage a future of more desperate international contests over resources. But the functional collapse of large nation-states occurring at exactly the same time and for exactly the same reason—shortage of critical resources and capital—would also compromise their ability to project military power in distant places. It is already costing the U.S. Army about $400 for each gallon of gasoline brought into remote Afghanistan. Large corporations could be subject to similar forces of disintegration—the inability to project economic control in far-flung operations. We may find ourselves at a certain point in history with the salvaged residue of whatever high-tech stuff we were able to manufacture in the first years of the twenty-first century and not much to replace it. Localities will do what they can with it, while much more attention goes into reorganizing farming, commerce, transportation, and some workable armature of civic life.

In *The Long Emergency* I wrote that if we want to keep the lights on there may be no alternative but nuclear power. That might still be technically true, but the earthquake disaster at Fukushima, Japan, and ensuing events seem to indicate we won't be going down that road after all. (The Germans won't be, anyway. They canceled their whole nuclear program in the spring of 2011.) One thing we learned from Fukushima after many years of complacency is that, in the event of trouble with a nuke plant, it's not a good thing when there is no auxiliary power.

At Fukushima, not only did several reactor cores melt down but the cooling also failed in the structures where the spent fuel was stored. When the cooling water boiled off, the old fuel, which was still highly radioactive, also started burning and melting. The Fukushima reactors were American-designed, of course. Here in the United States we have made no coherent plans for what to do if the electric grid were to go down for more than a few hours and our nuke plants were to run out of emergency power for cooling. Having never made provision for any permanent storage of spent reactor fuel rods, they are all still temporarily stored all over the country, on-site, where they were originally used.

The destiny of nuclear power in the United States is not just a matter of public unease over it. The growing scarcity of capital alone is enough to keep the country from embarking on a next generation of nuclear power plants. We're too broke, and we're getting a lot broker. Also, as economist Nicole Foss (writing as "Stoneleigh" at TheAutomaticEarth. org) has pointed out, if you are living in a disorderly, bankrupt society it may become difficult to operate existing nuclear facilities; workers must be paid regularly, and sufficiently, to keep up the rigorous maintenance and safety routines these installations require. You can't have nuclear plant workers showing up late or drinking on the job because they're depressed. In any case, ramping up a new generation of nuclear power plants in the United States would require five years, minimum, if there were no other obstacles and if a kind of national emergency mentality provoked the political will to get started. I think it's too late for that now.

That's not quite the end of the nuclear story, though. The latest so-called game changer is thorium, a less radioactive element than familiar uranium, used in molten salt reactors, typically a liquid fluoride thorium reactor (LFTR). Among the many touted benefits of thorium reactors is that the reaction can be run without building elaborate containment vessels; it could be used even in portable reactors manufactured off site; the process supposedly generates less radioactive waste (probably not true); it claims not to produce isotopes that can be used in weapons (also probably not true); and thorium is much more abundant than uranium and supposedly cannot melt down or run out of control. One catch is that you need a regular uranium fission reaction to kick-start a thorium reaction, so it's not as though thorium is a nonnuclear power process. The U.S. government experimented exhaustively with thorium reactors in the 1960s and eventually closed down experimentation as unpromising. Lately, China and India have restarted research and development toward deploying thorium reactors. Despite all the talk there are no commercial thorium reactors in operation now. Whatever the political system, they require substantial government subsidies, since a thorium reactor will typically cost more than $2 billion. If oil prices go back into the $100 a barrel and above range, they will cost even more, since the fabrication is highly fossil fuel dependent. Even under ideal circumstances development of the first reactors would take years, and they will be net energy losers.

I discussed hydrogen at length in *The Long Emergency*. None of its problems or limitations have been overcome. It's still a net energy loser. It takes more energy to make the stuff than you get from making it. Loose talk about using hydrogen persists in alt.energy circles, but I maintain what I said about it in 2005: fuggedaboutit.

Biofuels still attract a lot of interest, considerable press, some investment, and big government subsidies. While it's true that you can grow something and turn it into something else, a credulous public has been fooled into thinking that these procedures are economically sound and can easily scale up to the Walmart level, even though the most ballyhooed biofuel project, ethanol from corn, is a well-documented and thoroughly discredited net energy loser. The competition that biofuels set up with food crops is a recipe for social disaster, as every bushel of corn or rapeseed that ends up running a motor vehicle somewhere will increase food prices or scarcity for the world's poorer people, including the poorer people in the United States, who will become increasingly desperate too. Social unrest over high food prices has already shown up in the North Africa and Middle East political revolts of 2011. The year 2010 happened to be a very bad year for wheat crops in Russia, which customarily exports large amounts of grain to the Middle East. Because of the massive crop failures, Russia declared a ban on grain exports in 2011. Meanwhile prices of other staple grains soared on the commodity exchanges. At the same time, in 2011 Congress extended subsidies to ethanol producers.

My guess is that in the future we will use ethanol and biodiesel to run small engines, mainly for agricultural chores, and not much else. In this realm I'd include the possibility of animal waste–based methane gas generators on a limited basis, around individual farms, perhaps for cooking or small-scale food processing activities (maple sugar evaporators, grain drying operations), but there would be limits to storing organically generated natural gas without the special equipment and machinery for compressing the stuff in tanks.

Around the time I was writing *The Long Emergency*, a process called thermal depolymerization was making a splash in alt.energy circles. It was based on a new kind of distillery technology that, theoretically, could accept just about any kind of waste at one end—turkey offal, old plastic crap—and produce something akin to petroleum at the other end. Notice that you probably haven't heard anything about it since then. Likewise, I doubt that the latest experiments with algae-oil products will ever get past the science project stage because they will not work at the large scale and, given the necessary complexity, they will not be worth doing on a small scale. We are not going to run the trucking system, not to mention the plastics industry, on algae-oil secretions.

Clean Coal and Smart Grids

There really is no such thing as clean coal, despite relentless advertising from the coal mining industry during what's left of the nightly news hours on TV (when voters tune in). "Clean coal" refers obliquely to the wished-for technology known as *carbon dioxide sequestration*. The idea is that you capture the CO_2 from the smokestack of your electric power plant and jam it underground, or marry it chemically to inert compounds, in such a manner that it will not get out into the atmosphere and aggravate climate change. That way, America gets all the electricity it wants and the coal mining industry gets to sell all the coal it can to the electric utilities. Since 54 percent of America's electric power comes from burning coal, and because America has a lot of coal—though of diminishing quality—there is the implication that we need not worry anymore about our energy problems. There is the further implication, depicted graphically in some of these TV spots, that we will be able to run all our cars on electricity and, therefore, we can be carefree about how we live in this country and all our investments in suburbia. Clean coal is a marketing scheme, not a reality.

The likelihood is that we will continue burning coal for electric power as long as possible, because we will have no better choices for keeping the lights on, but even this will face some severe limitations. Right now, the economics are such that we still have reliable supplies of affordable diesel fuel to run the operations of coal mining, including the massive machinery of the western open pits and the endless line of freight trains that bring coal from Wyoming to the power plants east of the Mississippi. The coal industry may not function so well if the oil supply is reduced or constrained and this is sure to happen. We could run the trains on electricity, or on coal itself, but at the current scale of our national electric production that could make electricity a lot more expensive. Another possibility is that serious trouble in the oil markets would lead to a substantial contraction of the U.S. economy or so much disorder that our interdependent networked systems, including the aging American electric grid, would simply be unable to function.

Because comprehensive contraction will require all systems in the United States to get smaller and local, and given scarcities of capital and basic resources such as copper—indispensable for electric transmission—we will probably have to make other arrangements for our electric power, perhaps do without it in some places. Our smart-grid wishes are grounded on the idea that we will continue to enjoy broadly distributed electrical service that will be managed more effectively with computer technology. I'm not convinced we will ever get to that. And if we don't, we face the challenge of trying to remain civilized minus the most distinctive feature of modernity.

Fusion

Atomic fusion, a controlled nuclear reaction that combines atoms rather than splitting them—as in the process that keeps our sun burning—has long been touted as "the energy of the future" and it always will be.

A Disquieting Conclusion

I'm quite sure that we will try to use all the alternative and renewable energy systems that we can in order to maintain the familiar activities and comforts of modern life, at least for a while. People do what they can until they can't. I'm not against using what we can. But I have a feeling that whatever we can do with wind turbines, solar electric rigs, and the other systems will be a transitory phase of history. Our longer-term destination is a society run at much lower levels of available energy, with much lower populations, and a time-out from the kinds of progressive innovation that so many have taken for granted their whole lives. It was an illusory result of a certain sequencing in the exploitation of resources in the planet earth that we have now pretty much run through. We have an awful lot to contend with in this reset of human activities. If it leads to the intermission from technological advance that I believe is in store, then we'll have plenty of time to reflect on what we've done and where we go from here.

EIGHT

INSULTS TO THE PLANET
AND THE PLANET'S REPLY

Not even people who are preoccupied with climate change like to think about it anymore. The more you explore the problem, the worse it seems and the more hopeless you feel. A lot of people like myself who *do* think about it remain plugged in to the fossil fuel economies that are responsible for this set of problems. I suppose we're free to blame ourselves, for all the good it may do. I can't speak for others in my position but I feel that I am a hostage to this economy. To say that it is the only economy I've known my whole long life may sound like a lame excuse. More to the point, perhaps, there is no post–fossil fuel economy yet to—forgive me for putting it this way—plug your life into, no *World Made by Hand* that represents the kind of immersive reset of daily life that would allow someone to function in a different context.

There are foreign cultures outside the whirring fantasia of America where human beings live more closely attuned to a solar economy, that is, an economy that uses just what the day's sunlight affords, including wind and running water that are by-products of that solar activity. But at this point of course I can't move to the Kalahari desert and volunteer to join a clan of bushmen. Even if they didn't laugh when I stepped out of the Range Rover and presented myself, I would surely fail miserably at living among them. I don't have the skills to forage, to stalk and kill other animals without firearms, to find water where it is not self-evidently right in front of me. I don't have the fortitude to sleep out under stars every night in all weather without fancy engineered gear. I could never pull my weight. They'd have to abandon me to the hyenas, like a hopeless old cripple, and just move on to their next seasonal stop.

Not to say that one would have to go back to a hunter-gatherer mode of existence in order to live on a solar budget. Pick any preindustrial culture you like, or pick the best or most relevant parts from any of them to get on with daily life, for instance the habitations of Edo Japan, the division of labor of the Inca, the diet of the Florentines, the animal husbandry of Georgian England, the costumes of the Ming dynasty. Surely one could contrive life on a solar budget from these modes of daily endeavor and put together a satisfying existence that would amount to being civilized. Anyway, a great many of the useful inventions that made life comfortable and interesting were developed before we began using fossil fuels, quite a few of them in China alone. Add to that some additional knowledge that the human race has acquired since those historical periods, perhaps only the germ theory of disease, and you could enjoy a decent living standard.

Anyway, that's a theory. History does run backward now and then, and the centers of civilization shift from one place to another, but we've never seen anything like what we face: the crash of a turbocharged cheap energy economy along with an ecological catastrophe perhaps beyond the biblical scale. History is also not symmetrical; you don't necessarily go down the same way you came, recapitulating earlier arrangements in the same sequence backward. What we might get instead could be just a one-way ticket to Palookaville instead of getting to relive the sixteenth century.

These scenarios surely call into question what it means to be modern, and by that I do not mean the fashion sense of the word, of being on the cutting edge of human development, which I regard as quintessentially narcissistic and dumb. Rather, I would aver that to be modern means only to be at the end of a historical chain of consequence that has brought the human race to the present moment. Which brings me back to the point I have strayed from: that we are arguably forcing conditions that might make the only planet we call home uninhabitable. And, of course, even if catastrophic climate change were not due to the recent human habit of pumping fossil fuel wastes into the earth's fine-tuned atmosphere, the question still arises as to what we would do to cope with the kind of climate changes that appear to be upon us.

Now, I happen to subscribe to the theory that human activity is responsible for driving the changes that are presently observably occurring, such as the measurable parts per million (ppm) of carbon dioxide in the composition of the air we breathe. At the least, this suggests that if perhaps we ceased pumping so much additional carbon dioxide into the air, the process of catastrophic climate change might be halted or averted. Alas, other observable data suggest that certain feedback loops have been set in motion that may possibly be irreversible, such as the reduced reflectivity of polar sea ice, the albedo effect, wherein the ice-free, darker ocean now absorbs more of the sun's heat.

In any case, the distaste for accepting the horrors of climate change, denial, stupidity, fecklessness, whatever you want to call it, has spawned a lively industry in climate change denial that is a wholly owned subsidiary of the oil, gas, and coal industries and a political sub-culture in its own right, aimed at defeating any policy consensus that would reduce the use (and sale) of oil, gas, and coal. Climate denial also happens to work nicely for that big chunk of the public at large that does not want to entertain any comprehensive change in the way we currently do things. And so the debate about what to do about climate change decays into incoherence as the deniers deliberately distort the facts while the science-minded are buffaloed by such mendacity and frustrated by a public that isn't interested in the facts.

This dynamic led, in one instance, to the now infamous Climate-gate scandal of 2009, which was exquisitely timed by its engineers to break one month before the December UN climate change conference, better known as the Copenhagen Summit, and thus to sabotage any agreements on reducing carbon emissions (which would, of course, require nations to burn less fossil fuel). The incident involved the hacking of a thousand e-mails and many more assorted documents from the Climate Research Unit (CRU) of the University of East Anglia (England), by parties unknown, in an attempt to debunk a three-thousand-page report by the UN's Intergovernmental Panel on Climate Change (IPCC) that was a cornerstone of the Copenhagen meeting. The CRU functioned as a sort of clearinghouse for climate scientists working on the United Nations study. In the event, the scientists were accused of making several errors including a miscalculation of the amount of land below sea level in the Netherlands and the time frame for the melting of Himalayan glaciers. More controversy was manufactured over routine but esoteric disagreements between scientists trying to reconcile tree growth ring data with ice core data. The hacking itself was suspiciously routed through a computer server in Russia and the material was posted to the Internet via a Web site located in Saudi Arabia.

A principal agent involved in publicizing Climategate was the Science and Public Policy Institute (SPPI), a right-wing climate change denial think tank run by the Virginia attorney Robert Ferguson, formerly connected with the Exxon-Mobil-funded Frontiers of Freedom Institute.[1] The PR front for SPPI was the chief policy adviser Lord Christopher Monckton, a British right-wing journalist and adept media entertainer. Also active in the attack on "climate alarmists" was Patrick J. Michaels, senior fellow at the Cato Institute, a conservative think tank funded by the Koch brothers, who are major funders of the Tea Party. Koch Industries is the largest private company in the United States, involved in enterprises ranging from oil and gas to fertilizer, chemicals, timber, paper, gypsum, and more. They are aggressively against any political action to limit CO_2 emissions as well as many other government environmental initiatives

---

1. SourceWatch, the Center for Media and Democracy (www.sourcewatch.org).

in the public interest. Cato's Patrick Michaels made more than 150 appearances in the mainstream media during the months when both Climategate and the Copenhagen Summit had the public's attention. Climategate rather spectacularly sabotaged the Copenhagen Summit, especially because so much of the meeting's success hinged on America's willingness to go along with CO_2 reduction standards, and legislation about it was moving through Congress at the time. The Climategate misinformation was seized on by the right-wing media and flogged mercilessly by so-called conservative political figures including former veep nominee Sarah Palin and Oklahoma senator James Inhofe, ranking member of the Senate Committee on Environment and Public Works (and oil industry errand boy), until all the pending legislation was disabled. The IPCC report and the scientists involved in the East Anglia University e-mails and documents were eventually absolved of any professional wrongdoing, and the fundamental assertion that climate change was for real and likely caused by human activity was once again substantiated by investigating panels ranging from the American Association for the Advancement of Science and the National Academy of Sciences to the British House of Commons.

Unfortunately the damage went beyond the Copenhagen Summit. Climategate demoralized the scientific community, which had been operating on the perhaps naive assumption that, when all was said and done, the leadership layer of American society was composed of rational people who would make sane decisions and policies if presented with the plain facts, especially about a situation that conceivably threatened America's well-being, civilization, or the survival of life on earth. Some scientists of lofty repute such as James Hansen of NASA, Stephen Hawking, and James Lovelock, who co-created the Gaia theory, were retailing some very dire conclusions about climate change, and there was plenty of reason to think that politicians would take them seriously. One question the denial industry couldn't answer was: why would all these scientists make this stuff up?

The bad news about what was happening to humanity's only planet obviously freaked out the public and gave deniers and their self-interested brethren in business and politics more reason to contest the facts, by any nefarious means. It also turned out that the crucial years of the climate change tipping point, which we are now living, happened to coincide with the peak oil situation, and the peak oil situation coincided with the grave economic contraction and its attendant banking crises—arguably even caused it. The great recession, or second depression, or whatever you want to call it, brought on tremendous, persistent hardship among the American middle class. Any political action aimed at reducing carbon emissions was demagogued by rabid free-market conservative politicians as a further threat to the wished-for economic recovery. The U.S. Chamber of Commerce claimed that carbon taxes and other restraints would prevent businesses from creating jobs when in truth it was all about corporate profits and the cost of doing business.

On balance, the American public was seemingly too horrified by climate change even to think about it, and the nation's elected officials were too willing to pander to the frightened public and too deep in the pockets of corporate interests to do so. The public consensus on climate change was that it was best ignored, with the hope that it would go away, like a case of poison oak. Ordinary people already felt hopeless about the things they were conditioned to believe they had control over, such as the idea that gainful employment would find those willing to work. Now they were expected to not only comprehend but learn lessons from a science-fiction story about the end of the world? It was too much. They tuned out. (Ironically, even those pious Christian fundamentalist Republicans who trafficked in apocalyptic stories tuned out on the climate change issue.)

Demoralized scientists could not overcome the politics and the majority of them decided just to shut up about it for a while and keep on doing the science. So we arrive at the position where our society has chosen to do nothing about what is among the gravest problems that the human race has ever faced.

What's Happening Now

An overwhelming majority of scientists who have looked into the matter agree that global warming is under way and is probably caused by people burning fossil fuels. This is the meta-fact hovering over all the details. After all, in burning so much coal, oil, and gas we've released 460 million years of sequestered carbon into the atmosphere in a mere two hundred years. There are consequences for doing this. The trajectory of climate problems has gotten only more severe since I discussed the issue in *The Long Emergency* in 2005. Greenhouse gas emissions have exceeded predictions. The IPCC report expects a sea level rise of at least three feet by 2100; James Hansen of NASA says possibly seventeen feet. If that is the case, there would be no need to argue over the finer points of how many square miles in the Netherlands would be under water—you could just kiss it good-bye, along with Bangladesh, many Pacific islands, most of Florida and the Mississippi River Delta, Houston, Jacksonville, Key West, and thousands of other places. Remember, most of the people on the planet live near the world's seacoasts.

A Stanford University study released in 2011 reported that "rising greenhouse gas concentrations will result in a new, permanent heat regime in which the coolest warm-season of the 21st century is hotter than the hottest warm-season of the late 20th century."[2] Warming seems to be accelerating. The IPCC report concluded that the past decade has been the warmest since modern record keeping commenced around 1850. The polar ice caps and glaciers are visibly melting. Extreme weather events—floods, drought, wildfires, tropical storms, tornadoes, and even blizzards—are more frequent (yes, blizzards, because the phenomenon of winter is still extant, though changes in the jet stream cause precipitation patterns to shift). The tropic zones are expanding

2. Noah S. Diffenbaugh and Martin Scherer, "Observational and model evidence of global emergence of permanent, unprecedented heat in the 20th and 21st centuries; A letter." *Climatic Change*, Springer Science and Media, Berlin, May 16, 2011.

and getting hotter. In turn, they are pushing desert zones into new territory. Ocean temperatures are increasing and seawater is acidifying. Coral reefs are dying all around the world and many plant and animal species face extinction. Warming is linked to insect invasions and diseases of the forests. Bird migrations have shifted northward, and not all bird species adjust easily to habitat change.

By 2100 we can expect an overall temperature rise between 3 and 7 degrees Fahrenheit, according to the U.S. Environmental Protection Agency. The net effect will be extreme hardship for the human race, crop failure and starvation, mass demographic shifts, water scarcity, and about as much political instability and disintegration as anyone can imagine. These effects fall short, however, of the dreadful predictions made by Hansen, who warns of a "runaway global warming" that would make the earth inhospitable to life, like our neighboring planet Venus. It's scary, and Hansen has a lot of cred, though some scientists firmly in the climate-change-is-real camp disagree with him in the particulars. But it's easy to see why so many ordinary people don't want to think about it. Climate change *is* depressing.

It's harder to understand why so few people in positions of responsibility would actively campaign to do nothing in the face of this, especially when it's so clear that choosing to pump less CO_2 into the air could make all the difference. There's an outside chance that Lovelock's Gaia theory is even more profound than he himself has imagined: that the peak oil and peak capital situation currently under way will create conditions that curtail our ability to run industrial economies and therefore to burn fossil fuels at the rate we have been in recent decades. In other words, Mother Nature smacks us on the head and forces us to behave differently. (Note, climate change deniers tend also to be peak oil deniers.) This outcome would be more like the scenes I've depicted in my novel *World Made by Hand* and its sequels, a much more austere economy, postindustrial for practical purposes, lacking in most of the conveniences and luxuries that we associate with modernity. I'd take it in a heartbeat over a dying planet. How about you?

Complications and Confusions

Even if there is little question about climate change happening per se, it is true that climate science is complex and difficult to model. You may start with the familiar measurable trends: CO_2 in the atmosphere, ground temperatures, ocean temperatures, shrinkage of glaciers, rainfall, shoreline heights, wind speeds, numbers and intensity of storms, et cetera. But there are many other forces and factors, cycles and cycles within cycles, pendulum swings between one state and another, and smaller pendulum swings within these.

For instance, the Milankovitch cycle, which has to do with variations in the combined movements of the earth's elliptical orbit and the angle of its rotational axis, correlates with the amount of sunlight that ends up reaching the planet's surface. Sometimes the earth's orbit is more round, sometimes less round. Sometimes the earth is closer to the sun than it is at other times. The angle that the earth presents to the sun changes slightly over geologic time. These days the axis is tilted at a 23.45-degree angle. We have evidence that it has varied from 21.45 degrees to 24.45 degrees over the ages. This alters the seasonal difference between the northern and southern hemispheres. You get warmer summers and cooler winters. Get enough cooler winters in a given cycle and you're in an ice age. Get enough warm ones and you're ready for Jurassic Park. Milankovitch models posit a 100,000-year cycle and a 400,000-year cycle. They are not well understood though they appear to have a relationship with the ice ages of the past few million years. Our sun also has an orbit around the galaxy, and little is known about how it affects us. All these various forces are interrelational, of course, and over longer periods of time they are subject to other forces and cycles, with different outcomes for life on earth.

Another variable has to do with sunspot activity, which comes and goes in roughly eleven-year cycles. Since they do not leave any traces beyond what human beings can observe, sunspots have been tracked systematically only during the past four centuries as astrology morphed into the science of astronomy and optical instruments made it possible to follow the doings on the sun's surface. (Past sunspot activity can be inferred indirectly from carbon-14 dating, tree ring measurements, and other gradients, though conclusions are hypothetical.)

Among the sunspot observations made since the ascent of scientific study is an anomaly referred to as the Maunder Minimum, after astronomer Edward W. Maunder (1851–1928), a seventy-year phase (1645–1715) of unusually low sunspot activity that corresponded with the historical period we call the Little Ice Age (which extended on both ends of the Maunder Minimum, from the fourteenth century to the mid-nineteenth), when winters in the northern hemisphere turned noticeably harsher. Within the period of the Maunder Minimum, observable eleven-year cycles continued but sunspots were sparse. The Little Ice Age stands in contrast to the preceding Medieval Warm Period (950–1250), when vineyards flourished in England and the Vikings established colonies in Greenland. It also coincided with extreme drought in what is now the southwest United States. Astronomical observation from this episode is scarce, and the evidence is inferred from mud sediments, oxygen isotope samples in mollusk shells obtained from core samples, and the anthropological record. The actual scale of temperature rise during the medieval-era warming is believed to be comparatively less than the records now show from the current warming episode running from the late twentieth century to the present.

All of these various episodes occurred in just the past thousand years of the Holocene epoch, which itself has been a brief 12,000-year interval following the previous glaciation. As such, it comprises just a small slice of the modern human species' sojourn on the planet—going back some 150,000 to 200,000 years to Mitochondrial Eve, or 2.5 million years before the first record of hominid tools. The previous interglacial warm period lasted 28,000 years, and there is no firm estimate of exactly how long the current one will run, even if carbon dumping by humans were not an issue. The causes of ice ages are not well understood, though feedbacks between plant growth, carbon dioxide, and oxygen are likely involved. Volcanic activity is another complication in the larger climate picture. Eruptions spew dust into the atmosphere, partially blocking sunlight. Volcanoes located near the equator seem to have the greatest effect, as in the 1991 eruption of Mount Pinatubo in the Philippines, estimated to have released about 10 cubic kilometers of ash into the atmosphere along with 20 million tons of sulfur dioxide, which formed a sulfuric acid haze in the upper atmosphere that was visible as spectacularly colored sunsets and caused the global average temperature to drop about 1 degree Fahrenheit that year. Volcanic ash was launched twenty-one miles up into the thinnest layer of the atmosphere at the height of the eruption—the mountain literally blew its head off. Pinatubo represented the largest injection of aerosol particles since the 1883 explosion of Krakatoa in the Sunda Strait off Java (estimated to have shot 21 cubic kilometers of rock and dust into the air). Average global temperatures dropped about 2 degrees the year following and effects were felt for five years. The single greatest volcanic eruption of the twentieth century, the 1912 Novarupta event in Alaska, was greater than Pinatubo but, being well out of the equatorial zone, did not affect global weather as much; likewise the 2010 eruption of Iceland's Eyjafjallajökull, though it interfered with airline service for several weeks. One other notable global weather aberration was the 1816 "year without summer," thought to be caused by a combination of low sunspot activity and the 1815 eruption of Mount Tambora, also in the neighborhood of Java. It decreased global temperatures as much as 1.3 degrees Fahrenheit and resulted in acute food shortages in Europe and North America.

At the continental level, for North America, the weather picture can be greatly influenced by the El Niño / La Niña phenomena. The names refer to pools of warm or cool water in the Pacific ocean that affect the jet stream and the dispersion of moisture. They run in cycles that seem to average about five years. In general, an El Niño pattern tends to produce warmer winters with low snow and rainfall in most of the United States except the Southeast, which gets wetter. Hurricane activity is reduced. The cooler La Niña phase brings above average snow and rainfall to most of the United States, except the Southeast, which is subject to drought. La Niña increases hurricane activity in the South Atlantic and the Caribbean. The causes of El Niño / La Niña are not completely understood, but the dynamic swirl and interplay with warm and cool ocean currents is affected by changes in the earth's average temperature.

Rainfall over landmasses has increased by about 2 percent through the twentieth century. Global warming increases the evaporation of moisture from oceans. It eventually precipitates out as rain or snow. Greater rainfall in the U.S. heartland combines with more intense melting of Rocky Mountain snowpacks and results in floods through the Missouri–Mississippi river system, as we saw in 2011. The drama of the earth's climate, and of the weather, the local and seasonal manifestations of climate, is driven by countless feedbacks like these. We know enough about them to be concerned, and we have reason to believe that the human race has contributed to these feedbacks. We know enough to be anxious about our future, but not enough to do anything to change our behavior, especially our habit of dumping CO_2 into the sky.

Carbon dioxide is the earth's thermostat. It makes up 0.04 percent of the gases in our atmosphere. It's necessary for life on the surface of the planet and it is the vehicle for carrying on the ceaseless carbon exchange between the oceans, the land masses, the plants, and the other organisms. Carbon is stored in soil, oceans, and in the crust of the planet (e.g., coal, oil, natural gas). Trees and grasses convert CO_2 into carbohydrates through photosynthesis and give off oxygen. Animals thrive on oxygen and give off CO_2 and methane. CO_2 and methane are greenhouse gases. They act as insulators in the earth's thin atmosphere and trap heat from the sun that would otherwise just radiate out into space. Theories about the history of the earth's atmosphere suggest that the development of plant life pumped oxygen into the atmosphere making possible the emergence of animal life. This helped set up the feedback relationships that have allowed life on earth to continue and to evolve. The aberration of human carbon dumping by burning off about half of the 460 million years of stored solar energy embodied in coal, oil, and natural gas has altered the balance of this planetary carbon budget. It has tripped off additional feedbacks that may be deadly and irreversible. For instance, the additional heat trapped by liberating CO_2 into the air causes the melting of methane clathrates (methane trapped in ice crystals) that have been lying in permafrost for eons. Methane is an even more effective heat-trapping gas than CO_2. It takes many years for greenhouse gases released into the atmosphere to reenter the other end of the carbon cycle and return to the soil and the oceans. It certainly won't become coal or oil again anytime soon. Scientists worry that the cycle just feeds back on itself until the earth becomes inhospitable to all life.

This has prompted schemes for a kind of solar shielding with which to mitigate warming by injecting particles into the atmosphere or other techno-grandiose strategies to ward off climate change. In fact, apart from the CO_2 issues, anti–air pollution protocols had been quite successful in lowering particulates in the atmosphere, which allowed more sunlight to reach the earth, increasing the temperature. Meanwhile, we had been making the atmospheric insulation more effective with our carbon dumping and methane releases. So various ideas were hatched in labs and campuses to release benign particles into the upper atmosphere in order to reflect away warming sunlight, or make clouds more reflective, or spread algae-inducing particles into the ocean to enlist more plant life in absorbing CO_2.[3] So far, none of these projects have gone beyond the laboratory stage.

This sort of unprecedented tinkering with the earth's atmosphere gives off more than a whiff of unintended consequences. If nothing else,

---

3. The whole range of these schemes is addressed by Jeff Goodell, in *How to Cool the Planet* (Houghton Mifflin Harcourt, 2010).

heaping extra complexity on top of existing out-of-control complexity seems the very essence of too much magic. The sorcerer's apprentice now wants to bring a cosmic chain saw into the picture to cut up all those multiplying broom handles he had mistakenly set into motion. There's an excellent chance he'll cut off his own head in the process.

From the Margins Inward

The most immediate, critical effect of climate change for people is food scarcity. When the weather turns extreme or unpredictable crops fail and people go hungry, starve, and die. A population rising remorselessly above the capacity of agriculture to provide for it and weather conditions that push agriculture to the margins of its limits to provide is a very bad combination. Add to this one hundred years (since oil-powered tractors were introduced) of aggravated soil erosion from the overuse of machinery, the depletion of aquifers (composed of fossil water left by retreating glaciers) that cannot be recharged by rainfall cycles, the degradation of rivers, expanding desertification, the diversion of corn to ethanol for fueling cars, the global reemergence of crop-plant diseases such as wheat stem rust that were thought to have been defeated or controlled, the approaching absolute depletion of phosphates and potash fertilizers, and a feedback of growing political instability that will only make it more difficult for settled people to succeed at the difficult task of farming successfully. Haiti, North Korea, the Horn of Africa, Lesotho, Egypt, Pakistan, Nepal—these are some of the unfortunate places on the margins of human existence where hunger is extreme and common. But food scarcities will soon move inward from the fringes to the economic center, where industry struggles against overwhelming limits and jobs evaporate. People who have had only lifestyle worries for a generation or more will be very surprised to find themselves worrying about the basics.

Just as the latest technological advances have compromised the planet's health and destroyed the resilience of human support systems of trade, transportation, and capital finance in this decade of peak oil, so have the diminishing returns of industrial farming blown back on the world in so many damaging ways. Perhaps the most ironic repercussion at this moment in history—Gaia's dark joke on humanity—is the epidemic of obesity that has radiated from America to many other nations, a result of our success at industrial-style corn production and its transmutation into engineered processed food products that have spread metabolic disorder to every corner of the globe where candy bars and Big Macs are sold. People gorging on hamburgers, sugary snacks, and soda pop balloon in size like cartoon characters at the same time that they become victims of malnutrition. A pandemic of insulin disorders including deadly diabetes comes with that, along with a greatly reduced capacity to work, to think clearly, or to take the kinds of actions that would prepare individuals, families, and communities for epic changes in daily life.

The unfortunate citizens of the United States may not overcome this terrible insult to their health until the population simply contracts by attrition. Only a tiny minority of Americans has any idea that the processed food industry is killing the public by a steady overdose of corn syrup derivatives and, of course, that minority is regarded as un-American and elitist for saying so. For everybody else, the evolution of cultural habits has erased the memory of what it is like to eat real food and what a normal mealtime is. Eating has lost its ceremonial trappings of communion with other people and become a furtive, solitary pursuit, a sugar addiction with overtones of nutritional masturbation. Mandatory motoring through psychologically punishing roadscapes furnished with fried food sheds and convenience stores promotes relief seeking via mindless snacking. It has made the public stupid and weak, and cultural phenomena ranging from omnipresent TV advertising to the policies of the U.S. Department of Agriculture reinforce it incessantly.

The medical establishment shares the responsibility and the blame for failing to aggressively battle the snack industry and instead just treats the symptoms of its depredations with therapies that have exceeded the nation's ability to pay for them. Soda pop is the number one source of calories in the American diet. A USDA survey shows that the average American is consuming about twenty teaspoons of sugar per day. Seven percent of the U.S. population visits a McDonald's burger shack every day, and about a quarter of Americans go to some kind of junk food joint daily. Ninety percent of Americans' food dollars are spent on processed foods.

The rest of the world has been catching up with the United States, even such paragons of good nutrition as the Japanese, and in Japan and elsewhere bariatric surgery on children is no longer unknown. Meanwhile the Malthusian equation of population growth exceeding the expansion of the food supply has finally caught up with the human race after the head fake of the so-called green revolution. If the world managed to produce a lot more food through the twentieth century than was previously believed possible, you can attribute that largely to cheap oil and natural gas, not to the genetic engineering of crops or to better land management. In effect, the world has been eating oil transformed into wheat, rice, and soybeans. Malthus was right after all. Human beings reproduce exponentially and food production does not. The combination of reduced oil and gas by-products, an extreme shortage of phosphates, less capital available for industrial-scale growers, and soil degradation is colliding with climate change to produce the perfect conditions for food shortages.

Severe drought, heat, and wildfires provoked epic crop failures in Russia in 2010 and led to a yearlong ban on grain exports to the Middle East and Africa. High food prices a few months after the harvest set off the political crisis in Egypt and other North African countries in 2011. Heavy rains cut back Canada's wheat harvest in 2010; Germany's wheat production fell 10 percent. Floods in China reduced the 2010 rice crop. In 2011 Texas endured the worst drought since the dust bowl, including the hottest June ever recorded. Two million acres of cropland were simply abandoned. In all, over 40 percent of the entire United States was subject to drought the same year. Extraordinary heat in Australia's adjoining states of Victoria and New South Wales led to devastating wildfires in 2009. Drought in Western Australia severely reduced the wheat crop from 2009 to 2011, affecting exports to China especially (yes, the Chinese eat wheat; think *noodles*). The great Queensland floods of 2010–11 caused $30 billion in damage to Australia's GDP; 10 million tons of wheat were damaged and the coal mining industry had to write off 15 percent of its annual production. During the same period, Australia repeatedly suffered locust plagues, keyed to unusual extremes of warm, wet, and then dry conditions. A one-kilometer-wide locust swarm can eat ten tons of crops in a day, amounting to a third of their combined body weight.

Other parts of the world are going through severe drops in their water tables. Saudi Arabia got into the wheat-growing business as its oil industry grew, pumping its fossil water as aggressively as its fossil fuel. The short-lived experiment in one of the earth's harshest environments is ending as the water table runs dry. In 2010 the kingdom had reduced its wheat crop by two-thirds. In the wet parts of India, longer dry spells and shorter sudden heavy showers are replacing the three months of continuous rain that has characterized the Indian monsoon. India is the world's leading consumer of groundwater. The World Bank reported that 60 percent of the aquifers in India will be in critical condition in fifteen years. Water is being pumped into irrigated farmland faster than rainfall can recharge it. The result will be a collapse of agricultural output, sooner rather than later, even while the population continues to grow—remember, even hungry people have sex.

The water crisis in China continues to match pace with its decades-long economic boom. China's reserves of freshwater dropped 13 percent between 2000 and 2009. A chronic drought is causing the Gobi Desert to creep south out of Mongolia. The Yellow River is too polluted for human consumption. The aquifers of northern China are drained. The solution for the world's most populous nation is the South-North Water Transfer Project, an insane scheme to reengineer the entire hydrology of China, diverting water from the more southerly Yangtze to the basin of the northerly Yellow River. The diverted water will require hundreds of new treatment plants to make it fit for drinking. Officials in the city of Tianjin on the seacoast near Beijing are so skeptical of the project's water quality that they've proposed building desalinization plants in any case. As this has occurred, more than 20 million acres of farmland have been taken out of production for industrial or urban development, much of it due to widespread illegal land sales, itself the result of entrepreneurial autarky among officials in a massively corrupt central government.

On the salty side of the water equation, the damage to ocean ecosystems around the world has no precedent. The industrial-scale vacuuming of wild fish stocks by advanced, giant trawlers has succeeded in pushing 69 percent of commercial fish stocks to the edge of extermination. The equilibrium of natural food chains, habitats, and local ocean ecosystems may be permanently damaged. There is no way to regulate the carnage in terms of meaningful international fishing protocols. In fact, as food problems mount up generally, there will be more incentive for the nations that can overfish to continue their predations. The peak oil situation will eventually limit commercial fishing but probably not soon enough.

International conflict is a better bet, though that cure for the world's oceans is about as severe as anything else. During the Second World War, codfish stocks in the North Atlantic recovered from prewar commercial overfishing, but the trawling technology prior to 1945 was primitive compared to today's and the catches back then a fraction of recent years. Personally, I will purchase only farmed fish, and not much of that either, because the practices behind it are increasingly dubious.

Massive stresses on the world's food system, including problems associated with climate change, have combined with peak oil and economic contraction to reach an inflection point. We've run out of techno tricks for goosing the food supply upward, and we've overdrawn the natural resources from water to good soil to nonartificial fertilizer. Organized societies can endure a lot of hardship and still carry on, but when populations go hungry all bets are off for cultural cohesion and political stability. If world events follow their usual perverse course, food shortages and other resource scarcities will express themselves indirectly in quarrels that may seem to have little to do with the pertinent issues: conflicts over abstractions such as interest rates and currencies, trade wars, revolutions, fights over boundaries and islands, nationalist chest-beating displays, and religious warfare of the jihad and crusade variety. There may be little public acknowledgment or even consciousness of the reasons behind one outburst of trouble or another.

We can conclude that the earth is a fickle place for all life, not least the human project of civilization. We maintain a most uncertain toehold in our narrow niche of comfort here, with a vast community of other living things on a planet that might have a self-regulating life of its own. I'm not altogether convinced by the Gaia theory, but there's plenty of reason to believe in a form of cosmic equilibrium that amounts to rough justice. There are consequences for our doings, and when we cross the frontier into the realm of too much magic cosmic judgment may come thundering through our little lives like what our distant ancestors thought of as the wrath of God.

In 2010, the United States spent just $1.7 billion on international climate change financing, far less than we spend on air-conditioning in the various theaters of war. The psychology in our politics is revealing. Again, note that climate change deniers also tend to be peak oil deniers. It's probably more accurate to say that they are reality deniers. It's another of the universe's jokes on us that the humans who call themselves conservatives tend to be the most avid for squandering everything the planet affords us to live. Though many of these same people happen to be religious fundamentalists, I'm not even sure how much they believe their own scriptured end-of-the-world notions. More likely, they are just plain stupid.

NINE

SOCIAL RELATIONS
AND THE DILEMMAS
OF DIFFERENCE

Years ago I had a girlfriend whose family owned a place on Lake George, a liquid memento of the last ice age that cuts majestically through the eastern Adirondacks. It wasn't just a house; it was an impressive compound of the type called a camp in the local vernacular. By this they did not mean a children's summer camp, or a bivouac for loggers, but a very substantial and permanent establishment built for a single family. It had several outbuildings but not quite enough of them to qualify for the uppermost category of these things, a "*great* camp." Only a dozen or so Adirondack great camps were ever built for a very few superplutocrats of the nineteenth century. They gave them fanciful names, their way I suppose of imbuing these grandiose dwellings with some historical afterglow as a counterpoint to their actual raw, bright, perhaps ill-gotten newness. J. P. Morgan called his Uncas, after the noble sachem in *The Last of the Mohicans*. The Vanderbilts owned Sagamore next door (one lake over, that is). Collis P. Huntington of the Southern Pacific Railroad enjoyed himself at Camp Pine Knot on Raquette Lake.

The great camps were built in the log-and-twig style, both inside and out, and operated like medieval villages, with their own workshops, gardens, dairies, laundries, stables, and other practical dependencies to support the lords of capital so far from the regular swim of civilized life. In those days, you didn't just drive to the Walmart with a shopping list. And of course there were hordes of servants, everything from hunting guides to liveried waiters, gardeners, valets, nursemaids, cooks, and scullery girls, many living on the premises. Before the age of labor-saving machines, some people saved the labor of other people. To the generations that followed, the unfairness of that system may seem outrageous. I'm not so sure it was worse than the current disposition of things in the United States.

My ex-girlfriend's family place was not such a great camp as to have had a storybook name, though it did eventually acquire some historical luster. It was built starting in 1898, over a period of a few years, mostly in the wintertime, when a horse-drawn sled could transport materials and workers across the frozen lake to the remote site on a point of land otherwise inaccessible by road. The great-grandfather who built it was a successful paint manufacturer from Long Island. He allegedly dallied with Broadway chorus girls at the Lake George place when Great-grandma wasn't around, and there were stories about finding lots of champagne bottles stashed in the basement long after his demise.

Inside, the place had seven bedrooms and one bathroom. Under the circumstances any indoor plumbing in such a remote spot was a kind of miracle, though the toilet drained into a leach field that surely ended up percolating into Lake George. The bedrooms were spacious and airy, with beadboard wainscoting throughout. The kitchen was a dark room at the rear of the house, mostly the realm of a domestic worker. Preparing meals in 1900 was not the artistic recreation it has been for us; it was work. The place was designed to operate with servants. This was an era when 6 percent of the working people in America were domestic servants of one kind or another. Without them, the place eventually slid into a long cycle of dereliction.

When I came along around 2004, the few outbuildings on the property were in various stages of decrepitude. There was a boathouse, where a sclerotic 1930s-era mahogany motor launch could be kept out of the rain, and a fieldstone toolshed with a leaky roof where a jumble of old saws, wrenches, and hammers had all rusted into a single undifferentiated orange lump of oxidized iron. Next to it was a stone generator house, which had once contained a diesel-powered electric turbine that kept the whole place lighted, pumped water to a holding tank up the hill, and allowed for a refrigerator and a radio. The generator had been installed in the 1920s and was finally carted off in the early 1970s. A marvelous little windmill house with the steel pylon and rotor coming out of the top had once automatically pumped air to a bubbler system around the boathouse to prevent ice from forming near it in the winter, which otherwise tended to smash things up. The windmill compressed the air in a storage tank, which, in turn, rationed out the release, so the bubbler operated continuously, even if the wind stopped blowing and there was nobody around.

What fascinated me most about this place was the fact that these state-of-the-art amenities, which we associate with modernity, were so long gone that they gave you the strange impression the modern era itself was actually long gone too. Now, in the early twenty-first century, the age of the microchip, the iPod, and genetic engineering, almost nothing in the house worked anymore. The electric generator was gone. There was no running water. You could use the toilet if you fetched two buckets from the lake and lugged them upstairs. All kitchen water had to be fetched too, of course. If you wanted it hot, you had to heat it on the kitchen stove, a handsome, green-and-cream-colored enamel hybrid that burned wood but also had several gas burners. The wood-burning part was useless, hopelessly gunked up. Nobody had bothered to clean it for decades. But a couple of gas burners still worked. The quaint old electric lamps were useless, of course. I wouldn't have dared hooking up a new portable generator, since the wiring all through the house was that ancient stuff with paper insulation and was turning to dust. At night now it was either candles or kerosene lamps and apparently neither my girlfriend nor her four grown sisters (there were no brothers) who used the place had ever learned how to clean a kerosene lamp, since the glass chimneys were all blackened. Even the fireplaces were useless, for years the abode of squirrels, hornets, and bats.

There was one last little outbuilding, which the family called "the Bin," a one-room cottage about fifty yards from the main house and only a few yards above the lakeshore, with a porch poised over the rocky shore. This had been the summer dwelling of a husband-and-wife team who looked after things in the place's heyday. Their names are lost to history. They stayed there through the whole summer season while family and guests came and went. The woman was the housekeeper, cook, laundress, and nursemaid and the man kept the electric and water systems running, brought in plenty of wood for the fireplace, took care of the grounds and the small vegetable garden, made periodic runs to the town of Bolton Landing in the boat to fetch necessities including diesel oil to run the generator and bottled gas for the stove, and picked up the family at an appointed hour when they rolled in on the train from New York City. When the family finally stepped off the launch onto their property, everything was meticulously in order and they could turn their attention strictly to matters of leisure. Thus was an upper-middle-class household organized in a day now bygone.

By the time I came along nobody had stayed in the Bin for decades. Mice, yellow jackets, and fungal microorganisms were feasting on it. The big house itself was a near ruin. Magnificent as it was—and the location was mind blowing, including a lovely, sheltered, private cove to swim in—staying there was more like camping out than visiting a civilized country house. Even the rattlesnakes that had been driven to near extinction around their Tongue Mountain microhabitat were regularly turning up again. What impressed me most was how a place built to endure had so sadly, utterly failed to. An air of desperate neglect and incompetence engloomed it. Nobody took care of anything anymore. The social structure it was designed to exist within had dissolved too.

Things Un-Happen

The sad gestalt of the situation always put me in a mood to reflect on the current state of American society. The United States, like the house on Tongue Mountain, had become a kind of wreck. Nobody took care of anything. The whole nation was sliding into dereliction and ineptitude. The old gag that "you can't find good help anymore" was not so funny now. Even relatively well-off, intact families lived in chaotic households, with both parents off working to service mortgages, car loans, and revolving credit card debt, with the laundry piling up and no regular mealtime, just everybody eating alone by raiding the refrigerator. If you wanted household help, you pretty much had to hire an illegal alien, and that didn't work so well on a casual labor basis since a certain quasi-familial allegiance is needed to cement mutual trust.

America looked like hell, the product of a zillion bad choices over many decades. Too many shitty buildings, too many paved-over corn-fields, and now the whole kit and kaboodle was past its design life. The shabby physical condition of the United States in the twenty-first century mirrored its social condition, just as the outward appearance of so many citizens signified frightful breakdowns, abuses, imbalances, and patholo-gies in their bodies. A range of social and political forces had especially deconstructed the lower echelons in the division of labor so that the few remaining available adult roles to choose between were 1) minimum-wage employee of a cruel and remote supergigantic corporation such as Walmart or McDonald's; 2) social services client, hostage to a cruel and remote bureaucratic "safety net" system including food stamps, minimal medical care, and meager cash handouts; 3) participant in the outlaw underground economy, trafficking in drugs, sex, usurious moneylending, and other crude larcenies. America in 2011 had huge pretenses about social equality and equally huge tensions over the inequities that, indeed, actually separated vocational, ethnic, and regional groups despite the great social justice campaigns of the late twentieth century. The living conditions, diets, daily routines, and social relations of today's hard-up classes may in fact be a lot worse than those of yesteryear's servant class. America was never without social distinctions, of course, but for a brief while in the mid-twentieth century the stars lined up in such a way as to compress the economic divides between the categories. Among the many wonders and marvels of the period after World War II, when our country dominated the world economically, was the astounding rise in standards of living among social classes who had hardly ever known leisure or had a dollar to spare on the accoutrements of it. If the hunter-gatherers enjoyed more pure equality in their little bands, it was mostly because they possessed next to nothing in material wealth. The rest, in a word, is history. Once civilization got up and running the story was nothing *but* class, for our complex societies required many layers of organization in the making, moving, and caretaking of things, and some persons enjoyed more favorable roles in that process than others.

Industrial civilization enlarged the middle class without necessarily relieving the misery of the lower classes, which also grew, shifting their labors from the farm to the factory. Marxism was an effort to reform industrial society by inciting the lower classes to make war on all the classes above them. It failed because it eliminated the necessary incentives for producing industrial wealth in the first place, namely, the legal right of persons to call it their own and accumulate it, and it failed additionally to abolish privilege among the politically connected. So in the Soviet Union, for example, privileged persons simply worked around the artificial impediments to a superior lifestyle, while the masses toiled in squalid and resigned futility.

The situation in the United States after World War II, on the other hand, was favorable to an extreme never dreamed of in Karl Marx's most hyperbolic fantasies. The U.S. continental homeland went unscathed. Our factories, mines, oil fields, harbors, and railroads stood completely intact while everyone else's was devastated. Our possession of the world's greatest oil industry, in particular, and the staggering reserves of the stuff, was itself a powerful mechanism for restarting other industrial economies shattered by war. We set out immediately to supply the rest of the world with the manufactured goods necessary to resume civilized life and lent them plenty of money to buy our stuff. Once this program got under way in earnest, one of the side effects was a fabulous enrichment of America's working classes.

These classes — the assembly-line workers, the road builders, the house framers, masons, plumbers, electricians, auto mechanics, truck drivers, and on and on — entered this miraculous new age straight from the lengthy sequential traumas of Depression and war. Their expectations were modest. Many were just grateful to have made it home alive from the canebrakes of the Solomon Islands and the beaches of Normandy. There was a lingering anxiety that without the artificial stimulus of war production America would again sink back into the economic doldrums. This worked out otherwise. The factories easily converted from tank building back to carmaking, William Levitt figured out how to mass produce the suburban house, starting a real estate boom, the American oil industry got the world's motors up and humming again, and the big cleanup of Europe and Japan's war-torn landscape commenced.

American managing classes had returned from their stints as officers in the armed forces with equally modest expectations for the rewards of being in charge of things in civilian life. The military had conditioned them to a subculture assembled by rank, but had prudently allocated privilege, so as to keep up morale through all the ranks for the greater good of winning the war. The officers turned executives in peacetime brought these values into postwar corporate life for the greater good of winning a durable prosperity. By the same token, the lower ranks came out of the war with a fund of respect for the authority that had engineered their victory. It erased much of the resentment and grievance that had festered in the Great Depression.

And so, by 1956, the president of a toaster company might be paid several multiples more than the guy on the assembly line but not obscenely more. In 1956, both would certainly be owners of American cars (a Cadillac versus a Ford Fairlane) and might well have owned their own homes in greater or lesser suburbs. But their standards of living would seem, from today's standpoint, strikingly similar. Both families would have had TV, perhaps one versus several, but both families also went to the movies at the Loew's Theater and democratically took their seats first come first served. Ditto the ballparks and football stadiums in the days before luxury corporate boxes. Both upper- and working-class families ate the standard supermarket victuals of the day, because the dietary stratification of America had not yet happened, with morbidly obese snack addicts at one end and anorectic vegan gourmets at the other. The families of working people and managers might well have sent their children to public primary schools, with divergence only later on into high school and prep schools. Both fathers may have been Sunday golfers, though on different public and private courses. And so on.

Now, politically, the situation I describe in postwar America would seem to be very desirable, perhaps ideal, considering all the cruel and unjust social systems that had existed before and elsewhere. The American system in those years was fairly equitable and appeared to be stable. But like all good things deriving from industrial civilization this social leveling process had some strange diminishing returns. One was that the lower ranks of American society were able to despotically impose their tastes on everybody else, if only because there were so many of them, with so much money to spend. They begin to occupy and modify the terrain of America in a way that lower classes never had been able to in any country before—not even in the Soviet Union's workers' paradise—using the prime artifact of industrial civilization to accomplish that takeover: the car. They disfigured the physical landscape and took over the cultural landscape with a bottomless demand for simpleminded entertainments, provided cynically by their social higher-ups in the showbiz industry, which eventually drove truth and beauty in the arts so far underground that the sheer memory of it, let alone truth and beauty themselves, may be unrecoverable. The common denominator of idiotic TV shows, relentless advertising, and ceaseless consumer manipulation democratically overwhelmed and crushed anything even aspiring to be intelligent and independent, especially in thought. The response in the fine arts was alienation and irony. They divorced themselves from the tyranny of common culture and produced artifacts increasingly designed to offend, mock, attack, and confound it: Warhol's movies, John Cage's music (e.g., his symphony for twelve radios), the porn lit of William S. Burroughs, and the like. Among educated people American pop culture was certain to inspire cynicism, as embodied in what came to be called camp: the elevation of the banal and vulgar to high art status. The intellectual damage has been permanent in a society that is now incapable of generating either sincere artistry or intelligent responses to today's great crises.

Acting Out

The tendency for symbolic behavior in human beings is impressive. Although we are not conscious of it, we are naturally metaphorical beings, especially as our technological culture has evolved and we have developed more prosthetic extensions of our powers. By the 1960s, when America's industrial smokestack economy was at its zenith, cigarette smoking was at its peak too. Forty percent of the adult population smoked, each smoker behaving like a little factory, expelling the byproducts of combustion at all hours of the day and night. It was practically required as a mark of adulthood. It was at least an entitlement. You could smoke on the job and in the college classroom. You could smoke in the doctor's waiting room. You could smoke in your seat on an airplane—an ashtray was provided right there in the armrest—and nobody had a right to complain about it. Every middle-class household had ashtrays deployed around the living room, even if the householders were themselves nonsmokers. In those days, smoking was more central to socializing than sharing food. Tobacco advertising largely supported TV broadcasting. Smoking defined the character of movie stars: Humphrey Bogart expressed the entire range of human emotion in the way he handled his beloved Chesterfields, though eventually they killed him. In the middle of Times Square, a mechanized billboard with a hole in it blew smoke rings of steam out over the masses parading below on the sidewalk, as if instructing them how to act. The adult population had plumes of smoke coming out of its collective mouths and nostrils the way that our society had smoke coming out of its cities and mill towns. Cigarette smoking has waned in lockstep with the decline of the American smokestack industry. It has lately been legally banned in barrooms and even public parks. In private homes these days, not only are ashtrays absent but smokers now have to furtively step outside to light up. Bogart would have been very surprised.

Cigarette smoking was a mass phenomenon in a mass society that had been undergoing accelerating atomization. The diminishing returns of hypercomplexity now erode what remains of mass media. We have hundreds of cable TV networks, including many that purport to offer news, which is no longer news. Rather, it has evolved into a universal shouting match of irreconcilable positions by increasingly desperate and irate political factions roughly representing what remains of the left and the right in a time of incomprehensible change. Printed newspapers rapidly sink into oblivion—including the so-called newspaper of record, the *New York Times*—and with them goes both the solemn authority and legitimacy of something like truthfulness in reporting or a reality you can trust. The book publishing industry is threatened as content shifts to electronic media. For the moment, an artifact about the same size as a book (in word count, let's say) has moved to electronic readers, Kindles, Nooks, iPads, phones, and other devices. Nobody should assume that this is the final outcome of the process. In fact, I warn the reader to consider that electronic media may be the most ephemeral of all. If our technological society is overtaken by the kind of resource scarcities I have predicted, then electronic media will be rendered inaccessible. We will be left with the physical books that already exist, and all but a tiny fraction of them are printed on paper with a relatively short design life. Something similar can be said of our modernist libraries with their stored digital media and their flat roofs that are certain to leak sooner rather than later.

The Internet is now assumed to be a permanent fixture of human life. I doubt it will work out that way. It has been interesting while it lasted but I'm persuaded that it will not last very far into the future. Our resource limits are too stark and pressing. The electronic server "farms" composed of massed computers require too much electricity. Networked computing is unlikely to shift soon enough (if ever) to less energy intensive nanomachines, or computers that run "biologically," or anything else currently on the wish list for new leaps forward. The computer industry shows little interest in our fundamental resource limits. All this will come as a huge and unhappy surprise for people accustomed to thinking of technological progress as both inevitable and a kind of entitlement. We've been so dazzled by the magic of computers that we were not paying attention to what has happened in the background. A greater irony is that the Internet, including so-called social media and cell phones, is facilitating the first stages of epochal social unrest that will synchronize with the contractions in energy and economic activity that await us presently. Angry youth may be out rioting in the streets when their cell phone service goes dark for good.

Hollywood is dying a slow death as the cineplexes shutter and the diminishing returns of technology make even the large-format high-definition flat-screen video experience at home less compelling than the previous system of projecting analog film images onto a theater screen. Anyway, movies have become sadly irrelevant. Vanishing incomes prompt the cancellation of cable TV service, even as the cable networks compete to produce cheaper and more idiotic reality entertainments, which are based mainly on categories of Americans (housewives, rich kids, horny young proles) humiliating themselves, an interesting formula for a shameless culture.

The video game industry has overtaken motion pictures in capital revenues—at least, that is the situation these days. The time will come when there is not enough juice for the Xbox and the Wii and not enough leftover income to squander on new programming. For the moment, though, and for a decade or so leading up to this moment, the mayhem of video gaming has formed the cognitive experience of a great many boys and young men. It offers them a simulacrum of magical abilities for projecting power and inflicting death, arbitrarily, casually, and with sadistic overtones. It also imparts feelings of omnipotence that are, of course, unreal fantasies and, in addition, tend to compensate for the economic and social marginalization they face in the contracting economy of the real world.

The self-presentation of young men for at least a decade has been simultaneously infantile and barbaric. The clothing is essentially infantile: pants that fall down or appear several sizes too large or baggy shorts that hang to the ankle combined with oversized shirts. The effect is of a human body with very short legs and a large torso, which is exactly how little children are proportioned. A hat worn sideways and gigantic clunky sneakers with trailing laces complete the picture of a male human being who has somehow missed several stages in development. This kind of costume is reputed to derive from prison culture, and no doubt some of it originates in that milieu, with threatening body language to match. Note, too, that historically certain fashions are designed to advertise that the wearer does not expect to do any physical labor. This is probably the case with pants that appear to be falling down (and, in fact, are).

There is no analogous baby costuming for young women in the same culture, though there are suggestions of a certain kind of work that might be performed: prostitution. If anything young women present a look of hypersexualized adulthood, including premature sexual development for girls who are unprepared for motherhood. The combination of men who act like babies and young women advertising their sexual availability has produced a predictably terrible outcome: more children who grow up in chaotic conditions with defective parenting.

A fad for body piercing and tattoos for both young men and women has added some interesting notes of barbarism to the image of young adulthood in our time. The contest for tattoo status is reaching certain limits now with full "sleeve" treatments and new territory claimed on the knuckles, neck, and head. It is hard to imagine how these self-mutilations will advance anyone's economic interests in the future. It may just be a way of saying, graphically, that you have written off your economic future. It's sad and unfortunate but, after all, it represents a choice that someone has made and must be responsible for. Life is tragic.

The idea that so many members of a younger generation may feel written off ought to be very troubling to the rest of us. Surely there is at the same time a spectrum of other young people who don't feel defeated, some bubbling with self-confidence, some idealists, some ardent revolutionaries, some earnest toilers, some warriors, some clear thinkers who have not written off their future. However, the sum of it all will add up to generational warfare, one way or another. The young people of today who make it to maturity all have one thing in common: they will never forgive us for passing on such a damaged world.

The Social Order

After I published my first two novels set in the post-collapse American future (*World Made by Hand* and *The Witch of Hebron*), I got a lot of mail from indignant women readers who felt that I depicted a future in which the victories of feminism had been nullified. They were especially upset that men seemed to be back running things, as if all the political advances of our day had never occurred. I didn't construct my fictional society to undo the flow of history, but I did try to imagine what would actually happen. What struck me about their complaints was their refusal to imagine a world in which drastically altered economic relations had produced social relations strikingly different from the forms and manners of current times. It was not unlike the dogmatic position of people who can't believe that technological progress will not solve all our problems. Well, this entire book is about the manifold failures of all kinds of people to anticipate the changes we face—politicians, economists, corporate executives, professors—so it's not awfully surprising that some feminists think the arc of history leads only to more and better feminism. I'm not convinced that it will.

The reset of the economy in North America is sure to alter the divisions of labor that we take for granted today. The current arrangements have enabled women to compete for positions with men and to justifiably ask for equal compensation. The results are often attributed to the triumph of feminism. It may have had as much or more to do with the need for a second income in the household to make up for stagnating wage levels post-1970 and to cover the growing monthly expenses of multiple car payments, hefty mortgages on ever larger houses, and tuition costs for baby boomers (and their successors) trundling off to college. Expanding corporate and public bureaucracies also contributed to the trend by creating jobs that could be performed by either men or women. In the universities, where sexual politics were practiced much more overtly and strenuously, women accomplished a takeover of department chairs and administrative posts, yielded easily by tractable academic men looking for brownie points by giving ground. By the 1990s the growth in available teaching posts had leveled off and a scramble was on to secure tenure in existing jobs. Women now represent a clear majority in overall college enrollments.

Well-paid blue-collar jobs for men were among the greatest losses in the global outsourcing process, and they were never replaced. The housing bubble diverted some of these male workers into construction for a few years but they were left high and dry when that bubble burst. By the early 2000s a lot of the office work that could be done by either men or women was also being outsourced to foreign lands, or else replaced by robots. Meanwhile, the extremely lopsided earnings of a few thousand high-testosterone "masters of the universe" in Wall Street banks did not compensate for the demoralization of more than one generation of ordinary men who could not find a self-respecting place in the economy or support a family. The losses keep adding up in family dysfunction and social discontent. A lot of that damage has remained hidden, as shameful things often do, or is channeled into angry extremist politics. It will express itself dynamically in the years ahead in ways that may not be so comfortable for our society.

The failures, weaknesses, and turpitudes of men in positions of power have tracked not only the decline of the American economy but the ethical decline as well. Abandonment of principle and a vacuum of rectitude in leadership of every type has been standard operating procedure for years. Think of the men who have been in charge of important things the past decade: Bush, Cheney, Alan Greenspan, Ben Bernanke, Robert Rubin, Larry Summers, Timothy Geithner, Barney Frank, Harry Reid, John Boehner, and of course Barack Obama. Look where they have led the United States. They lack not only conviction but also apparently the sheer will to do the right thing where it could be done (such as replacing an SEC director who won't enforce the law), and if they are reputed to be intelligent they give that quality of mind a bad odor. It's no wonder that half of the human beings in this country think that men are incompetent and dishonest. As it happens, conditions have allowed them to compete successfully for positions of leadership—though indications coming in from the careers of Sarah Palin, Michele Bachmann, and a couple of other female whackos who were not elected last time around suggest that women can be every bit as incompetent politically as men.

Conditions are once again changing in the landscape of work and livelihood. As unemployment mounts in the collapsing cheap oil economy, there may be fewer glass ceilings around for women to break through. I would not be sanguine about the survival of the corporate structures we take for granted today, since anything organized at the giant scale is likely to get into trouble and even fail as contraction accelerates along with resource and capital scarcities. It may be difficult to imagine the demise of behemoths such as Amazon, Google, Exxon-Mobil, American Airlines, or any other large enterprise, but I think we will be surprised to watch them wobble and fall. Similar disturbances of scale will ripple through government, colleges, giant health care companies, service organizations such as pension funds, and all kinds of institutions that employ people at desks. The result could be fewer jobs in which women are interchangeable with men. The loss of this framework for understanding social roles in relation to work will come as a shock to people ideologically programmed by past experiences in the twentieth century. I'd even go so far as to predict a wave of nostalgia for competent, honest male leadership in the years ahead.

The notion of a job itself may give way to different ideas about what work is. It was not so long ago that half the people in the United States spent their days farming. I doubt that they went about their routines thinking they were holding *a job*. In fact, a job was more likely to mean a particular task—getting in a crop or fixing a piece of machinery—not a career. Nonfarmers in an earlier time might have referred to their daily activities as a trade, a vocation, or a calling. Servants were recruited for positions, which to my mind means about the same as a job does today. And in one way or another, many people who toil for big corporations today are the equivalent of servants, even if they are paid a lot and enjoy benefits and protections. Like a lot of other elements of contemporary society, we regard the corporate armature of work as something basic to everyday life. I suggest we prepare for most of it to go away as economies become more local.

As it occurs, we'll be faced with different modes for the organization of work in the future, and indeed for the organization of everyday life generally. Expect hierarchical arrangements to change. The very rich will become a lot less rich as the swollen financial part of the economy dissolves in debt default and vanishing ghost assets. If the wrong political choices are made, hyperinflation could follow, but the bottom line in any case will be a poorer society overall, with *different* differences between people. A process that usually attends these economic upheavals is called *the circulation of elites*. One group gets knocked down and is replaced by a new cohort. The previous elite is usually subject to persecution and confiscation of property. In our situation it's hard to say exactly what kind of property will remain as paper investments melt away. McMansions on the beach and Lamborghinis may not hold their value. As our economy refocuses from the ephemeral to what's tangible, wealth is likely to revert to things such as productive farmland, commodity resources, and control of transport routes. Some current social status signifiers, for example, being an entertainment celebrity or a sports star, are surely headed for extinction.

Powerful distant corporations will give way to powerful local individuals who command the allegiance of people struggling to feed and shelter themselves, and a social hierarchy will organize around them emergently, whether it be a household or a geographic realm. I believe it may come to resemble the feudal structure of preindustrial times. America has been averse to aristocratic titles and that is likely to continue, but everybody will know where he or she stands. These days, even the term "mister" is a high honorific. Edwin Drake, the man who first drilled commercially for oil in the United States (1859, Titusville, Pennsylvania), was called "Colonel" though he had never been one (he was previously a train conductor). Whatever the lexicon of this new hierarchy turns out to be, the strata will be overt and unlike the superficial egalitarianism we've been familiar with recently. There will be no pretending that everybody is equal, even if relative differences in wealth are less extreme than today's. There may even be new social stigmas, such as being related to anyone who ever worked on Wall Street.

In my post-collapse novels, I depicted a character named Stephen Bullock who had consolidated the farms of many failed farmers around him unable to adjust to post-oil conditions. Bullock's success was based on his ability to reorganize the work of farming in a way that was consistent with the demise of agribusiness. Instead of machines run on cheap diesel fuel, work would require many laboring hands. Bullock welcomed men and women whose careers in the modern economy had evaporated to live on his consolidated property of several thousand acres and he allowed them to build what amounted to a village in the middle of it. The divisions of labor were different for the men and the women, though they had one thing in common: working alongside other people. Much of the work for both the men and the women would be considered hard by our standards. Bullock was extremely sensitive to the fact that he had become, in effect, a kind of feudal lord, the object of some resentment among the ordinary people in the adjoining town who were not subject to his authority or largesse. Those who came to live on Bullock's "plantation" gave him their labor and loyalty in exchange for security, reliable supplies of food, and other goods. One additional benefit for them was a firm sense of social structure in a time when so many familiar supports for daily life had catastrophically fallen away.

I don't know if this will become the model for everyday life in the future but it is one way of organizing a society that has become extremely local. In fact, my post-oil novels posit several social arrangements coexisting in the fictional locality I imagined. There was Bullock's establishment but also the fairly normal small town of Union Grove, New York, and, within the town, the cult group of New Faith Christians (about seventy in number) who came to inhabit the decommissioned high school and functioned like a commune, with some overtones of a monastery in the way that workshops and skill sets were organized. Most of the dramatic velocity of the story derived from the friction between these three modes of social organization, and the characters were keenly conscious of the conflicts that arose as a result. The characters were also sharply aware of the losses they had endured, including the loss of their faith in technology, the loss of the corporate armature for work, the loss of goods and daily routines, the loss of basic institutions—from government to education to the courts—and the loss of their illusions about social progress, including the absolute equality of the sexes in all things.

Demographic Booby Traps Await

The whole planet is in a crisis of human population overshoot. The problems around it are accelerating. Since human beings have sex even under conditions of hardship, it's likely that the population will keep growing for a while, past the point when resource and capital scarcities combine with climate problems to force the issue via food shortages, social upheaval, and perhaps even war. As this occurs, people will be on the move all over the world, trying to leave places where things are not working out so well. The United States does not have to take in everybody who wants to come here, nor should it. We'll have plenty of problems of our own, including demographic shifts within our borders as, for example, life gets difficult in the cities of the desert Southwest and Florida, the provisional suburban nature of which will lead to manifold system failures. I've already stated that we're not likely to pass any policies or protocols in the way of birth control in this country. But we could get serious about reforming our immigration laws and then enforcing them. While this is a nation of immigrants, our laws about admitting newcomers have not remained static through history. We are extremely unwise to pretend that we can continue to absorb large numbers indefinitely.

Both major political parties have been dishonest about the immigration issue from every angle. Both have supported the status quo of doing nothing on either reform or enforcement, though they pay lip service to it. Since the largest numbers of illegal immigrants come from Mexico and Central America, both parties have pandered blatantly for the Hispanic vote. Both parties are equally unserious about defending borders. The right wing favors a continuous flow of cheap labor for agribusiness and industry. Their motive is simply greed. The left wing works actively to shield so-called "undocumented workers" from legal procedures that would send them home and to assure them of public services that they should not be entitled to. Their motive is to get brownie points for occupying the multicultural moral high ground (and win minority group votes). In any case, both political parties act with disregard for the law and, like other enforcement failures these days (e.g., misconduct in banking), the net effect is corrosive to the rule of law and the legitimacy of government itself.

In the late nineteenth and early twentieth centuries the United States depended on immigration to supply cheap labor for burgeoning industry. The rate of industrial expansion in the country during that period was like nothing the world had ever seen before, and much of America was still sparsely populated, especially the industrial band around the Great Lakes and the Pacific Coast. New arrivals were transported and processed with the kind of epic efficiency that characterized the American factory system, including all the now mythologized story lines about crossing the ocean in steerage on giant ships, being greeted in the New York harbor by the astounding, bristling office towers of lower Manhattan, and getting sorted out on Ellis Island with the inspiring Statue of Liberty hovering in the background. In the early 1920s, after a sharp depression that followed the First World War, Congress changed the immigration laws, with quotas necked down to nearly nothing. The old-line Anglo establishment had gotten nervous about its hegemony in culture and party politics. An even worse depression settled over the country a few years later, then a second world war, and it was not until the 1960s that the immigration laws were updated again. It coincided with the campaign for racial justice in the United States, and the new round of changes included more liberal quotas for non-Europeans and nonwhites. The immigration laws have not been revised substantially since then, though the American economy is nothing like it was.

One reason the door remains so wide open is that both political parties came to realize that population growth in and of itself was a way to keep up the appearance of economic growth even when so much genuine productive activity, like manufacturing, was being offshored. The new jobs in enterprises such as fast food, chain stores, motels, and other manifestations of the so-called service economy paid less than the factory jobs exported outside the country. But there were a lot of these service jobs and they were associated with one of America's remaining boom industries: sprawl building. Ultimately, the sprawl-building racket was tied into the bubble machine of financialization, since the suburban houses as well as all the strip malls and commercial buildings made up the collateral for the torrent of mortgage-backed securities and their derivatives that helped puff up the banking sector from around 5 percent of the economy in the 1970s to 40 percent of it in 2007 when it all started crashing down. Where jacking up the nation's population was concerned, the housing scene became a game of musical chairs. People getting rich off the sprawl building and the highway construction and SUV sales and mortgage-hawking and banking scams and all the other dizzying money-grubbing of the day upgraded to bigger new houses in more distant exurban subdivisions while the older inner suburbs were increasingly occupied by immigrants, minorities, and other striving groups.

At the end of the bubble, of course, all sanity evaporated as giant new McHouses were sold to anyone, even illegal immigrants, financed by so-called NINJA loans (*no income, no job, no assets*) — and it all, inevitably, collapsed. A few years later the sprawl economy and the banking industry stand in ruins and the illusion that perpetual population growth leads to perpetual prosperity ought to be discredited.

If anything, high unemployment has come to be seen as structural, that is, a now chronic feature of a system in decay. The situation will improve when the public realizes we face a restructuring of our economy along the lines I have already suggested: relocalized, downscaled, moving away from fossil fuels and toward much more modest energy use based on solar income. Surely a much larger percentage of the total population will be engaged in food production at every level, and both old and new craft trades will occupy people who can acquire the skills. We won't get all our goods from halfway around the world forever. The American economic scene will be as different in the decades ahead as the now bygone heyday of manufacturing looks to us now in the old photographs. The sexual divisions of labor are apt to become less flexible than they have been for several generations, as there will be fewer kinds of work that can be done by just anybody. I don't believe there will be big quarrels about it; it will be accepted as self-evident.

The current phase of globalism is winding down as well. There have been others through history. They come and go. Let's hope we can make the transition peacefully. As it occurs, expect an economy much more internally focused on what we can produce and trade in North America. By the way, this is not an argument for creating a larger nation that combines the United States, Mexico, and Canada, a fantasy of many conspiracy freaks. That will not happen. If anything, the three big nations of North America may break up into smaller self-governing regions, a subject I covered at length in *The Long Emergency*. The same problems of scale that apply to corporate enterprise also apply to governance.

The Multicultural Dilemma

Ideologies and belief systems don't necessarily provoke cultural change. Often they simply ratify changes that have already occurred. I suspect that this was the case with feminism. It was not the angry protests of women in the 1970s, or the debut of *Ms.* magazine, that got women into the workplace. They were already flowing in there because incomes for men had begun to stagnate. Before long, the two-income family became the norm. After the fact, the results were often attributed to the triumph of feminist politics, but sexual politics mostly came into play only later, in disputes over pay equity and other fairness issues once women were already on the job. Then, of course, came the sad discovery that plenty of jobs, even with equal pay, are boring and unsatisfying for anybody, no matter what the gender.

In the same way, the ideology of multiculturalism followed the fact of it. It was a way of saying that the demographic makeup of the United States had changed a lot and now everybody ought to get used to it and try to be nice. Once the fact was established, the political left formalized an ideology around it. Then they used it for a moral high ground "teachable moment" and made themselves obnoxious with sententious shibboleths and hyped-up identity agendas. In so doing, they revealed a problem: multiculturalism is okay for a while, perhaps when your society is trying to adjust to new conditions, but sooner or later if you want to have a unified nation it helps to have something identifiable as common culture so that a consensus can form about standards of behavior and values. With ideological multiculturalism members of different groups were entitled to different standards of behavior and competing values. This made for a certain amount of confusion and resentment and in any case was impractical over the long term.

In the previous major wave of immigration spanning the late nineteenth and early twentieth centuries, a consensus of expectation required newcomers to learn the English language and adapt to established behavioral norms, in short, to assimilate into a common culture. The outcome then was pretty successful. Within a short period of history people from eastern Europe, Russia, and Italy were participating fully in American life, eventually running companies, getting elected to high office, entering professions and becoming economic elites. There was no question in the New York of, say, 1912, that children of immigrants would go to school and speak English there. No one dared argue about it. It was self-evidently necessary. The result was rapid acculturation. In the case of Catholics and Jews, quite a few restrictive old prejudices yielded in the years that followed, meaning the established culture had to give some ground in the face of people who had obviously met their obligations. You couldn't keep Jews out of hotels anymore and a Catholic was elected president in 1960.

Now, on the verge of a very tough economic transition, there is a rather flimsy sense of common culture, and the politics of multi-culturalism are an impediment to getting through the transition. As a nation we would benefit a lot more from common culture, from broad agreement between all cultural groups about what is okay and what is not okay, than we would from insisting on different prerogatives based on background and identity. The trouble is it may be too late. I'm not so sure we will find our way back to a national common culture. The United States is balkanizing in strange new ways.

Race: America's Wild Card

America elected a half-Caucasian, half–African American president in 2008.[1] Senator Barack Obama was poised and self-possessed. His Republican opponent John McCain represented a party in terrible standing, picked a divisive running mate, and campaigned erratically during a profound financial crisis caused by his political associates. Obama astounded the world by winning the election. (I voted for him.) Many Americans felt it was the capstone moment in the long campaign for social justice, demonstrating, at last, our essential national moral uprightness. The right wing behaved rather churlishly toward Obama from the get-go, seeming to disdain him on racial grounds alone, without ever really saying so—a cowardly position.

1. The old "one drop rule" predisposes our culture to label anyone who is only partly black as "black." One might as easily label Barack Obama "white." Incidentally, rumors long followed the twenty-ninth president, Warren G. Harding (who served from 1921–23), that he was of racially mixed origin; they were never confirmed.

In any case, history is cruel, life is unfair, and Barack Obama has not done so well in his term of office as of this writing. He came along at a very difficult time in our national history. The economy is wobbling again for reasons this president has never adequately articulated (and which are the subject of this book), despite his renown for eloquence. And despite his genial disposition and adult demeanor he can be faulted for failing on many issues, including botched health care reform, a dumb energy policy, keeping two of the longest wars in our history going, and not reestablishing the rule of law in banking in the face of arrant misconduct. There's a fair chance that he will not be reelected. I worry about what may happen to the social fabric after Obama, if the voters reject him. I worry that the African American minority will be discouraged and angry, that the large and growing reactionary elements of white America will behave badly in response to them, and that serious conflict will ensue.

For someone who came of age in the 1960s, with all its political, generational, and racial tensions, recent times in the United States have seemed eerily placid. People of all ethnic groups are suffering unusually intractable economic hardship and yet for the moment they appear to have internalized their emotions. If the dominant emotion is shame or humiliation, then I believe there is a natural human inclination to keep it inside, to conceal it. After all, feelings of shame are shameful. But there is often a point where emotions transmute, especially at the political scale, and shame turns to rage and blame.

The tensions across this sore beset republic can be felt in the tent cities and in the ghettos, the people living in cars in the Walmart parking lot, those still living in houses they haven't made payments on in a year, those bankrupted by some medical catastrophe, those cast aside and forsaken, and even those somehow still getting by who endure constant anxiety about what humiliating nightmare this long emergency will plunge them into.

Coda: A Systematic Misunderstanding of Reality

A few months ago, American astronauts flew what appears to be the very last space shuttle mission. The shuttle vehicle will be retired (after two blew up). NASA has no next-generation manned space exploration vehicle offstage. Officials have talked about developing a new rocket to put *something* out there, but the chatter sounds pretty vague and demoralized. I'm not persuaded that it will amount to anything. The end of the shuttle era was a poignant moment in American science, full of sad resonances for dissolving dreams of adventure in other worlds. The government is out of money, and capital will only get scarcer as our fossil fuel energy inputs decline. Space travel will probably prove to have been another product of the cheap oil age, retrograde as that sounds. The truth works backward and forward, and sometimes it hurts.

The first U.S. moon landing took place so long ago now that it seems more like ancient history than science fiction. We may never go back there again (though our successors the sapient cockroaches or fruit bats might). Looking back, I regarded it as a kind of horror show, a fantastic bundle of surreal banalities, a memento wholly of its time and place. I was twenty years old, having an adolescent nervous breakdown in Provincetown, at the tip of Cape Cod. How I got there is not important but it was all sort of a blunder. I had a summer job as a line cook in a restaurant called the Penny Farthing. We were working the dinner rush when the *Eagle* landed.

The Apollo 11 mission went to the moon with less computer power than the average cell phone now has. I guess the math needed to go there wasn't all that hard. In our current mood of techno grandiosity we forget what an excellent computer the unaided human mind is. Descending to the lunar surface in the landing module, the puny onboard NASA computer went haywire and the mission commander Neil Armstrong had to guide the clunky-looking spacecraft down manually. Can you imagine? Flying by the scat of your pants . . . to another world? (Since then, by the way, Commander Armstrong, the first human being to step on the moon, has led a life as obscure from public view as the giant squid of the Aleutian Trench.)

Once parked safely upon the Sea of Tranquillity, Armstrong suited right up and ventured outside to make his bland utterance about "one giant leap for mankind" in keeping with the culture of Wonder Bread and television that he represented. Then, he and his sidekick Edwin "Buzz" Aldrin bustled about on the surface for two and a half hours carrying out a meticulously scheduled roster of chores. They planted a flag, bored some core samples from the lunar ground, had a chat by telephone with President Nixon, deployed a video camera, shot some still photos of each other like tourists at Yosemite, and scooped up about fifty pounds of rock and dust to take home. Then they retired back inside the landing module for a scheduled seven hours of sleep before the blastoff to rendezvous with the command module *Columbia*, high above in lunar orbit, manned by the lonely third crew member Michael Collins.

That's one part of the adventure I still have trouble with. They went to sleep before blastoff! I'm sorry, but I fail to comprehend how any person might fall asleep in a tin can parked on the moon (prior to a dangerous return trip to earth) without a huge dose of soporific drugs, which I very much doubt that either Armstrong or Aldrin took, since they needed to be sharp for their next scheduled task and the sleeping meds of that day were rather crude. Nor can I imagine what went through their minds as the disembodied voices from Mission Control in Houston radioed in seven hours later and they spiraled up from the innocent raptures of their childlike sleep to find themselves . . . parked on the moon! Holy fuck!

These anxious ruminations probably reveal more about my own skittish state of mind that busy, spooky summer of 1969 than the condition of U.S. culture forty-odd years ago. The whole Apollo 11 moon landing, from start to finish, gave me the creeps. We tend to forget that the extravaganza lasted for a week, from the initial blastoff atop a Saturn rocket on July 16, 1969, to the splashdown on July 24, so there was a huge buildup to the Big Moment itself. The whole nation was riveted. I didn't even like *hearing* about it in casual chitchat it made me so uncomfortable.

We had a little black-and-white TV set up on top of the reach-in fridge in the restaurant kitchen where I worked. All the other employees—the chef, the waiters, the dishwasher—were glued to the set, grinning, high-fiving, shooting thumbs-up signs, and enjoying the show. I didn't even want to watch the broadcast, but I was stuck there on the job. Armstrong made his famous utterance while I was breaking down the garnish station. My cold and trembling hands fumbled with the lemon wedges as he bounced down the landing module's steps. While I recognized that the moon landing was an amazing deed in the annals of science, I wanted to run shrieking from the room. For years afterward I couldn't bear the sight of the moon pinned up there in the velvet sky.

All of this is to say that I was very early in life inoculated against the triumphs of technology and imprinted instead with a respectful hypersensitivity for its implications. Though I am no longer afflicted with adolescent anxiety attacks, this conditioning has led me much later in life to take an extremely skeptical view of what is commonly regarded as "progress." By an odd coincidence, I have also found myself later in life in a society that is crumbling under the weight of its investments in technology (and tortured by the unintended consequences and diminishing returns of these investments), not to mention the agony of its ongoing fantasies about a technological rescue from the very predicaments already spawned by the misuse of technology.

A Hopeful Future

My auditors often call me a "doomer," a label I reject. I'm actually a pretty cheerful person, considering the things I feel compelled to write about. I think the human race has many more innings ahead, but I am convinced that the terms for daily life can change sharply, and have historically, and will again. If you are inclined to despair about being alive in this world of mystery, you could find plenty of reasons to sulk even if we weren't in for the rigors of climate change, peak oil, resource scarcity, geopolitical conflict, and a crashing standard of living. Plenty of Hollywood stars have been miserable in their hermetic luxury, and lots of lowly peasants have been infused with the light of gratitude for being.

A fortunate person will come to terms with the anxiety that being alive in this world presents. My own anxiety took its most dramatic form in adolescence, with all my frights and fears about things like space travel, but behind all that melodrama was the simple question of my own competence. I was not very well prepared to become an adult and had to figure out many things for myself with no guidance. It took me a little longer than average. The younger generations today are less prepared than I was. Their elders, in particular leaders and authority figures, have made a point of not telling them the truth. My generation especially, the baby boomers, has engineered a systematic misunderstanding of reality. That "hologram," as the late and great Joe Bageant called the hallucinatory globe of falsehood that envelopes us, is crumbling but something else is moving in to take its place.

I certainly believe in facing the future with hope, but I have learned that this feeling of confidence does not come from outside you. It's not something that Santa Claus or a candidate for president is going to furnish you with. The way to become hopeful is to demonstrate to yourself that you are a competent person who can understand the signals that reality is sending to you (even from its current remove offstage) and act intelligently in response. We once were exactly that kind of people: brave, clear-eyed, resourceful, resolute, competent, and confident. Generations will soon come into their power feeling differently about themselves than we do now, and in their reenchanted lives they will wonder about us and what we did to their world and what we thought we were doing.